# THE DOCTRINE OF GOD

## GERALD BRAY

CONTOURS *of*

CHRISTIAN

THEOLOGY

---

GERALD BRAY
*General Editor*

INTERVARSITY PRESS
DOWNERS GROVE, ILLINOIS 60515

© 1993 by Gerald Bray

Published in the United States of America by InterVarsity Press, Downers Grove, Illinois, with permission from Universities and Colleges Christian Fellowship, Leicester, England.

InterVarsity Press® is the book-publishing division of InterVarsity Christian Fellowship®, a student movement active on campus at hundreds of universities, colleges and schools of nursing in the United States of America, and a member movement of the International Fellowship of Evangelical Students. For information about local and regional activities, write Public Relations Dept., InterVarsity Christian Fellowship, 6400 Schroeder Rd., P.O. Box 7895, Madison, WI 53707-7895.

Unless otherwise stated, quotations from the Bible are taken from the British edition of the Holy Bible: New International Version, copyright ©1973, 1978 and 1984 by the International Bible Society. Published by Hodder and Stoughton Ltd.

ISBN 0-8308-1531-7

Printed in the United States of America ∞

**Library of Congress Cataloging-in-Publication Data**

Bray, Gerald Lewis.
    The doctrine of God/Gerald Bray.
      p.    cm.—(Contours of Christian theology)
    Includes bibliographical references and index.
    ISBN 0-8308-1531-7
    1. God.  2. Trinity.  I. Title.  II. Series.
    BT102.B718   1993
    231—dc20                      93-19204
                                      CIP

| 17 | 16 | 15 | 14 | 13 | 12 | 11 | 10 | 9 | 8 | 7 | 6 | 5 | 4 | 3 | 2 | 1 |
|----|----|----|----|----|----|----|----|---|---|---|---|---|---|---|---|---|
| 07 | 06 | 05 | 04 | 03 | 02 | 01 | 00 | 99 | 98 | 97 | 96 | 95 | 94 | 93 | | |

# Contents

# Series Preface

*Contours of Christian Theology* covers the main themes of Christian doctrine. The series offers a systematic presentation of most of the major doctrines in a way which complements the traditional textbooks but does not copy them. Top priority has been given to contemporary issues, some of which may not be dealt with elsewhere from an evangelical point of view. The series aims, however, not merely to answer current objections to evangelical Christianity, but also to rework the orthodox evangelical position in a fresh and compelling way. The overall thrust is therefore positive and evangelistic in the best sense.

The series is intended to be of value to theological students at all levels, whether at a Bible college, a seminary or a secular university. It should also appeal to ministers and to educated lay-people. As far as possible, efforts have been made to make technical vocabulary accessible to the non-specialist reader, and the presentation has avoided the extremes of academic style. Occasionally this has meant that particular issues have been presented without a thorough argument, taking into account different positions, but when this has happened, authors have been encouraged to refer the reader to other works which take the discussion further. For this purpose adequate but not exhaustive notes have been provided.

The doctrines covered in the series are not exhaustive, but have been chosen in response to contemporary concerns. The title and general presentation of each volume are at the discretion of the author, but final editorial decisions have been taken by the General Editor of the series in consultation with IVP.

In offering this series to the public, the authors and the publishers hope that it will meet the needs of theological students in this generation, and bring honour and glory to God the Father, and to his Son, Jesus Christ, in whose service the work has been undertaken from the beginning.

*Gerald Bray*
*General Editor*

# Introduction

This book on the doctrine of God forms volume 1 of the series Contours of Christian Theology. So vast a subject is obviously too demanding for a single volume, and inevitably much of the discussion in these pages has had to be curtailed, and some topics have been virtually omitted altogether, in order to keep within the dimensions of the series as a whole.

One of the major difficulties with the subject is that, broadly speaking, there are two quite distinct aspects to it, both of which demand our attention. The first of these may be called the doctrine of God's nature, which covers all aspects of his being in relation to things outside himself. These include such questions as the proofs for his existence, election and predestination, creation and providence, and so on. As these matters will be dealt with more fully in other volumes in this series, it was thought best to refer to them here only in passing, and leave the major treatment to those volumes.

This has allowed more space to be devoted to the second aspect of the doctrine of God, which is his personal, trinitarian subsistence. The present volume goes into this subject in some detail, and tries to connect the evangelical understanding of the doctrine to the wider Christian tradition. Readers will doubtless notice that an unusually large amount of space has been devoted to the Eastern Orthodox understanding of the Trinity, which may be explained as follows. First, it is of intrinsic interest and importance, although it has been sadly neglected by the Western world until recent years. Second, it has some curious points of affinity with the evangelical outlook which need to be pointed out, especially in these days of ecumenical contact and discussion. Third, one of the stated aims of the series is to explore new ground in contemporary theological discussion, and the rise of interest in Eastern Orthodoxy since 1945 has been nothing less than phenomenal. This does not mean that the approach taken here is naive or uncritical; on the contrary, it seeks merely to do justice to a tradition which has been unjustly neglected for too long, and to explain in what ways evangelical Christians may accept as well as dissent from it.

It should also be said that although the present volume is a defence of evangelical theology, as this is generally understood by conservatives in the English-speaking world, it is far from being uncritically dogmatic in its presentation of that position. Indeed, one of its main aims is to point out that evangelical theology has long neglected certain areas of discussion and has suffered as a result. At the same time, objections to other forms of Christianity have not been concealed, and at times they may have been pressed in a way which may seem to be unfair to adherents of a different point of view. If this is so I wish to apologize for any misrepresentation of an opposing position, and would welcome correction on this score. At the same time I would also ask potential objectors to consider the ways in which they may have misunderstood the evangelical position as presented in this book, and to recognize that I have taken a critical position with regard to it whenever I have felt it necessary to do so. This is particularly evident in the last chapter, which is intended as a plea to evangelicals to return to serious theology at a time when experiential forms of religion threaten to snuff it out altogether.

In preparing this manuscript for publication much time

and many hands have been needed. Particular thanks must go to Mrs Alison Wilkinson (*née* Jones), who typed various portions of the text, and to the Rev. David Kingdon of IVP. In addition, I would like to thank those who read the manuscript in draft for IVP and made many valuable suggestions. Of my students, I must make special mention of the Rev. Graham Wintle and the Rev. Ambrose Mason, who together offered some acute observations on the chapter dealing with Calvin, and also to the Rev. Roderick Doulton, who is responsible for a number of alterations in content and presentation. Thanks are also due to the General Theological Seminary in New York for offering me generous sabbatical leave, during which the final portions of the manuscript were completed.

Finally, to all readers I recommend that this book be read and understood as an introduction to the study of Holy Scripture, from which all true doctrine must be derived, and to the Christian tradition, which through the ages has sought to be faithful to the record of God's revelation of himself to the world. As I lay the fruit of my own study and research before the Christian public, it is my hope that those who read this book may find themselves drawn more deeply into this study and be more willing to offer praise to God himself.

*Gerald Bray*

# 1

## OUR KNOWLEDGE
## OF GOD

Is it possible to know God? Opinion polls occasionally tell us
that a large majority of people believe in God, or at least in
some kind of supreme being, or supernatural force. But when
the same people are questioned on the finer points of Christian
belief, far fewer are prepared to go along with what the church
has traditionally taught. For most people, it would seem that
belief in God has little to do with organized religion or with the
'official' Christian faith. On the other hand, we are also
familiar with small groups of committed believers who are
prepared to press their version of belief in God as if it were the
only possible option. One difficulty with them is that there are
many such groups, and that their ideas are usually quite
different. They cannot all be right, but how are we to distinguish the true from the false? Is it not easier to conclude either
that all are wrong, or that some may be right, but we cannot be
sure which? Those who take the first option may call themselves
atheists, whilst those who take the second may prefer to be called
agnostics, but in the end it makes little practical difference.
Whoever God is, and whatever he may be like, he is essentially
unknowable, and speculating about him is a waste of time.

Convinced Christians, of course, cannot agree with this kind of thinking. To be a Christian is to believe that it is possible to know God. More than that, it is to believe that God has made it possible for us to know him by revealing himself to us. This special (as opposed to the revelation of God in the created order of which Paul speaks in Romans 1:18–20) revelation began about four thousand years ago, and was initially connected with the history of the people of Israel. This history, Christians assert, came to a climax in the life, death and resurrection of Jesus of Nazareth, who lived in Palestine about two thousand years ago and who claimed to be the Son of God. Furthermore, Christians claim, this belief is not just a matter of opinion. It can be held with the same conviction as any other belief about what we call 'reality', and can be supported by arguments which use the same rational criteria as those found in other scientific disciplines. Of course there are differences between believing that there is a God and believing that the world is round, but the mental processes which we use to defend each of these beliefs are essentially the same. In other words, Christians claim that God belongs to the same framework of reality as the universe does. He is not an illusion, nor is he a being who can be approached only by a special procedure which has been revealed to true believers but which is otherwise unknown.

At the same time, Christians are forced to admit that their belief in God is not widely shared outside religious circles. Most people believe that the world is round, but it makes little difference to their lives. Many of the same people may also believe in God, but if that belief makes no difference to their lives, a Christian would argue that it is essentially false. To believe in God, a Christian would say, is to know God, and if we know God, then it is inevitable that he will change our lives and become the most central part of our life-experience. For Christians it is impossible to be indifferent to the supreme being; the God we worship is a person whom we encounter and who changes human lives.

But how do we know such a God? How can we explain him to people who do not share our beliefs? Can we prove his existence in a way which an open-minded outsider would have to accept? These questions make us ask what kind of

14

knowledge we can have about a being who is not accessible to us by any of the normal scientific criteria, and whose existence can be doubted or denied with no apparent effect. Clearly there is something about our knowledge of God which does not fit the normal scientific pattern, and unless we accept this, we are unlikely to make much headway.

How is Christian belief different from other kinds of knowledge? We have already said that God makes himself known to us by *revelation*. This means that unless he tells us about himself, we cannot know him. This may seem unacceptable to those who think that God should be available for investigation in the same way as the roundness of the earth is, but if we think about it a little more we shall see that we are talking about two different kinds of knowledge. If God is a personal being, it is not surprising that we can know him only by revelation, since the same is true of every person. Other people know us only to the extent that we reveal ourselves to them. This does not necessarily mean that we have to speak to them directly, but knowledge which has been picked up in other ways may have to be corrected by direct explanation. We all know that it is possible to observe another person in action and draw the wrong conclusions, and so we should not be surprised to discover that the same is true of a personal God. We may have our ideas about him, which we have picked up by observation, but in the final analysis our perceptions must be open to correction by what he tells us about himself.

When asked to explain how God has spoken to us, Christians answer that this has happened in and through his Word. The Word of God is understood in two distinct, but related senses. In one sense it is applied to the texts which we have in the Bible, the sourcebook of Christian teaching. In another sense, it is applied to Jesus Christ, who is the fulfilment of the Bible's teaching and the focus of Christian faith. Some people believe that these two sources of knowledge may be contradictory, but that when they are, we must choose one over the other. To choose the Bible over Jesus makes little sense, since Jesus is what the Bible is all about, and so most people are inclined to think that Jesus should be preferred to the Bible, if the latter disagrees with him, though this approach is not as simple as it seems. One of the main problems with it is that the Bible is the only source of our knowledge of Jesus, so that to cast doubt on its reliability is to cast doubt on whatever knowledge of him we may claim to have.

For better or for worse, Christians have always maintained that there is no real contradiction between Jesus and the Bible. The one explains and illuminates the other, and the two must be kept in balance if we are going to have any true knowledge of the God whom they both reveal. Working this out is the special task of theology, a word which means the study of God. Over the years theology has come to be understood as containing a number of other subjects, like church history, ethics, liturgical studies, homiletics, Greek and Hebrew, which may all be taught as part of a degree course in theological studies, but they should not be confused with theology in the strict sense. Even Biblical Studies, important though they are, are not theological in the true sense of the term![1]

Many people will assume from this that theology, narrowly defined, means the study of Christian beliefs or doctrine (which means teaching), but even that is not a totally accurate description. The study of doctrine certainly plays an important role in theology, but it also covers matters which are theological only in a secondary sense. The nature of man, the structure of the church, the meaning of the sacraments and the last judgment are all part of Christian teaching, but in so far as they are not directly concerned with the being and nature of God, they are dependants of theology and not component parts of it.[2]

It is also true, of course, that theology need not be Christian, since the word can be used to mean the study of the god or gods of any religion. Yet it is surprising to what extent the emergence of systematic theology as an academic discipline is unique to Christianity. Not even Judaism or Islam, both of which are related, monotheistic religions, has a corpus of theology or a corps of theologians to compare with the Christian one.[3] Still less can we discover anything similar in Hinduism or Buddhism, and it is remarkable that even heretical offshoots of Christianity, like Mormonism, have seldom troubled to construct a rival theological system. Only Christians have consistently maintained that God can and must be known in a way which can bear comparison with any other type of philosophy or science.

In the pages which follow, we shall consider first, what kind of knowledge it is that Christians claim they have about God. Then we shall examine the origin of Christian theology as a systematic exposition of the Bible. After that, we shall look briefly at Christianity's historical links with ancient Greek philosophy and with Roman law, two disciplines which have frequently been cited as having influenced the development of Christian theology in a non-biblical direction. Finally, we shall look at how classical Christian theism came into being, and consider the ways in which the Protestant reformers and their successors have adopted and modified that tradition.

## What kind of knowledge can we have?

It is when we come to define the nature of theology more closely that we run into difficulties. On the one hand, it is possible to argue that because Christians believe that there is a God who has revealed himself in ways which make him available to our minds, Christian theology is a science, similar to biology, geology, dendrology and other subjects which apply the mind to the study of objectively existing things. Christians have developed a science of theology which examines the data of revelation, *i.e.* the statements made about God in the Bible, in much the same way as a biologist examines plant and animal life. The theologian employs the same techniques of analysis which may be found in any other discipline, relying on the same logical processes to elaborate a system of thought which can function without internal contradiction. At times he or she will be obliged to acknowledge, as any scientist must, that in our present state of knowledge there are tensions and paradoxes which cannot be fully resolved (*e.g.* the apparent contradiction between God's love and the presence of evil in the world), but without conceding that such a dilemma is insoluble in principle. Theologians will insist that further knowledge can and will resolve the paradox, either by adding further data to the system(s) we already

17

have, or by replacing our inadequate system(s) with a better one, which restructures already known data on a different principle.[4]

Looked at in this way, it would appear that theology can indeed be called a science, and the systematic theologian works on that assumption. Yet from another point of view, there are great differences between theology and the other sciences, which seem to bring this definition into question. The most fundamental of these is the problem of epistemology, the principle of knowledge. Where do our data come from and how can we be sure that they are reliable? Christianity has always maintained that theological data come from the Bible, which is believed to be God's revelation of himself to human beings. Yet virtually nobody would wish to argue that the Bible is an *exhaustive* source of theological knowledge. Opinions differ even about how *exclusive* it is.[5] Some theologians have wanted to supplement it by appealing to the natural sciences, to commonsense, and to personal experience. But in spite of these differences all agree that the biblical revelation is fundamental, and most would want to justify their appeal to other authorities on the ground that the Bible itself allows this, as for example, when it praises the natural order as an expression of the glory of God (Ps. 19).

But unlike theology, the other sciences rely for their information not on revelation, but on experiment and discovery. It is quite true that scientific progress sometimes occurs as a result of brilliant guesswork, but in the natural sciences, intuitive genius must always be supported by empirical evidence if it is to be accepted as established fact, and few scientists would regard genius of this type as miraculous, or as an example of God's self-revelation. The result is that the natural sciences have a different database, a different procedural method and a different attitude to unresolved paradoxes. Where theologians will bow in agnostic reverence before a mystery which they cannot penetrate, because they know that their database will not increase this side of eternity, scientists will continue to look for a solution to their problems. Given that they belong to the time-and-space order of creation, they will assume that an answer lies within their grasp if only the right key to the puzzle can be found.

18

Some people argue that it does not matter if theology uses a very different method from that of the other sciences because, they say, its subject matter is also very different from theirs. People have the power to analyse things which are inferior to their own being, but they cannot treat their Maker in the same way. As Paul said to the Romans (9:20) '. . . who are you, O man, to talk back to God? "Shall what is formed say to him who formed it, 'Why did you make me like this?'"' But although there is substance in this argument, matters are complicated by the fact that when the modern academic disciplines were founded, and for many centuries thereafter, both theology and the natural sciences *did* in fact use the same approach to their respective material – an approach which theology alone has continued to find appropriate.

In the Middle Ages it was generally believed that all knowledge could be found in ancient books, and education usually meant little more than learning classical texts by rote. In one or two cases, like Euclid's study of geometry, these texts are still accepted today, but on the whole, the scientific work of Aristotle, Ptolemy, Galen and the rest is now seen to have been primitive and unsound. As most modern historians of science understand the matter, it was not until the authoritative status of the ancients was overthrown that the natural sciences could be established on the right foundations.[6]

This scientific revolution began about 1500 and was complete by the end of the eighteenth century. Many of the greatest scientists were clergymen and some of them were accomplished theologians, but for a variety of reasons, the scientific developments they encouraged soon left theology behind, and even led some of them into conflict with the church. The most notorious example of this was the case of Galileo, who in 1633 was condemned for saying that the earth revolves around the sun, contrary to the apparent testimony of the Scriptures and the decided beliefs of the Roman Inquisition. Today everyone recognizes that Galileo's judges were using the Bible to support a Ptolemaic astronomy which the biblical writers themselves had never heard of and were not concerned with. But this recognition usually goes hand-in-hand with the belief that Scripture speaks about both God and the natural order in a non-scientific way – in other words, the Bible can no more be used to construct a scientifically valid systematic theology than it can be searched for the data of astronomy.

Because of all this, even Christian theologians are now likely to admit that theology is not a science like biology, although they are not always agreed as to how it should be classified among the academic disciplines. It is obviously closely connected with philosophy – so much so that many historians would argue that without the stimulus of the Graeco-Roman philosophical schools, Christian theology would never have come into being. There may be an element of truth in this belief, but two important qualifications need to be borne in mind. First, it cannot be claimed that the influence of Greek philosophy drove Christians to develop a corresponding theology; Jews and Muslims were exposed to the same influences, but with very different results. This suggests that there is something in the nature of Christianity itself which led to this development, quite apart from external influences. Second, the Christian theological tradition has always included a strong mystical element which is the declared enemy of Greek philosophy, but which has usually been regarded by theologians as lying close to the heart of their own discipline. The link between theology and philosophy cannot be regarded as inevitable, even though theologians have always borrowed philosophical terms and concepts with great freedom, and have even regarded philosophy as the handmaid of theology. The two disciplines meet in the sense that theology can be said to have put a name to the underlying principle of the universe, which philosophers have always tried to discover and understand. This meeting of disciplines has sometimes been harmonious, although usually the harmony has been the product of a conflict which has been resolved only by mutual accommodation (synthesis). Thus, for example, as long as most philosophers believed that the absolute principle of the universe was a static being, it was possible for theologians to talk of God as the absolute substance, the source of all existence, and so on. The supreme being thus described was not necessarily the Christian God, as both believing Christians (like Pascal) and unbelieving philosophers (like Spinoza) were ready to point out, but the possibility of a harmony between the demands of natural reason and the data of revelation was not ruled out by the broad mass of informed opinion.[7]

Things began to change when the old picture of the universe gave way to new ideas. Belief in creation was replaced by theories of evolution which purported to make creation unnecessary. The idea of an absolute substance was replaced by theories of relativity based on random energy. Above all, the once common affirmation that behind the universe there lay the mind of a supreme being came increasingly to be denied by philosophers, and it was declared irrelevant by many scientists. The age-old link between theology and philosophy came to look more and more like the link between astrology and astronomy – a pseudo-science popular among the superstitious and the uneducated, doing battle with its intellectually respectable replacement. Once the concept of a unifying intelligent power behind the universe began to be questioned, there was no more room for theological study among the academically accredited scientific disciplines, and its continued survival in the universities became a problem.

Theologians often found themselves isolated in a hostile intellectual climate, and many of them sought to justify their continued existence either by becoming specialists in historical or comparative religion, or by defining theology as an art akin to music and poetry. According to them, the dogmatic tradition of systematic theology represents a false development of material which is not scientific fact but *myth*.[8] Myth is not to be understood as falsehood but as storytelling – an attempt to explain the meaning of reality in terms which ordinary people find comprehensible, but which correspond to scientific fact only in a metaphorical sense. In the Bible, they claimed, reality is explained by the myths of creation and redemption, which were borrowed from pagan sources but modified and purged by an ethical monotheism, which claimed to be in harmony with reason. Today these myths have largely lost their power, and the task of the theologian is either to help humanity to live according to a moral standard without mythology, or to construct new myths which modern human beings can find plausible. If such a theologian is a Christian, he or she will presumably try to reinterpret the

21

biblical picture of God and Jesus Christ along lines which are comparable with belief in a relativistic universe held together by the power of creative energy.

This attitude towards theology appears to be very modern, but in fact it takes us right back to the earliest, and virtually only pre-Christian, use of the term. The word *theologia* appears for the first time almost by accident, in Plato's *Republic* (379a). The passage is sufficiently interesting to be worth quoting at some length:

> — My dear Adeiamantus, you and I are not poets, on the present occasion, but founders of a state (*polis*). Now founders ought certainly to know the genres (*typoi*) in which their poets are to compose their myths, and from which they cannot be allowed to deviate; though they are not required to write myths themselves.

> — You are right, but these genres as you put it – what should they be in the case of theology?

> — They should be as follows ... It is surely always right for God to be portrayed as he really is, whether a poet describes him in epic, lyric or dramatic verse.

> — Yes, of course.

> — Then surely God is good in reality, and should be described as such?

> — Of course.

This dialogue is extremely interesting because it brings out the prehistoric link between poetry and the divine in a way which finds some close parallels in modern thought. Adeiamantus assumes without question that theology is a literary topic which must be expounded in poetic myth, and wants to know only which type of poetry is most suitable for the purpose. Socrates (= Plato) replies that any genre will do, as long as God is portrayed as he is – good. We are still a long way from a theology rooted in divine self-disclosure, but it is important to note that Plato believed that God's greatest attribute (as he saw it) could be defined as a statement of fact, without recourse to myth in any form. In other words, belief in a good God is not a myth; it is the hard core of truth around which the myths were to be constructed. It is this basic substance of truth, not the poetic expression of it, which constitutes the subject matter of *Christian* theology, and distinguishes it from Platonic or modern mythological interpretations.

Interestingly enough, Plato went on to use this non-mythological principle to study the literary sources of ancient Greek theology – Homer and the classical dramatists, especially Aeschylus. When they were found to be inconsistent, or below the standard set by the Socratic tradition, they were criticized as corrupt and misleading. Eventually Plato got to the point where he wanted to drive poets out of his ideal Republic, because their myth-making could never be an adequate representation of reality (*i.e.* the basis of Christian theology). This was his reason for attacking *theologia* (= mythology), which makes him sound more like an orthodox Christian theologian than like a modern liberal![9]

Plato's objections to poetic mythology became part of the philosophical tradition named after him, but his successors did not create a rational theology to put in its place. Partly this was because pagan religion was too bound up with mythology to be easily separated from it, and partly it was because the practice of this religion was more or less devoid of the ethical content which was so central to Platonism. As a result, the Platonic tradition developed an ethical and aesthetic belief in the Supreme Good, without identifying this too closely with popular ideas of the gods, although we can detect a move in some quarters to make the Olympian Zeus the personification of the Good, and thereby identify him with the true God. In dealing with classical poetry, the Platonists developed the technique of allegory, which was a device used to get round the inconsistencies and immoral activities of the pagan gods. It is important to remember, however, that allegory was not used arbitrarily, as so many people today think. Its specific purpose was to reconcile theological difficulties, like the immoral behaviour of the gods, with a very specific picture of the divine. When it was

23

not needed it was not used, although the mythical character of the relevant literature meant that it occurred fairly frequently.[10]

We ought therefore to remember that modern attempts to connect theology with poetry and mythology are not an advance in understanding, but a retreat to a more primitive stage of culture, from which even Plato and his successors were struggling to be free. For a theologian to go back to it, even with the aid of the sophisticated jargon of modern anthropology, is an abdication of responsibility. It is better to rest in an uncomfortable, scientific agnosticism than to reconstruct theology in a way which was discredited even before the time of Christ.

What then should we make of theology as an academic discipline? It has certain affinities with the natural sciences and with philosophy, but it cannot be identified with either. It has borrowed words and ideas from, and occasionally loaned them to, other disciplines, but as we shall see, these words and ideas have been modified by the genius of the subject – not the other way round. Theology now is quite simply what it has always been: the study of God which presupposes, as a condition of its existence, that such an activity is both possible and meaningful. Those who disagree with that belief will see no need for the discipline; those who accept it will maintain that it is the most important study on which any human being can engage. At bottom, modern controversies about the subject are not questions of definition but questions of faith, for the heart of all theology is nothing less than to know God, and to make him known.

## The origin of Christian theology

When Christians want to explain the origin of their theological tradition, they do not look primarily to the ancient Greeks, who invented the word *theology*, but to the Israelites, who worshipped the God of whom Christian theology speaks – the God whom we have met and known in Jesus Christ. It is true that neither the Old nor the New Testament contains a systematic theology of the type which developed in later Christian tradition, and not a few scholars have interpreted that fact to mean that systematic theology is somehow a corruption of the biblical message. As we have already indicated, at one time the emphasis was put on the influence which Greek ideas had supposedly exerted on the first Christians, to make then turn away from their Hebraic roots. More recently, stress has been laid on the literary character of the Bible, which is supposed to be written largely in 'story' form, a feature which apparently makes it resistant to dogmatic systematization.[11]

As far as the Old Testament is concerned, the Christian theologian is preoccupied with two main problems. The first is whether the text as we have it presents a logically consistent picture of God, or whether there is a development of theological sophistication in different historical periods, with correspondingly different pictures of the divine. The second is whether the literary genre of the text makes logical systematization an inappropriate, if not an impossible, means of analysing its meaning.

To the first of these questions we may answer that the Christian theologian is committed to a belief in the theological unity of the Old Testament *because this is what Jesus assumed and what the New Testament writers taught.* This does not preclude the notion of a development in theological understanding from one age to another, but it does rule out any suggestion that the God of Abraham was a different being from the God of Moses or the God of Isaiah. Orthodox systematic theologians draw a firm distinction between the idea of a progressive development of revelation in the sense of a deepening relationship with God and a growing understanding of his ways (which they accept as a valid interpretation of biblical history), and the idea of a progressive development of revelation in the sense of a 'higher', 'purer', more morally elevated conception of God's being (which they reject because it gives the earlier stages of this development an inferior value in religious terms). The Old Testament must remain accessible to Christian theologians in all of its parts, although due regard must certainly be given to the context and literary style of each particular chapter and verse.[12]

As far as genre is concerned, the careful scholar must be

wary of claiming that the entire Old Testament is 'story'. Some of it quite clearly is not – the Proverbs, for example, or the Psalms. Then too, the conventions of Hebrew poetry must be given their due, as must poetic licence in other parts of the text. This is particularly important because it was a Hebrew habit to express emotions and feelings by referring to different parts of the body. This imagery is also applied to God in what are known as anthropomorphic figures of speech which, if taken literally, would produce a ridiculous and quite unbiblical picture of God.

At this level, the need to respect literary convention is obvious, but we must be careful not to falsify the text as a whole by calling it myth or drama, even if we agree with Hans Frei that biblical storytelling is 'realistic' in character.[13] The theological core of the Old Testament is not poetry but *law*, a category which is matter-of-fact and historical, without necessarily being rationally scientific. Law in the Old Testament serves to reveal the character of God, and the 'story' element is proof that he really does exist and is active in the life of his people. The distinction between realistic narrative and historical fact, which Frei and the proponents of the 'New Yale Theology' have suggested, goes against the inner logic of the text itself, which demands a correspondence between legal precept and historical fact (as in the reference to the Exodus at the beginning of the ten commandments) as proof that the God of Israel's claims are valid ones. Moreover, the pattern by which God reveals his character in historical events can be observed right through the historical and prophetic books. It may be less obvious in the Wisdom literature, which has a curiously 'secular' tone, and often seems to be more concerned with human behaviour than with the being of God; but it is equally true that it is in Wisdom writing that the narrative element linking God's self-revelation to historical fact is most wanting!

The point which we need to bear in mind is that the *acts* of God are always subordinate to his *character*, and are explained by it. It is not enough to say that the ancient Israelites gave a theological colouring to their national epic; they existed as a nation because God had bound them in covenant to himself. His character as a God of mercy and faithfulness was not only the explanation of what had happened to them in the past; it was also, and more importantly, the guarantee of what would be given to them *in the future*. In this important sense, the prophets of Israel were not historians but theologians, offering the people a knowledge of God and an insight into his ways which was designed to sustain them through the trials of the present, as well as those to come.[14]

When we turn to the New Testament we find that the main themes of the Old Testament recur, though in a rather different way. The 'story' element is now the gospel, though once again the narrative is subservient to the didactic purpose, which is closely tied to the law. Jesus came to teach his disciples a new way of reading the Old Testament, which went against the received wisdom of the Pharisees, but which claimed to be a faithful repetition of the beliefs of Abraham and Moses. Jesus claimed to fulfil the sacrificial demands of the Mosaic law and to break down the barriers which restricted the extent of the old covenant. His life, death and resurrection bore witness to the claims of his teaching, and sealed their validity in the eyes of his disciples.[15]

This understanding is brought out quite plainly in the epistles, which have often been treated as the most obviously theological part of the New Testament. It is quite clear from the letters of Paul, Peter and John, not to mention the Epistle to the Hebrews, that there is a body of Christian teaching which must be learned, and its implications understood. The difficulty is that the epistles do not generally give a systematic exposition of this teaching, although they frequently dwell on its implications, so that the task of the exegete, as much as of the theologian, is to reconstruct the underlying dogmatic framework. On closer inspection it turns out that the same is true of the gospels, where the narrative conceals – and at the same time reveals – a complex set of theological presuppositions which need to be elucidated and systematized if we are to understand the 'story'.

In short, Christian theology began as the exposition of Scripture, and developed its systematic character because of the nature of the God of whom it speaks. The unity of God, his self-consistency and his logical plan of self-disclosure have

27

all determined that Christianity should have a systematic theology, quite apart from any influence which Greek philosophical ideas may have had. That Christian systematic theology should have developed the complexity it now has is due to the belief that the God of the Old Testament became man in the person of Jesus Christ, and that now he dwells in our hearts in the person of the Holy Spirit. But how can God become human? How can he subsist in three persons, without ceasing to be one? These complex questions, which no philosophy can answer, form the twin poles of Christian theology. They have to be resolved if the message of the New Testament is to be credible. In short, a systematic, theological exposition of the Bible is imposed on us by the nature of its contents, which demand from us an intellectual effort equal to the task of explaining the logic which underlies and sustains our faith.

## Christianity and Platonic philosophy

If the principles which made the development of a Christian systematic theology inevitable are present in the New Testament, the process by which this was achieved is not. That belongs rather to the history of the church, which can be written very largely in terms of the theological controversies which divided it.

In the first few generations of the church's life the pattern established by the apostles continued to flourish more or less unchanged. The heart of Christian teaching was conveyed orally, with a growing emphasis on detailed instruction before baptism. When things went wrong, letters were despatched to the churches concerned, instructing them as to how to put their house in order. During this period the cultural diversity of the New Testament church lessened, with the eclipse of the Jewish Christians after the destruction of Jerusalem (AD 70). After about AD 100 there would have been hardly anyone in the church with a knowledge of Hebrew and of Judaism comparable to that possessed by the apostle Paul, and which he assumed to exist among a significant percentage of church members.

The loss of contact with Judaism had a considerable effect

on the church, in that converts from paganism no longer had the controlling influence of the Hebraic tradition to guide them in their interpretations of the Bible. Not everybody went as far as Marcion (d. *c.* 144), who denied the validity of the Old Testament revelation, and claimed that Yahweh was a God inferior to the Father of Jesus Christ. But large numbers of Christians were tempted to regard the Scriptures as a kind of puzzle, concealing the truth about God in a form of human language which only the initiated could decode.

By AD 150 a large number of quasi-philosophical systems of theology were circulating which purported to unlock the mysteries of the Bible and lead the initiated into a higher, spiritual knowledge (*gnōsis*). These systems played on words like 'mind' (*nous*), 'word' (*logos*) and 'fullness' (*plērōma*) and combined them in ways which had little or nothing to do with biblical teaching. The so-called 'gnostic' systems were invariably rejected by the church as a whole, but their existence pointed out the need for a systematic explanation of what the Bible was saying about God, creation, humankind and salvation.[16]

Church leaders took up the concept of *gnōsis* and sought to develop it in an authentically Christian way. A leading figure in this development was Clement of Alexandria (*fl. c.* AD 200), who relied for his inspiration on the work of Philo (d. *c.* AD 50), an Alexandrian Jew who had sought to harmonize the Old Testament with Platonic philosophy. To achieve his goals, Philo naturally had to resort to extensive use of allegory, because the Bible described God in ways which seemed to him to be incompatible with Plato's idea of 'the good'. References to God having 'a body, parts or passions' had to be explained away, as did a number of events which seemed to be immoral, or unworthy of the divine majesty.

Philo's allegorical exegesis is very similar to that which pagan Platonists applied to Homer, and it seems that by the time of Clement it was possible to put Homer and Moses in competition over against each other as authorities on the divine. In this conflict though, Moses was bound to win in the end, not merely because he was a more ancient

29

authority, but also because of the historical and legal character of the Pentateuch, which made it more like Plato than like epic poetry, *i.e.* more applicable to everyday life.

Signs that Moses was indeed gaining the upper hand begin to appear about AD 180. Sometime before that date, a pagan philosopher called Celsus wrote a refutation of Christianity which he called *True Reason* (*Alēthēs Logos*). His main argument was that Platonism could supply all the positive teaching of Christianity without the latter's materialistic, religious elements (*e.g.* blood sacrifice). According to him, Christianity was no more than a pseudo-philosophy masquerading as a way of salvation, and a confident Platonist had nothing to fear from it. Celsus' defence of his philosophy is interesting, not only because he realized the need for philosophers to do battle with their Christian challengers, but because he implicitly accepted the main teachings of Christianity, including its theology, and sought to demonstrate that a revamped Platonism could match it point for point. In other words, he tried to accommodate Platonism to Christianity, not the other way round.[17]

On the Christian side there was a certain amount of sympathy for the Greek philosophical tradition, though naturally not for the view-point of people like Celsus. Justin Martyr (*c.* AD 100–65) and Athenagoras of Athens (*fl. c.* 170–80) had both been prepared to recognize Socrates and Plato as forerunners of the Messiah among the pagans, and compared their writings to the Old Testament. But of course, they accepted Greek philosophy only as a *preparation for the gospel*, not as an end in itself, and it was at this point that conflict with the likes of Celsus was inevitable. Christians believed that the Platonic tradition had to be superseded by the New Testament just as Judaism had been, and this conviction remained central to their theology even when they later borrowed heavily from Greek philosophical sources.[18]

The next stage in the interaction between Christianity and Platonism is closely associated with the name of Origen (*c.* 185– *c.* 254). Origen not only refuted the work of Celsus, but responded to it by trying to establish working principles for the development of a biblical theology. He had inherited the allegorical tradition of Philo and Clement, but systematized it in a new way. He drew a careful distinction between the literal sense of Scripture and the spiritual sense, and tried to establish rules for deciding when the former must give way to the latter. Origen generally preferred the literal sense of the text, so long as it presented a consistent picture of God. Moreover, as far as he was concerned, the literal sense was sufficiently clear to provide the church with its basic doctrine of God. When the literal sense was obscure, meaningless or unworthy of God, as he believed it was in large parts of the Old Testament, it was necessary to resort to allegory to discover the spiritual meaning of the text. *But the doctrine of God revealed in the literal sense was the factor which controlled the use of allegory.* In other words, allegory was a device designed to make the obscure parts of Scripture harmonize with the passages whose meaning was clear – a principle of biblical interpretation which is still accepted today, even though the allegorical method has long since been abandoned in scholarly circles.[19]

Origen had been trained in Platonic philosophy and was much influenced by it, particularly in his understanding of the human soul. He also developed a doctrine of the Trinity which is very similar, both in conception and in vocabulary, to the theory of his younger contemporary Plotinus (c. 204–70). Plotinus is generally regarded as the founder of Neoplatonism, a philosophy which was to play a key role in the intellectual formation of the leading Christian theologians in the centuries when the classical creeds and theological definitions came into being. Ought we not therefore to conclude, as many have done, that Origen's work represents the beginnings of what was to become a Neoplatonic takeover of the church?[20]

This view was widely propagated in the nineteenth century, especially by the great Adolf von Harnack (1851–1930), and it has taken root in many wings of the church, both conservative and liberal. But it is a view which, at the scholarly level, has come under increasing attack in recent years, and we must now consider seriously whether or not it should be abandoned altogether.

The main points which have to be born in mind are these. First, Origen's theology was very influential until about AD 400, when it came under suspicion, largely because he believed in the transmigration of souls (re-incarnation). At first this condemnation did not stick, and there was a revival of interest in his thought in the early part of the sixth century. But after the Second Council of Constantinople in 553, his writings were once more condemned and his influence was gradually expunged from the mind of the church. What is so interesting from our point of view is that this happened just when the influence of Neoplatonic thought on Christianity was at its height, which suggests that Christians were more resistant to it than has traditionally been thought.

Second, it is certain that Plotinus was deeply influenced by Christianity in his youth, and it is possible that he was himself a Christian at some stage. In his reworking of the Platonic tradition it is at least likely that he was as much influenced by Christianity as Origen had been influenced by Plato, so that to picture the interaction between the two schools of thought as a one-way street is basically wrong.

Third, and most important, the pressure was on Platonism to adapt to the challenge of Christianity, not the other way round. We have already seen this in the case of Celsus, and what is true of him is *a fortiori* even more true of Plotinus. The fact that Plotinus does not mention Christianity by name must not fool us into thinking that he had no interest in it. His apparent lack of interest is certainly feigned, and when we examine his philosophy its obvious similarities to Christianity make it more than probable that he was making the modification of Platonism which was needed if it was to compete succcessfully against the new religion. In other words, classical Platonism was transformed by Christian ideas at least as much as the resulting Neoplatonism was later to influence Christian thought.

Another indication of this is the sudden reappearance of the word *theologia* in the sense to which we are now accustomed. It is true that there are one or two odd references to the term after Plato's time, in Aristotle and in Philodemus (first century BC) for example. But it was the rise of Christianity which brought the term into general use, among Platonists as well as among Christians. It was Origen who first made wide use of it, not least in his polemic against Celsus, and from that time on it recurs frequently. If the Platonic tradition is examined without reference to Christianity, the

32

reappearance of *theologia* after a gap of some six centuries seems very odd, as does the sudden interest in finding a solid philosophical foundation for it. The likelihood that Platonism would have moved in that direction spontaneously is not very great; certainly it did not happen until Christianity became a major threat to its continued existence. The balance of probability therefore is that Neoplatonic interest in theology is a direct (and characteristic) offshoot of its contact with Christianity.[21]

## Mystical theology

Of course it is true that if we look at the relationship between Neoplatonism and Christianity at a somewhat later stage, a different picture emerges. In the fourth and fifth centuries large numbers of pagan intellectuals became Christians, although others developed an increasingly bitter hostility to the new religion which did not disappear until after 529, when the ancient philosophical schools were closed. One result of this was that most of the leading theologians of the classical period of Christian dogmatic development had received a Neoplatonic education. Like their predecessors in the second century, they were inclined to regard their philosophy as a preparation for the gospel – an assumption which in the case of Neoplatonism was plausible, even if it was historically inaccurate. Certainly it is true that many individuals moved back and forth from one to the other without noticing any great difference between them, and there must have been many Christians whose faith was scarcely distinguishable from Neoplatonism, just as in the nineteenth century there were many churchgoers who identified Christianity with middle-class morality and Western civilization.[22]

That there was a certain symbiosis between Christianity and Neoplatonism is indisputable, but we must be very careful before we assume that the latter exercised a normative influence on the definition of Christian doctrine.[23] For it was at the highest reaches of theology that the conflict between the two systems was most acute, and it was at that level that the essential difference between them was most

33

clearly perceived. To put it bluntly, Neoplatonism thought of God as an abstract *thing*, an object which could be analysed in terms like goodness, beauty, oneness and so on. Christianity on the other hand, thought of God as a *person*, or rather as three persons, who could not be defined in abstract terms but with whom it was possible – and necessary for salvation – to have a personal relationship. In the language of the time, Neoplatonists called God *to on*, 'that which is', but Christians called him *ho ōn*, 'he who is', a subtle difference which on investigation turns out to have been an all-important distinction.

When Christian theologians began to examine the presuppositions of Neoplatonism they found that it was inadequate at two crucial points. First, its abstract picture of deity made an intellectual idol out of the supreme being, and actually blocked the way to an encounter with the living God. Second, the Neoplatonic system of contemplation was a rational construction of the human mind, a work of human beings which denied the fundamental biblical principle of revelation. Revelation was logical, in the sense that it held together as a systematic whole, but it was not rationalistic, because its basic principles could not be harmonized with any secular philosophical way of thinking.

God could be known only by meeting him personally, an experience which went beyond the boundaries of created existence, to which philosophy was inevitably limited. It was therefore wrong to say that the God of Jesus Christ was merely *ho ōn*, as if this were no more than a personalized version of *to on*. To avoid this equation, it was necessary to be more precise, and say that *ho ōn*, who revealed himself to Moses at the burning bush was not the equivalent of the Platonic *to on*. In Platonic terms God could be described only as *to mē on*, or non-being, because he far transcended even the highest conception of the unaided human mind. His sign was not the knowing mind of a philosopher, but the cloud of *un*knowing, which appeared at crucial moments in biblical history (*e.g.* the exodus, the transfiguration and the ascension) to remind us that in its depths, the divine reality was not accessible to human speculation.

The mystical theology which thus developed reached its classical expression in the writings of the unknown sixth-century monk who goes by the name of Dionysius the Areopagite (cf. Acts 17:24).[24] The Pseudo-Dionysius was deeply conversant with Neoplatonism, and it is often thought that he became a Christian in order to preserve this philosophical tradition after the closure of the pagan philosophical schools, by passing it off as the work of one of Paul's Athenian converts. This view, or something not too different from it, is now fairly standard in Western theological circles, although defenders of the mystical tradition, many of them Eastern Orthodox, tend to take a rather different view. Vladimir Lossky (1903–58) and Dumitru Staniloae (1903–), as well as the Roman Catholic theologian Hans Urs von Balthasar (1905–88) have argued that the Pseudo-Dionysius, far from copying the Neoplatonists, was trying rather to *correct* them, along the lines mentioned above.[25]

Furthermore, they argue that the full development of mystical, or 'apophatic' (negative) theology did not take place until much later, when its opposition to Neoplatonism was made far more explicit. Lossky points out that the Pseudo-Dionysius did not enter the mainstream of theological thought until his writings were interpreted by Maximus the Confessor (c. 580–662), who revamped the entire mystical tradition as it had developed since the time of Origen. Maximus, whose achievement is only now coming to be understood in the West, struggled against the anti-materialistic streak in Platonism, and sought to do justice to the created order as part of human spiritual experience.[26] Later this tendency was pushed even farther by John of Damascus (c. 675–749), Symeon the New Theologian (940–1022) and especially Gregory Palamas (1296–1359), all of whom rejected the dichotomy between body and soul/spirit which is so characteristic of the Platonic tradition.[27] More than that, they all affirmed that true theology was possible only when God disclosed himself in the sovereignty of his all-powerful and all-knowing grace – a theme which would also characterize the work of the great reformers.

## Christianity, Stoicism and Roman law

Platonic philosophy was not the only intellectual discipline to leave its mark on Christianity in the formative centuries of the classical theological tradition. Equally important was the influence of Roman law, which in many ways took the place of philosophy as the chief intellectual pursuit in the Latin (Western) half of the Roman Empire. It is well known that the Romans were a more pragmatic, practically-minded people than the Greeks, and that they generally avoided theoretical discussion for the sake of it. The Romans were attracted to certain types of Greek philosophy, but usually only to those which had a marked 'down-to-earth' quality about them.

At the time of Christ's birth, Roman intellectuals were divided between two types of materialism: that of Epicurus, and that of Zeno and the Stoics. At first Epicureanism had the upper hand, and the philosopher-poet Lucretius actually composed what might be called an anti-theology, an explanation of *The Nature of Things* (*De Rerum Natura*) which did not include divine intervention. Later on, though, Stoicism gained the upper hand, and from the time of Cicero (106–43 BC) to the time of Tertullian (*fl. c.* AD 196– *c.* 212) it was the most popular creed among educated Romans. The Stoics regarded Epicureanism as individualistic, hedonistic and irresponsible, whereas Stoicism was believed to offer an ethical way of life which could sustain a man of affairs and comfort him in both private and public misfortune.

For a long time it was believed that Stoicism had little influence on Christians who were supposedly more attracted to the non-material spirituality of Plato, but this belief has now been shown to be false.[28] Platonism did not gain much of a hearing in Christian circles until the end of the second century, whereas Stoicism was being actively considered long before. There is even a set of letters which purports to be the correspondence between Paul and the Stoic philosopher Seneca (3 BC – AD 65) which, although it is a forgery, is not as fantastic as one might suppose. Paul was in Rome and in touch with the imperial palace (*cf.* Phil. 4:22) at the time when Seneca was Nero's chief adviser, so it is not beyond the bounds of possibility that the two men could have met one another, especially if Paul was tried before Nero in about AD 62. Tertullian certainly believed that Seneca's philosophy was very near to Christianity in many places, and he himself found little difficulty in borrowing from the Stoics when the occasion offered itself.

One reason for this, apparent in Tertullian's writings, was that the materialism of Stoicism made it possible to hold body and soul/spirit together, whereas Platonism interpreted 'salvation' as the liberation of the soul from the body. Since Christians believed in the resurrection of the body, and not just in the salvation of the soul, Stoicism could appear to be more akin to the New Testament than was Platonism. Another reason was that Stoicism conceived of the deity as rational fire, a highly etherial substance out of which everything had come and to which everything would return. To a Stoic, the human soul was a spark of the divine fire, which shared the substance of God in lesser degree.

To the early Christians it must have seemed that this idea received a surprising amount of confirmation from Scripture. Did the New Testament not state quite clearly that our God was a consuming fire (Heb. 12:29)? Jeremiah had expressed his prophetic calling by God as the power of a fire within him (Je. 20:9), and it was as tongues of fire that the Holy Spirit descended on the apostles at the day of Pentecost (Acts 2:3). God had even appeared to Moses in a burning bush (Ex. 3:1–14) and Elijah had called on him to send down fire from heaven, to consume the sacrifice on Mount Carmel (1 Ki. 18:30–40).

In many ways, fire seemed to have properties analogous to those found in God. It was self-generating (or so it appeared), it was in constant motion without changing its character, and it was active in the material world without being assimilated by it. The chief source of fire was the sun, and there were even biblical passages which appeared to describe God in that way (cf., e.g., Mal. 4:2; 1 Tim. 6:16). It therefore became common to use the sun as an image of God, and to describe the Son and the Holy Spirit as rays which emanated from him.

Nevertheless, there were important reasons why fire and

the sun could not really be identified with God, and in the
end these prevailed. First, fire was finite, and God was infinite
– a fundamental opposition which no amount of argument
could overcome. Second, fire was worshipped in pagan
religions, from which Christians wished to distance themselves as much as possible. Third, fire was generally believed
to be one of the four elements (the others being earth, air and
water), whereas God was the Creator of everything material.
Gradually it came to be understood that fire was used in the
Bible as a metaphor for God's power to cleanse and purify
men from sin and idolatry, not as a description of his essence,
and thus theological thinking moved onto a higher, more
spiritual plane.

By about AD 200 Stoicism was waning as a philosophy, but
it did not die without leaving its mark on the development of
Roman law. Stoic materialism appealed to the Roman sense
of practicality, and it was thanks to this that much of its
vocabulary entered Roman legal usage. This is particularly
true of the word *substantia*, which passed from Roman law
into theology in the writings of Tertullian. *Substantia* was a
translation of the Greek *hypostasis*, but was used in Latin only
in the Stoic sense of a corporeal reality. When Tertullian
applied it in his theology, he was obliged to say that God was a
single *substantia*, because he was only one thing. This was in
direct contrast with the Platonic use of the term *hypostasis*,
which normally meant the form in which the thing (*ousia*,
essence) was manifested. Origen could therefore say that in
God there were three *hypostases* in one *ousia*, and this language subsequently became traditional in Eastern thought.[29]

To describe the threeness in God, Tertullian used another
legal term, *persona*, which had never been used in philosophical discourse at all. *Persona* came from the theatre, where it
meant *mask*, or later *character* (*cf.* Shakespeare's *dramatis per-
sonae*). Cicero used it to mean a particular individual,
especially one who was involved in a legal transaction, and
from there it passed into general legal usage. When Tertullian borrowed the term for theology, he did so because he
realized that there was a close connection between biblical
and Roman ways of thinking. The Bible warned Christians
off philosophy, but reminded them that God was a God of

law. In the Old Testament he had given this law to Israel, but its provisions were adapted to the limits and limitations of a single nation. In the New Testament the law was fulfilled and re-established on a new basis, that of the gospel, which Tertullian called the *nova lex*.

In the gospel the principles of Israel's law were vindicated, but the dispensation under which it was administered changed with the coming of Christ and the sending of the Holy Spirit. What had previously been external and oppressive now became internal and regenerative, without altering the basically legal framework of the covenant. On the side of God there were three parties to the covenant, the Father, the Son and the Holy Spirit, each of whom played his own particular role (note the theatrical imagery) in its fulfilment. On the side of human beings were innumerable individuals, joined to God by personal relationship as parties to his covenant.

This legal imagery is fundamental to our understanding, not only of the term *persona* but of the whole development of Western theology. What, after all, is justification by faith, if not the (legal) declaration of God's forgiveness and restoration of the sinner? What is the meaning of sonship by adoption into Christ, if the legal background is discounted? Tertullian was a Roman who knew no Hebrew, but he had a clear understanding of the fundamental biblical concept of law, which has influenced the development of Western theology ever since.

The impact of Roman law on Western theology was much more far-reaching than the loan of a few words might suggest. Roman law was basically pragmatic, concerned with regulating and controlling the use of power, which has its ultimate source in God. Theology therefore came to be understood as the dispensation of divine power: in the work of the persons of the Trinity, in the structure of the church, in the means of grace. This emphasis can still be seen in the controversies which continue to divide the Western churches today. Almost without exception, they concern such matters as the existence and role of the ordained clergy, the authority of written documents and the validity of the sacraments – questions posed in legal terms about matters of authority and jurisdiction, which we regard as being of crucial importance for our access to the grace of God.

Today it has become fashionable to attack this tradition, both because it is supposed to be 'unbiblical' and because it tends to ignore the claims of mystical, contemplative thought. But although it has its weaknesses, the Western tradition has a fair claim to be closer to the meaning of the Bible than its most readily available alternative.[30] Rather than reject it, it is better to accept it in principle and seek to supplement its weaknesses by constant reference to the Word of God, remembering that it was precisely when discussing a deep point of theology that the apostle Paul was constrained to remark that: 'Now we see but a poor reflection . . .; then we shall see face to face. Now I know in part; then I shall know fully, even as I am fully known' (1 Cor. 13:12).

## The emergence of classical Western theism

We have seen above that by the third century AD the Christian church was developing two distinct theological traditions; one which was basically philosophical and engaged mainly with Platonism, and one which was fundamentally legal. To a great extent these traditions became typical of the Greek- and Latin-speaking worlds respectively, although each part of the Roman Empire felt the influence of the other. Neoplatonism, for example, entered Western theology in the writings of Marius Victorinus (fourth century) and it also influenced Augustine of Hippo (354–430), although to what extent is a matter of continuing scholarly debate.[31]

The Neoplatonism which made a lasting impression on the Latin mind, however, was not that of Plotinus. Rather, it was the thought of his fiercely anti-Christian disciple Porphyry (c. 232 – c. 303) which left its mark. Porphyry's views were not at all the same as those of his master, as we shall see. For the moment, it is enough to bear in mind that Porphyry's Neoplatonism was influential among Christians largely because it corresponded to ideas which were already current in the tradition inherited from Tertullian, so that Latin Christians felt that there was some affinity between his thought and theirs. On the other hand, nobody could fail to notice Porphyry's hostility to Christianity, and this was always a major factor in Christian assessment of him. Augustine was particularly hostile to him because of this, so that we must be careful not to assign to Porphyry too great a role in the formation of Augustinian thought.

For many centuries after the time of Augustine there was little further development of theology at the level of basic principle. Eastern Neoplatonism made a brief intrusion in the work of John Scotus Eriugena (d. *c.* 877), but on the whole, Augustine remained the model until the twelfth century. The main interest of Western theologians during this period was concentrated on the need to evangelize the pagan peoples of Northern Europe, by giving them a solid grounding in the basic principles of Judaeo-Christian theism. The Germanic tribes were particularly impressed by manifestations of power, and this, combined with an attachment to magical practices, determined the approach which Christian theologians were obliged to take.[32]

At first Germanic religion was christianized in a superficial way, particularly at the popular level, where magical ideas were never far from most worshippers' imagination. But as far as serious theology was concerned, paganism of this kind had to be answered by a deeper penetration into the nature of God as this was revealed in the Bible. A great scholar like Alcuin of York (730–804) was forced to consider what omnipotence, immortality, impassibility and omniscience might mean, as attributes of God, and to apply them to the practical needs of everyday religious life. In many ways he was covering the same ground as John of Damascus, whose teaching we shall be examining in some detail later, but he had a very different end in view. John's purpose was essentially apophatic, concerned to point the believer away from created realities to the experience of the uncreated being of God. Alcuin's aim was to deflect a crude theology away from magical tendencies, whilst preserving a strong emphasis on the reality of divine power at work in the world.

The difference of approach reflected in these two theologians was later to become a subject of controversy and division in the long debate about the double procession of the

Holy Spirit. But this issue, which was of central importance in Eastern theology, tended to remain on the periphery of Western concerns. It troubled Anselm of Canterbury (c. 1033–1109), but only because others had problems in accepting it. His own theological purpose was merely to provide a rational explanation for points of difficulty or confusion in Christian doctrine. His belief, that every theological question could find an answer compatible with reason, continued to exert its influence on succeeding generations, even though they increasingly lacked his serene confidence that the answer lay in a faith which went in search of understanding (*fides quaerens intellectum*).[33]

The later twelfth century was a time when the church was outwardly triumphant but inwardly torn by doubts and questions which confronted its understanding of the faith. The reappearance of Aristotelian philosophy was particularly unsettling because it challenged the structure of authority on which the mediaeval church was built. Aristotelianism had appeared on the theological scene before, in the school of Antioch, which had flourished from about 300 to 484, when its surviving professors had been expelled to Persia. It had produced the arch-heretic Arius, and then Nestorius, whose views were finally condemned at the Council of Chalcedon in 451. Its main thrust had been to emphasize the humanity of Christ and to question whether God could really become man, an approach which later commended itself to Muslims, and helps to account for the popularity of Aristotle in mediaeval Islam.

As a philosophy, Aristotelianism was rooted in the concept of a rational order which could be analysed by the human mind. It was not an atheistic philosophy, in that it recognized the need for a first cause, a prime mover of the universe, but its method did not sit well with belief in a revealed authority by which God played an active part in the affairs of human beings. When, as in Islam, there was no question of God merging with humanity, and no expectation beyond submission to the laws of the universe, Aristotelianism could take hold quite easily, in spite of the revealedness of the Qur'ān. But when God and humans were expected to live together in partnership, Aristotelianism could not readily cope with the transcendent quality of the divine, which naturally claimed authority over the secular realm. In this failure of minds to meet lay the roots of what was to become the conflict between faith and reason, between religion and science.

The classical response to Aristotelianism was worked out by Thomas Aquinas (1226–74) and his disciples in a system which is called Thomism, or (more accurately) Scholasticism, because it became the teaching of the great mediaeval schools which even then were developing into our modern universities. Thomas revolutionized theology by accepting the scientific method of Aristotelianism and claiming that it was the right way to explore the realm of nature. But Thomas argued that there was another order of reality which Aristotle could not explain – the realm of grace. Grace could be understood only by revelation, which was mediated through the church and its sacraments. According to Thomas it did not contradict or destroy nature; rather, grace perfected it.[34]

In order to achieve this harmony there had to be a real correspondence between the earthly and heavenly realities. This correspondence was achieved by the principle of analogy, which stated that heavenly things could be described in terms usually reserved for natural phenomena, on the understanding that the terms had to be defined within the context of the spiritual order. This sounds complicated, but an example will show how simple and apparently logical it is. In God there is a Father–Son relationship, the essence of which we can understand by comparing it with what we see in human families. The analogy, however, is not perfect. Not only is there no mother in God (although some theologians have tried to find a female principle in the Holy Spirit) but the details of the relationship do not correspond with that of any given human situation. This Thomas accepted, but he explained it by appealing to the legitimate difference between the spiritual and the material worlds, which corresponds to the difference between analogy and identity of being.

Following this principle, Thomas accepted that God was a substance, analogous to other substances, and that like them he had properties (*i.e.* attributes or characteristics). God was not non-being but the supreme being, who was also an active power. Thomas apparently equated God with Aristotle's 'unmoved mover', *i.e.* a being who set other things in motion without moving himself, which explains why modern critics have been so ready to attack the classical forms of theism on the ground that they support belief in a 'static' deity. Quite apart from the modern argument that the God of the Bible is 'dynamic' (whatever that is supposed to mean in this context), it appears to be a logical contradiction to say that a perfectly static being can perform any action at all, since even initiating motion in other beings would appear to require some form of movement.

Classical theism, as it was elaborated by Thomas, tries to maintain that the existence of God can be proved by arguments drawn from the physical universe. These arguments are a logical extension of the principle of analogy on which his theological system is based, and they are used by Thomists to show that this world is not self-sufficient, but points from within its own structure to the existence of a higher reality. The existence of beings, some of which are clearly 'higher' (*i.e.* more complex and powerful) than others, is held to point to the logical necessity of a highest being, embracing the essential traits of all the others. The phenomenon of cause and effect implies that somewhere there must be a 'first cause', which set the rest in motion, and so on. Whether these arguments are really convincing is nowadays a very open question. It is generally agreed that no single one can be regarded as conclusive, but although some theists are prepared to abandon the whole system as untenable, others are convinced that it can be preserved, either with modifications in the arguments or with a frank acceptance that although no one 'proof' can be regarded, as conclusive, the cumulative weight of all the 'proofs' taken together adds up to a convincing degree of probability.

This is the line being taken more and more by philosophers who have expounded, or in some cases turned to, classical theism as the most plausible form of belief today. It is characteristic of the theology of Richard Swinburne, whose Wilde Lectures, delivered at Oxford in 1976–77, have since been written up as a full-length study on *The Existence of God*.[35] It has also been followed, though to a lesser extent, by

Keith Ward and by Huw Parri Owen, both of whom have written very able defences of Christian theism in recent years.[36]

Among those who reject classical theism, mention must be made of Charles Hartshorne (1897— ) who has adapted the philosophy of Alfred North Whitehead (1861–1947) into a system known as 'process theology'.[37] This is a term which can be used somewhat loosely to describe a wide range of theological constructions which emphasize happening, becoming and relating, instead of the classical concept of substance, but in the narrower sense it applies especially to the school of thought inspired by Whitehead. This believes that God's being is dipolar. At one pole God is a loving reality who is absolute, necessary and immutable. But at the other pole is God's need for involvement in the changing states of humanity; a constant, unchanging love must continually be adapting itself to the changing circumstances of the cosmic evolutionary process.

In this way the classical 'dipolarity' of person and essence in God has been transmuted into one of constant and changing, each of which is perceived as an act within time, and God, who can be found in every observable reality, is the supreme example of every metaphysical principle which the human mind can devise.

## Protestantism and classical theism

The defenders of process theology argue that its emphasis on a dynamic God of love makes it a philosophical system which is particularly congenial to a Bible-based Protestantism. Their main line of defence seems to be that the Bible presents us with a functional God whose dynamic love is more important than any of the divine attributes which classical theism has tried so hard to define. But although there is undoubtedly some truth in this assertion, on balance it must be regarded as superficial. Protestant theologians may differ from Thomists on many points of detail and of method, but at the end of the day they have usually felt obliged to defend something very like classical theism. The reason for this is not far to seek. However we may conceive of the being of God, in the last analysis what he is capable of doing must logically depend on who and what he is. Because Christians claim that God is the ultimate origin of all things, his being must have an absolute character which cannot be relativized in association with other, lesser beings. Similarly, as the Creator, God's being must exhibit a perfection in itself, independent of whatever he has created. It is therefore more profitable for us to ask how and why the Reformers modified their Scholastic inheritance, rather than to claim for them an outlook which they would not have recognized.[38]

The Protestant Reformers were educated in pre-Thomist Scholasticism as it had been packaged for general consumption, *e.g.* in the *Sentences* of Peter Lombard (*c.* 1095–1160), and as it had been reworked by increasingly humanist and rationalist thinkers up to the fifteenth century. They made less use of Aquinas and the great Scholastics of the thirteenth century, who were out of fashion in their time, although it is unlikely that they would have found the Thomist system any more congenial than its somewhat simplified substitutes. Admittedly, they did not deny that God was a substance with attributes, but they relegated this aspect of his being to the background. Instead, they emphasized that God could be known only in and through his persons, each of whom fully reveals the others. Knowledge of the persons could not be had by speculation, but only by faith, a divine gift which operated exclusively in the context of revelation.

Revelation, so the Reformers believed, had been given to human beings in the Bible and in Jesus Christ, both being called the Word of God. Christ and the Scriptures could not be separated from each other, since the latter bore witness to the former, but the link between them could not be understood apart from the inner witness of the Holy Spirit. This witness was not a power which made itself felt, but a voice which called people to repentance and conversion. The personal dimension of revelation was all important to the Reformers. It ensured that the link between God and humanity would take the form of verbal confrontation, not analogy of being, or reception of power. Within the verbal encounter the Christian would come to a living awareness of both God's being and his power, but this was the *fruit* of the

46

relationship, not its cause or even it content. For the Reformers, true *theologia* could be only a theology of the Word (*logos*) by which God entered into a covenant fellowship with his people.

In saying this the Reformers were transforming the traditional theology of the church, even though they perhaps were not fully aware of it at the time. They preserved the classical structure of theistic doctrine more or less intact, but the shift of perspective which they expounded within the established framework was so great that it produced a radically different theology. The classical tradition had worked out a doctrine of God who was one nature in three persons (or vice versa). In general, the ancient and mediaeval outlook put the weight of emphasis on the nature of God, and regarded the persons as somehow secondary to it. It is true that the mystical tradition dissented from this to some extent and put a strong emphasis on the persons, but it did so in a way which tended to discount the biblical revelation. The main reason for this is that the mystics were usually concerned to emphasize the complete otherness of the divine nature, and the persons of the Trinity tended, as a result, to become modes of access to that nature, indeed almost intermediaries between it and us. For this reason, the mystical tradition is really just as nature-based as the Scholastic, in spite of appearances to the contrary.

It is nevertheless clear that the Reformers had strong links with mystical influences, and that their theology could not have come into existence without them. Like the mystics, they were concerned to emphasize the need for a personal experience of God; the difference was that they believed that this experience was a form of spiritual rapture which, far from leading to a denial or abandonment of the world, impelled them towards a deeper involvement in it. This change was possible because the Reformers did not believe that a personal relationship with God entailed an assumption in some way of a divine nature. The deepest meaning of the famous statement by Martin Luther (1483–1546) that he was a justified sinner (*simul iustus et peccator*) is that he could enter into fellowship with God as a person, without losing or changing his nature. The link between person and nature, which had wrongly been thought to entail the dependence of the former on the latter, was now quite clearly reversed. A process which had begun at the Council of Chalcedon in 451 was now at last given practical application to the spiritual life of the individual believer.

Luther's great discovery was revolutionary in its impact, but in the nature of things it could not simply stand still. To retain its power, it required a system, and this was provided by Luther's disciple, Philip Melanchthon (1497–1560). Melanchthon was trained in Scholasticism to a greater degree than Luther was and, much to the latter's distress, he moved his master's teaching firmly in that direction. The principle of justification by faith alone retained its central importance, but faith acquired an objective and legalistic significance which it did not have for Luther. The centrality of the relationship with God gave way to a more formal assent to doctrines, and eventually to a confessional system which matched Roman Catholicism point for point.[39]

Luther's original vision was captured by John Calvin (1509–64), who sought to provide a different system for it than the one worked out by Melanchthon. Calvin determined to provide the church with a doctrinal foundation which would serve primarily as a hermeneutical key to the reading of Scripture, and thus to the encounter with God by faith. He explained Luther's teaching both in relation to mediaeval theism and in connection with the tradition of the early church. He was especially fond of quoting Augustine, but many of his statements clearly reflect the outlook and concerns of the Greek Fathers as well. Here there is something of a mystery which defies attempts to resolve it. That Calvin knew the writings of the Cappadocian Fathers is beyond doubt, but that he should have had such a close affinity with them, whilst apparently clinging to the Augustinian tradition, is something of a puzzle.

Partly, no doubt, it reflects the fact that Augustine himself was closer to the Cappadocians than many of his later followers were, but this cannot be the whole story. Recent research has started to uncover possible points of contact between Calvin and the East, by pointing out the availability of certain of the great Eastern Fathers' writings to him, and the occasional use of things like Chrysostom's homiletic techniques by him and his followers.[40] As a result, the existence of an affinity between two apparently quite dissimilar traditions has come to be accepted in the scholarly world, though its true causes remain obscure. It may simply be that Calvin found 'Eastern' ideas in the Bible itself, or that his reaction to Scholasticism was bound to push him in what looks to us like an Eastern direction. On the other hand, he may have had – and made use of – Greek sources to a degree which is as yet undetermined. It is possible that future scholarship will explain what precisely the links are; for the moment, it is sufficient to recognize that they are there, and that they represent an important bridge between Eastern and Western ways of thinking.

Calvin's achievement was very great, but like Luther's, it was scholasticized in the next generation. The relationship between Calvin and the Calvinists who later dominated the Synod of Dort (1618–19) and composed the Westminster Confession of Faith (1647) is a subject of intense research and controversy, with strong views held on both sides.[41] Some believe that the Puritans betrayed the substance of true Calvinism; others insist that they did no more than systematize Calvin's thinking, although, of course, Calvin was already a systematic theologian in his own right. The truth probably lies somewhere between these two extremes, but there is no doubt at all that by the end of the seventeenth century Puritanism had run out of steam, leaving behind a rationalism which quickly led to a widespread abandonment of trinitarian belief.

The deism which flourished in the eighteenth century can be traced to a number of sources in addition to scholasticized Calvinism, including the revival of Platonism in the mid-seventeenth century, and the excesses of the more extreme spiritualists, whose confidence in the 'inner light' soon led them to trust their own judgment more than the teaching of Scripture.[42] In its early form, deism was closely linked to the natural sciences, especially to mathematics, and was rather like Thomism without revelation. Indeed, the phrase 'natural religion' became popular, and continued to be used by many so-called 'liberals' until the twentieth century.

49

Deism, however, eventually gave way to a theology rooted more in human affections than in pure rationalism. This was the achievement of Pietism, which was integrated into academic theology by Friedrich Schleiermacher (1768–1834), who is generally reckoned to have been the founder of classical liberalism. Schleiermacher had little time for classical dogmatics, and reinterpreted trinitarian theism in a way which we would call psychological, interpreting dogma in terms of religious experience. He argued that the emotional side of human nature could not be explained in the logical terms of an exact science; this was the domain of theology, which now became 'modern' in the sense in which this term is generally used today.

Schleiermacher's synthesis has been deeply influential in Protestant circles, and in recent years it has spread to Roman Catholicism as well (although modernism flourished briefly in the Roman Church at the turn of the century). As a result many modern analyses of theology begin with his work as the starting-point of a new intellectual era.[43] As Karl Barth (1886–1968) pointed out, the deepest cleavage in Protestantism today is between those who accept Schleiermacher's synthesis, at least in principle, and those who reject it in favour of the classical theological tradition. Barth himself belonged to the latter group, and was largely responsible for the greatest restatement of Protestant orthodoxy in the twentieth century.[44]

It is true that in comparison with theologians of an earlier age, Barth is disconcertingly vague about such key concepts as revelation and the Word of God. These are central to his theological system, but he never defines them in a clear and unambiguous way. He also casts doubt on some classical theological terms like 'person', which he wants to replace with the rather suspect phrase 'mode of being'. But in spite of these difficulties, Barth has done more than any twentieth-century theologian to resurrect what appeared to be the moribund orthodox tradition, and which is once more a serious contender for the leading place in academic theology.

Barth's followers, whether 'conservative' or 'liberal' are noted for their concern to make traditional theology living and relevant for today's church. Whether they will succeed in the long term remains to be seen, but what is quite certain is that the theological developments of the future will bear a greater resemblance to those of the classical past than might at one time have been thought possible.

## Summary

The following points will help us to summarize what we have said so far.

1. Christian theology is the systematic exposition of a knowledge of God based on personal encounter with him in and through his revelation of himself to us. It may be possible to supplement this revelation by independent observation, but the controlling factor in any analysis of God and his works can be only his own self-disclosure.

2. For practical purposes, God's self-revelation is found in the Bible, which speaks supremely of the person and work of Jesus Christ, the Word of God incarnate. If something is not corroborated by the Bible, or is contradictory to it, it cannot be regarded as a true statement about God. This does not mean that everything in the Bible is easy to understand, nor does it imply that everything the Bible says is necessarily a direct disclosure of God. What it means is that extraneous material must not be added to the biblical witness in a way that would distort it.

3. Historically speaking, Christian theology has developed in the context of ancient Greek philosophy and Roman law. These influences have produced traditions of thought which have been used to explain the teaching of the Bible. From them two different (though often complementary) traditions have emerged, each with its own strengths and weaknesses. Christians are constantly attempting to mould them by applying biblical standards and insights to their theological constructions. These traditions do not possess the authority of the Bible, but it is now impossible to speak about God without employing the terminology which they have contributed. Attempts which have been made to get away from them altogether have so far proved to be unsuccessful, and have

usually resulted in a type of theology which is regressive in that it represents a lower, rather than a higher level of development.

4. Systematic Christian theology is constantly renewing itself by a process of self-criticism which is rooted in spiritual experience. All Christians accept that intellectual formulations are not enough, and that our knowledge of God remains fundamentally mysterious. But at the same time, Christians recognize that this knowledge is a shared mystery; God does not reveal himself to one person in a way which is incompatible with his self-disclosure to others. What cannot be explained can nevertheless be understood by personal experience.

# 2

## THE NATURE OF GOD

## The two aspects of theology

The Christian doctrine of God contains two distinct, though obviously related, aspects. The first of these is concerned to answer the question: what is God like? The second answers the question: who is God? To put it a different way, the first aspect deals with God's *nature*. At this level, it is generally recognized that God is one Being, totally different in every way from anything he has created. It is therefore a study in contrasts, which has to overcome the problem of finding a way to describe a being who is literally indescribable, because his nature surpasses anything of which we have direct experience.

The second aspect concentrates on his personal identity. In sharp distinction from the first, it insists that God is not one person but three. It also emphasizes the fact that although God's nature is so different from ours, he nevertheless can, and wants, to enter into a relationship with us. This is made possible by what we call 'personhood', which is a characteristic of God that he has shared with us.

The present chapter is concerned with the first of these aspects. It asks what it means to call God a 'being', and discusses how we can claim to know and describe something which is completely different from us. It then goes on to look at the so-called 'proofs' for the existence of God. Most of these were devised by theologians as a means of demonstrating that Christian belief is rational and in tune with other branches of science. They have been frequently criticized, but their value as supporting evidence, if not as 'proofs' for God's existence, should not be underestimated.

The chapter then goes on to discuss the validity of analogy, a device which involves using one word to mean something else in a different context, but which preserves an essential conceptual link with its original point of reference. From there, it looks at the meaning of the different attributes (characteristics) of God, all of which are basically analogies, before considering the challenges to this way of thinking which have been presented by modern theologians. The chapter concludes with a brief summary of what we can learn from this so-called 'natural' theology, and reviews the reasons why it is inadequate as a statement of the Christian doctrine of God.

## God as a being

Nowadays, if someone asks what God is like, we usually begin by saying that he is a being who possesses certain definite attributes like goodness, holiness, righteousness and so on. We may think that God is not the only being who has these characteristics, but a Christian is bound to say that God possesses them in greater measure (quantity) and to a higher degree (quality) than any other being. In fact God's qualities are all by definition absolutely perfect, so that no higher form of any of them can be imagined. The belief that God is a being with an objective existence which can be clearly distinguished from that of other beings is deeply rooted in our minds, to a large extent as the result of centuries of Christian culture. It seems so obvious to us, that we are surprised and ill-equipped when we meet religions and philosophies which do not share this fundamental assumption.

On the one hand, there are systems of belief which maintain that *only* God has being (*ousia*), that everything else is a corrupt or an illusory emanation from the 'one which is'. Views of this kind may be found in Platonism and in Buddhism, although the latter, like certain types of Neoplatonic and Christian mysticism, tends to want to break the barriers of being entirely and find fulfilment in a higher reality, which can be described only as 'non-being'. Mainstream Christianity has rejected this way of thinking, and granted to the created world the status of real being. At the same time it has also argued that God is the absolute being, completely different from any creature because he is absolute, but linked to his creation, because as a being he is related in some way to other beings. On the other hand, Christians have also had to confront systems of thought which do not make any distinction between God and creation at the level of being. Hinduism, and certain types of Western philosophy, believe that all reality, both material and spiritual, belongs to a single order of being, which is in some sense divine. In a religion like Hinduism, it may be expressed in precisely this way, so that what results is a definite kind of pantheism. In the more secularized West, similar ideas usually adopt a more abstract terminology, preferring 'cosmic force' or 'energy' to 'God', but the effect is the same, and process theology has recently attempted to reconstruct Christianity along these lines.

Process theology identifies God with the life-force which keeps the universe in being, although it generally avoids merging this completely with the real universe as we experience it. The result is a dipolarity in which God's objective existence is forever engaging with the actual forms of the world *within* a single time and space framework. Charles Hartshorne (1897– ) has called this *panentheism* ('everything in God') to emphasize both the universal extent of this inter-action and the ultimate distinction which must be maintained between the permanent reality of God and the transient forms of life as we see it.[1]

Few Christians have any doubts about how their religion differs from pantheism, but the status of process theology is more controversial. This is largely because it has been developed along Western lines by thinkers who are professing

55

Christians, which makes it possible to argue that process theology is just another philosophical expression of a common faith. In defence of this position it can be said that the differences between dipolar panentheism and monistic pantheism can be explained by the awareness which process theologians have of the Christian theological tradition, and their reluctance to deny it completely. But at the same time there is no doubt that its main exponents have wanted to break with the basic tenets of classical theism. The debate therefore, is whether process theology offers a picture of God which is more faithful to the biblical source of Christian witness than classical theism is. In other words, does the Bible draw as firm a line between God and the created order as the one which has been generally drawn by most theologians since ancient times?

Process theologians are well aware that Christian theology shares its vocabulary of being (*ousia, physis*) with Platonic philosophy, with which it was very closely linked at the most crucial period of its classical development. They also know that in Platonism the absolute being is static, since part of its perfection is the freedom to dwell in uninterrupted tranquillity (*hēsychia*) without any danger that this might be disturbed. Furthermore, it is clear that many of these ideas were incorporated into Christianity, particularly the belief that God is free from suffering, or impassible (*apathēs*), and that they appear to be unbiblical in certain respects. When we add to this the modern liberal belief that Christian dogmatics is little more than a (corrupt) Hellenization of the pure, nondogmatic gospel, it would appear that process theologians have a stronger case than initial comparisons with oriental pantheism might suggest.

When we turn to the Bible itself, the evidence of the Old Testament appears to advance the case of process theology even farther. There we discover that the being of God, in so far as it is described at all, is explained in terms of his acts and, more particularly, of his power. God is omnipresent because he can act anywhere; he is absolute, because there is no power greater than his. Moreover, God's activity is not remote, or something which was completed after the six days of creation. On the contrary, he appears to be at work in the forces of nature as much as in the lives of human beings, sustaining the universe by the power of his Word. To the Israelites, this sense of God's presence was so great that they continued to speak of him in semi-human terms, despite the fact that they condemned every form of idolatry. Thus we find the Old Testament constantly referring to the hand of God, the eye of God, the right arm of God, and so on.

Volumes have been written about these anthropomorphisms.[2] Many scholars interpret them as elements of an earlier, cruder paganism, which the Israelites were slow to abandon completely. Some would even say that the more cerebral, or spiritual picture of God, familiar to us, began to dominate Jewish thinking only from the time of the Greek invasions (fourth century BC), and that the parts of the Old Testament which reflect this outlook most clearly may be assigned to the Hellenistic period – i.e. to a time after the traditional date for the closure of the Hebrew canon. If such views today represent the majority opinion, one of the main reasons is that they have been accepted without proper investigation. Nobody doubts, for instance, that opposition to idolatry was an important feature of Israelite religion, not least because of the dangers that surrounding religions presented. Equally, nobody doubts that anthropomorphisms frequently occur in poetry of a very high spiritual order, particularly in the Psalms, or that the functions they describe (e.g. vision, knowledge, action) are fundamental to the Israelite understanding of God. Is it not preferable, therefore, to regard the anthropomorphisms of the Old Testament as a form of poetic licence, designed to protect the important belief that God was really present among his people?[3] And does not process theology, with its stress on the energetic activity of God within a continuum which includes both his being and the universe, offer us an ideal explanation of this phenomenon in modern language?

As far as the first of these questions is concerned, there is little doubt that it gives us a solution to the problem of Old Testament anthropomorphisms which is preferable to the standard view of liberal scholarship, not only because it can be harmonized better with later orthodoxy (which, after all, emerged from earlier tradition) but also because it fits in better with the witness of the texts themselves, and avoids the inconsistency which the liberal theory introduces.

But whether one can then go on to say that divine ontology in the Old Testament is presented chiefly in terms of power, and is therefore closer to process theology than it is to classical theism, is a very different question. The orthodox answer to it is that God has always been understood in terms of power and activity; Christians have never thought of him as a 'static' being. In borrowing the language of eternity and impassibility from Platonism, Christianity did not borrow the Platonic concepts as well, but used the vocabulary within its own conceptual framework. The ancients were quick to spot theologians who did not make this basic switch. We are less sensitive, partly because we have tended to put words before ideas, and partly because we have inherited a revived Platonism whose main exponents have usually been hostile to Christianity, and disposed to regard it much as Julian the Apostate (340–63) did – as a grotesque perversion of philosophical ideals. In protesting against this caricature, however, orthodox theologians are also concerned to point out that God's activity does not simply extend, or spill over, into the created universe. In his own being, God remains wholly other – completely different from his creation, whatever analogies might be drawn between it and him. It is at this point that classical theism parts company with process theology, which now begins to appear more like pantheism than like Christianity, whatever its defenders might argue to the contrary.

A more subtle and delicate problem than that of process theology is the theory propounded by Eberhard Jüngel (1934– ), who says that God's being is in 'becoming'. Jüngel does not follow process theology in linking this idea to the creation, but he does regard it as fundamental to our understanding of God as he is in himself – an understanding which, by implication, goes against the main tenets of classical theism.[4]

To understand Jüngel's argument it is necessary to look at the biblical evidence and the way in which it has been expounded by the orthodox tradition. To some extent, the idea that being must be equated with becoming may be traced back to the name of Yahweh itself. If we accept the etymology given in Exodus 3:14 (which retains its significance for Israelite religion, even if it can be shown to be inaccurate in purely linguistic terms), the covenant name of God derives from the imperfective form of *hayah*, to be. This may suggest the idea of uncompleted being, *i.e.* becoming, although it is doubtful to what extent this argument can really be pressed along purely linguistic lines, since the same form must also be used for completed being which has not ceased to exist.

More significant than this is the way in which God's activity has been understood in subsequent tradition. It has always been accepted that Yahweh is a living God, whose being must reflect that fact. Life is generally thought to require motion, though what this might mean in the case of an omnipresent being is not altogether clear. Obviously God cannot be regarded as displacing himself in a way which is analogous to human movement; his motion must therefore be internal. This was actually stated by the fourth-century theologian, Marius Victorinus, who argued that in God being (*esse*) = motion (*moveri*), thereby locating actual movement within the divine being.[5] This movement fulfilled itself in the generation of the Son and in the procession of the Holy Spirit, which is also where Jüngel locates it. But whereas Marius regarded these movements as completed in the perfection of the divine eternity, Jüngel sees them as continuing parts of the everlasting life of God.

A second factor which has contributed to our understanding of divine movement is the distinction between *dynamis* and *energeia* which is characteristic of Greek theology. *Dynamis* is latent power, or potential; *energeia* is realized power, or act(ion). There is a real distinction between these things in created beings, but the Greeks regarded this as a sign and consequence of finitude (imperfection). In God, *dynamis* was fully realized in *energeia*, so that God's being might be described as pure act. This *energeia* does not refer to the creative acts of God outside himself, but to his own being – an important point, since it reinforces the absoluteness of God as he is, and refuses to contemplate the possibility that God might get bigger or more powerful than he already is.

The activity of God outside himself was described by

Marcellus of Ancyra (mid-fourth century) as *energeia drastikē*, which is perhaps best translated as 'applied energy'. According to this way of thinking, God does not act from his *dynamis*, since this would imply that the result of his action was an extension of his being, and lead to pantheism or to panentheism. He acts from his *energeia*, which is already self-sufficient in him. To translate this into simple terms, Marcellus is saying that God is perfect in himself and does not need the creation to fulfil his inner potential. From that point of view the universe is superfluous, yet at the same time, it is a fruit of God's work which reflects his already existing perfection. In God's work we are privileged to see the same *energeia* which constitutes the fullness of his own being.[6]

When we compare this with Jüngel or with process theology, we realize that the moderns have not recognized the distinction between *dynamis* and *energeia* but have subsumed everything under the former. In the case of process theology, even *energeia drastikē* has become an extension of *dynamis*, although it is doubtful whether Jüngel would go this far. Trained as he has been in the Barthian tradition, it would appear that he restricts *dynamis* to the saving work of God in the world, and does not extend it, as do the process theologians, to the sustaining of the universe as well. The orthodox tradition, however, finds the distinction between *dynamis* and *energeia* an important one which must be retained, and regards the extension of *dynamis* in modern theology as a departure not only from classical theism, but from the biblical revelation as well.

The terminology may sound unfamiliar, but it is the distinction between *dynamis* and *energeia* which lies at the heart of most modern debate about the being of God. Theologians who deny that the divine *dynamis* is fully realized in God, independently of his creation, often argue that the crucifixion of Christ and the subsequent redemptive activity of God prove their point. By allowing the Son to be put to death, God is supposed to have taken human suffering into himself. By the redemption of humanity, God's love is said to be expanding to take in the fellowship of the human race. The growth of God through suffering and love is then presented to us as a model, and as the justification for an analogous pattern of spiritual growth in our own lives. Presented as it is in the guise of making God comprehensible to us (at a time when many Europeans, in particular, feel alienated from traditional Christianity), this theology is bound to make some impact on the church.[7]

Nor is it easy to deny that the Scriptures lend considerable support to these ideas, at least on the surface. We cannot fail to admire the emphasis which is placed on God's identification of himself with sinful humanity in the suffering and death of Christ – an emphasis which goes a long way towards restoring the doctrine of the atonement to its central place in theology. Nor can we neglect the welcome attention paid to the reconciling work of the Holy Spirit which is such a vital part of any healthy Christian fellowship. These things are important and true, but still the orthodox tradition is compelled to reject this particular formulation of the matter as fundamentally unbiblical. Why?

The simple answer is that modern theologians who have rejected classical theism have also rejected, though perhaps without realizing it, the important distinction between the persons and the nature of God. The activities which they ascribe to God's being belong in reality to the persons of the Trinity, in respect of whom the orthodox tradition confesses much the same things as Jüngel, or even a process theologian might suggest. The difference is that the persons of the Trinity are carefully distinguished from the divine nature (*physis*) or being (*ousia*) of God. At that level, says the orthodox tradition, the Bible teaches that God is one, not three, and that he possesses all the characteristics of a perfectly fulfilled and self-sufficient being.

It is difficult to produce a series of proof-texts which would clinch this argument, but the consequences of pursuing the alternative to its logical conclusion will help us to see our way more clearly. A God whose *dynamis* (= potential) extends beyond his own being is one who relies on an external factor for his fulfilment. Yet there is no suggestion in the Bible that God created the world in order to satisfy some unfulfilled potential in himself, or even in order to manifest his love. The Bible does not explain what God's motives were, but neither does it even so much as hint that the created universe had made any difference to his own character. We are told that:

> In the beginning you laid the foundations of the earth,
>     and the heavens are the work of your hands.
> They will perish, but you remain;
>     they will all wear out like a garment.
> Like clothing you will change them
>     and they will be discarded.
> But you remain the same,
>     and your years will never end.
>
> (Ps. 102:25–27)

This poetic proclamation is repeated in Hebrews 1:10–12 in a context which makes it clear that the contrast between God and the world is as valid in the sphere of redemption as it is in that of creation. The Son is exalted, not because of his earthly achievements, but because he shares the nature of the eternal God. It is therefore very difficult to see how God's nature can be said to have grown as a result of the earthly work of Christ, and later, of the Holy Spirit.

A further consequence of the modern view would be that Christ's redemptive work would lose its definitive character. It would retain its central importance, but only as a catalyst, pushing God into a new sphere of self-awareness. If this has really happened, it would be quite logical to assume that the biblical witness has lost its validity for us, since God would now be quite a different being from what he was 2,000 years ago. For one thing, the experience of suffering and love might well have mellowed him over the years, so that the harshness of his ethical demands, not to mention his negative attitude to those outside the covenant, might have softened to the point where the teaching of Scripture would no longer apply. If this sounds fantastic, we need only consider what a powerful effect both the techniques of modern psychology and the concept of cultural relativity have had on our understanding of the spiritual life, and the role of the Scriptures in it. A little reflection will show that what has happened here, as so often, is that God has been made into a human image, and a new idolatry has been born.[8]

The Bible itself counters these ideas in two ways. First, Jesus and the first Christians identify themselves with the faith of Abraham in a way which makes it plain that Christianity is meant to be the fulfilment of the covenant promises in a way which Abraham himself would have recognized. The point is that both the patriarch and the apostles knew the *same* God; the Jews, to whom this knowledge had also been given, had preferred to obscure it with their own traditions. Had God developed in some way during the 2,000 years that separated Abraham from the beginnings of the church, Abraham would not have recognized him instantly, any more than we recognize people whom we have not seen for a very long time, especially if they have changed to any significant extent.

The second factor which the Bible introduces is the belief that with the coming of Christ we have entered 'the last days'. Whatever changes may occur in the outside world, Jesus Christ – by which the writer to the Hebrews means both the person and the work of the Son of God – is the same, yesterday, today and forever (Heb. 13:8). There can therefore be no question of God developing, either inside himself or with respect to the world; if God were really like that, this verse would cease to be true. The Bible makes too sharp a distinction between the stability of God and the changeability of the world for us to be able to regard the latter as essentially a manifestation of the divine *dynamis*.

Lastly it must be said that in making this point, classical theism is not asserting that God's being is 'static'. The equation of stability with inertia is a curious aberration which introduces a false comparison into theological discourse. The orthodox tradition does *not* believe that God's *dynamis* is fully realized in *apatheia*, as the Platonists claimed, but in *energeia*. The divine *energeia* cannot grow or change its character, but it can function, and indeed does function, both in creation and in redemption. Its resources have not yet been fully displayed (although one may say they have been revealed, in some sense, in the prophecies of Scripture) nor will they ever be exhausted, or even diminish, as created energy does. Like his *dynamis*, God's *energeia* is also perfect and working out its purpose. But to do this, God's *dynamis* must be fully involved, with its every aspect brought clearly into play. Indeed, only if his potential is completely realized in his being, can his *energeia* function with the absolute power which the Scriptures attribute to him. We are not dealing with an immature or underdeveloped God, but with one who has every power at his immediate disposal and whom we can trust not to change, whatever may happen to us or to the world at large.

## Knowing God's being

The problems which surround the definition of God as a being are obviously fundamental to the church, and it is not surprising that they have received so much attention in modern times. Yet from the standpoint both of history and of Christian experience, they pale into insignificance beside the much more important question of whether we can know that being, and if so, how. Here the ground on which we are asked to tread is so delicate that even the orthodox tradition is divided between those who take the fundamentally positive course advocated by the classical theism of the Scholastics, and those who prefer the mystical approach of the early church, with its basically negative outlook.

After all the lengthy discussions about God's *ousia*, *dynamis* and *energeia*, it comes as something of a surprise to discover that those most deeply involved in defining these terms and elaborating their meaning all believed that God, in his essence, was incomprehensible. He could neither be known nor defined in human terms, and to experience him it was necessary to go beyond the language of the mind to the realm of non-being (*i.e.* beyond concept) which was known only to the mystic in his state of ecstasy. The kind of theology represented by the tomes of Athanasius and Augustine was less a systematization of knowledge about God than an attempt to avoid the embarrassment of complete silence in the face of the divine. That theology was necessary was demonstrated by the proliferation of heretics who were unable to discern the hidden truth of the Scriptures, and by the simple-mindedness of ordinary believers who were easily led astray. But that theology could in any way be equated with knowing God himself was an error denounced by every

64

name under the sun, from absurdity to blasphemy.

The mystical tradition was generally discounted by the Reformers, who regarded the claim to ecstatic experience as a form of presumption (*cf.*, *e.g.*, Calvin's statements about the Pseudo-Dionysius, *Institutes*, I, 14,4), but like the mystics, the Reformers made little attempt to examine the essence of God in itself (*cf.*, *e.g.* Calvin, *Institutes*, I, 2,2). To know God was to know his works (in creation), to hear his voice (in Scripture) and to enjoy fellowship with him (in the persons of the Trinity). If these things were properly understood and mastered, said the Reformers, the problem of knowing God's essence would appear as abstract – and useless – speculation.

From this has developed the modern Protestant belief, articulated by Karl Barth, that God is wholly other, *i.e.* completely different from any other being. Unfortunately, however, this statement has not always been accompanied by a very clear understanding of how we can know God, and the result has sometimes been a rather curious form of atheism, for which Barth himself must be held partly responsible. The Reformers believed that God must be known in the persons of the Trinity, and although Barth shared this belief, he disliked the term *person* (because to him it was too anthropomorphic) and preferred to speak of *modes of being* instead. By doing this, however, he subordinated the persons of the Trinity to the essence of God, which was 'wholly other', and never satisfactorily explained how it was possible to have any real knowledge of this.

Many theologians have tended to follow Barth in this respect, but they have been unable to ignore the problem which belief in an incomprehensible deity presents. It is generally agreed that a being must be definable in relation to other beings, since if it is not, we would have no means of recognizing it. But if God is wholly other, there is no point of contact between him and us, by which we might conceive of his existence. It therefore follows that we have no means of knowing God, so that as far as we are concerned, he might as well not exist at all. We thus find ourselves with a mental outlook in which human beings have 'come of age' and must live without God (Bonhoeffer), even to the point of taking leave of him altogether (Cupitt). As Barth's critics have put it, there is no bridge between God and humanity which can maintain a living relationship between the two.[9]

In response to this problem, the advocates of classical theism put forward their own solution, which goes back to Thomas Aquinas and even beyond. Aquinas did not deny the mystical tradition which until his time had been universal in serious theological thinking, but he supplemented it with what he regarded as a subsidiary authority of his own. He agreed that the human mind was an imperfect counterpart to the mind of God, but he insisted that there was nevertheless a correspondence between them, as Augustine had also believed (*On the Trinity* [*De Trinitate*] IV). This correspondence he called *analogy*, and from it he argued that this phenomenon was part of a principle which could be applied to all theology.

In saying this, Aquinas did not believe that he was going beyond what Augustine had said. In his great work on the Trinity, Augustine had argued that Scripture itself used earthly examples in order to instruct our minds in the things of God (I, 1). By faith, the believer would be led from these external things to the contemplation of God himself. But whereas Augustine did not believe that there was any real correspondence between these things and the being of God, apart from the human spirit (which included the mind) which was made in God's image, Aquinas believed that there was. He therefore set out to prove the existence of God by deploying the principle of analogy along lines first laid down by Aristotle (384–322BC) and subsequently developed into a theological system which appeared to be the exact opposite of Platonism. Whereas Plato had started from universal ideas and argued from them to the existence of actual (but corrupt) matter, Aristotelianism began with the particular phenomena of observable reality, and argued back from them to the underlying universals. In Aquinas' case, this meant arguing for the existence of God from the data of sense experience – a procedure which forms the basis of what we now call natural theology.

## The proofs for the existence of God

Characteristic of Scholastic theology are the so-called 'proofs' for the existence of God. They have been presented in different ways at different times, and some of them are considerably more ancient than Scholasticism itself. Yet the association of the two remains firmly implanted in our minds, because it was from these proofs that natural theology was developed. Whether the proofs are still valid depends to a large extent on what one thinks of the fundamental procedure being employed. If, like Karl Barth, one assumes that a natural theology is impossible, then clearly no proof for God's existence will be of any significance. If, on the other hand, one accepts that there is some conceptual link between the Creator and his creation, one might also be inclined to suppose that the latter offers clues to the existence and nature of the former.

From a historical point of view, it is curious that although the proofs for the existence of God have all been refuted at one time or other, somehow they keep reappearing. In the twentieth century the dominant philosophical trends have generally been non-theistic, if not openly atheistic, and the proofs for the existence of God have been discounted accordingly. In theological circles, the influence of Barthianism has provided another reaction against the proofs, which has contributed to a general lack of interest in them among Protestant theologians. Yet all the while there was a steady revival of neo-Thomism in the Roman Catholic Church, which lasted until the Second Vatican Council (1962–65), and which attempted to restate the proofs in modern terms. Today, Roman Catholic theologians have largely abandoned these attempts in a welter of confusion, which makes many observers wonder whether Rome now has any definable theology at all. On the other hand, there are signs of renewed interest in the proofs among Protestants, who have recently become interested in them in a way which would have surprised the generation of Barth. Richard Swinburne's study, *The Existence of God* (1979), has sought to validate the proofs taken as a whole, rather than individually – *i.e.* not as decisive in themselves, but as stepping-stones to an argument from probability. Similar views are now being expounded by other philosophers of note, and it may be that the pendulum is swinging back in favour of an approach which only a short time ago seemed to be irredeemably discredited.

The scope of this book does not permit a detailed analysis of all the proofs, but some idea of what they are like, and why they have been objected to, may be set out briefly as follows:

## The ontological argument[10]

This argument was first developed by Anselm of Canterbury (c. 1033–1109), and it was later expanded by the great Scholastics. The basic premiss is that God is the being than whom no greater being can be conceived. This sounds reasonable enough, and most people would probably be inclined to agree with it in principle. Yet the premiss has two major weaknesses which make its usefulness somewhat questionable.

The first weakness is contained in the word *greater*. Is God greater than anything else quantitatively (*i.e.* is he bigger?), qualitatively (*i.e.* is he better?), or both? If God is merely bigger than anything else there is no real problem, unless a still bigger object can be found or imagined, which is always possible, since quantity can theoretically be increased to infinity. If *greater* refers primarily to quality, the difficulty becomes one of measurement. Christians would want to argue that God can be measured only against himself, but in that case, the outcome of the argument is decided in advance.

Greatness might be understood in terms of power, but that would not necessarily have implications for God's size or character. The atom, for example, is more powerful when split than almost anything else, but it is also smaller and lacks any moral nature by which its quality could be judged. Is God to be thought of like that? And what about forms of greatness which are conceived along lines which are incompatible with the being of God? It would be a poor theologian who would argue that God is the greatest liar or thief imaginable! Greatness suffers in the end from being too subjective a concept, and one which may be applied without reference to moral criteria.

The second difficulty with the ontological argument is the word *conceived*. To conceive of relative greatness is to assume that the scale is open-ended; it will always be possible to conceive of something greater than the maximum. These conceptions may not exist in actual fact, but we have no

68

means of proving this one way or the other. Conceivability also implies that there must be limits to God, and that in itself makes it highly suspect, as the mystical tradition reminds us. If we answer that this objection is not valid because we conceive of God as the absolute being, we are still left with serious problems of definition. How can we conceive of God as being omnipresent, if there are creatures which exist outside him? Or how can God be omnipotent, if other powers exist, some of which are actually opposed to him? What indeed can such terms mean if we have nothing to measure them against? It is one thing to say that human beings are inferior to God, but we cannot say that God is superior to humans to the point of being absolute, if our standard of measurement is human capacity alone. In the final analysis, the absolute cannot be measured except by itself – a conclusion which seems to invalidate the ontological argument for God's existence.

To be fair to Anselm, it should be said that his own approach to the question was based neither on speculation nor on purely human logic. At the end of the day, he rested his case on the revelation of God found in the Bible. For him, the highest conceivable being was not an abstract mathematical concept, but a living reality whom he worshipped and served. It was on the basis of this knowledge of God that he made his claims, and it is on the same basis that Christians today are inclined to agree with him. But as a proof for the existence of God which is designed to convert unbelievers, the ontological argument is weak and it is probably better to abandon it, rather than pursue it to its logical conclusion.

## The aetiological argument[11]

The aetiological argument, which is sometimes regarded as part of a broader cosmological proof, relies on the assumption that every effect has a cause. By tracing the chain of cause and effect back to the beginning, we are supposed to come eventually to the first cause, or prime mover, which by definition is neither moved nor caused itself. This very Aristotelian argument was used by Thomas Aquinas and it became a standard feature of classical Scholasticism. At first sight it looks very promising, but although it has convinced many unbelievers, it has its own problems, which in strict logic are insoluble. For example, if the prime mover and first cause is supposed to be itself unmoved and uncaused, how did it come into being? And how can it be the cause of something else without some kind of movement? Another problem is that this argument does not tie in very well with the belief that God is both different from and sovereign over his creation. If he were merely the one who set the ball rolling, would he not be just one end of a great chain of beings which together make up the universe? And then what would become of the idea of divine providence, or control over the created order?

An equally serious objection is the fact that the Augustinian picture of God goes against the aetiological argument on both counts. In Augustine's way of thinking, as we have already seen, God's being is motion, and the second and third persons of the Trinity, although they are eternal, nevertheless have a cause. To say that God is unmoved and uncaused brings this tradition into question, even if we agree that these adjectives apply to God's nature (substance) and not to the subsistence of the persons of the Trinity. The reason for this is that the second and third persons of the Trinity are supposed to have issued forth from the substance of God, thereby making them equal with the Father. Careful choice and use of language may avoid serious difficulties over this, but the existence and popularity of process theology, for example, shows how difficult this is. Like the ontological argument, the aetiological argument asks more questions than it answers, and in the final analysis it must be judged inadequate as a proof for the existence of God.

## The teleological argument[12]

This proof for the existence of God is twinned with the aetiological argument under the wider cosmological umbrella. It is different though, in that it focuses on the end of the universe rather than on its beginning. According to the teleological argument, everything which happens has a purpose. There is a design in the universe, aspects of which can be studied at every level from the subatomic to the human. Such complexity cannot be accidental; a design implies a designer just as surely as a watch implies a watchmaker. Furthermore, a design implies a purpose, and it is this which distinguishes the teleological from the merely aetiological argument. Furthermore, if the design is cosmic, as it clearly is, the designer must be greater still, *i.e.* a metaphysical being capable of constructing such an artistic masterpiece.

The teleological argument is more substantial than is either the ontological or the aetiological ones, but it is not without its flaws. For a start, it is not clear that there really is a single design which can be applied to the entire universe. Things sometimes happen which do not go according to plan, and even scientific laws are not infallible. Proponents of the teleological argument may easily find themselves denying miracles, for instance, and therefore defending a picture of God which is inferior to the one offered to us in the Bible. Christians hardly need defenders of that type! As for the end result of the design, it appears that the energy which sustains the universe is slowly winding down, like a watch, so it may be that its ultimate 'purpose' is nothing at all – once again, a denial of biblical teaching. Some thinkers advance the idea that the universe contains an inner dynamic, or necessity, which counterbalances chance occurrences and gives the world some semblance of order. It is a belief somewhat like this, however, which undergirds the assertions of process theology, and it excludes the concept of a metaphysical God by definition.

In spite of its many attractions therefore, the teleological argument must be rejected both as insufficient in itself, and as open to interpretations which are not in harmony with classical theism.

## The ethical argument[13]

The ethical argument takes us out of the purely physical and into the moral domain. Most people tend to assume that the latter is also spiritual, but it is important to understand that this is not necessarily so. Hedonists would deny it categorically, since for them what is pleasurable to the senses is right. But hedonism, although at times it has been widely practised, has always been considered immoral, and its few theoretical advocates have never been able to overcome this

71

prejudice for long. Materialists might also reject this assumption on principle, though in practice their objections are usually formal rather than substantial. In fact, they quite often incline towards a puritanism which demands a very high degree of spiritual self-discipline. As far as the historical debate about the proofs for the existence of God is concerned, there can be no doubt that the ethical argument has always been regarded primarily as a spiritual one, although it obviously has important material implications.

That humanity has a moral understanding of sorts is generally agreed, but problems come when we attempt to define it any further. Good and bad doubtless have a meaning, but as we have already seen in the context of the ontological argument, that meaning can be very subjective and arbitrary. One person's meat is another's poison, as the saying goes, and this is nowhere more true than in the spiritual realm. The widespread agreement about moral matters which has been evident over the centuries in Europe is very largely due to the benefits of a common culture and civilization; where these have broken down, or have never existed, the moral consensus disappears. Allied prisoners of war, for example, were treated by the Japanese with abominable cruelty, largely because their standards of morality were so very different. More recently, we have seen a similar clash of values in our relations with Muslim states, and with Islam in general. The spread of Western civilization, divorced from traditional Western values, whose influence is generally declining, poses a problem of conflicting moralities which is one of the greatest difficulties the modern world has to face. There is certainly no easy answer to this problem, but at least it ought to be clear from this that the old appeal to a 'natural law', approximating to Christian morality without its accompanying theology, and supposedly inherent in every human being, is no longer tenable.

It is probably still true that most people believe that good and evil are more than relative concepts, but proving that they are right is a very different matter. Even the Bible, which most people assume is crystal-clear in moral matters, contains a number of apparent anomalies on this score. Monogamy is taught as a creation ordinance, but it seems that

72

polygamy was tolerated quite happily, especially in pre-exilic Israel. Murder is forbidden in principle, but it was frequently encouraged in practice, even to the point where Saul was censured for not slaying the Amalekites (1 Sa. 15:12–23). Right and wrong do not seem to obey any rigorous law, which makes it extremely difficult to appeal to such concepts as proof for the existence of a God who is supposed to be both the supreme good in himself and also the lawgiver of creation.

As a matter of historical fact, Christian theology has never found it easy to live with a moral code. Jesus and his disciples condemned the Jews of their time for obeying the letter of the law and ignoring its spirit. Later on, Augustine summed up a Christian's moral duty as 'love God and do what you like'. At the time of the Reformation, Martin Luther could even tell his disciple Melanchthon to 'sin boldly', in the assurance that he was justified by faith, not by works! Of course, these statements should not be taken out of context; in each case they presuppose a spiritual commitment leading to a self-discipline far greater than anything a moral law could impose. Such noble ideals have certainly been misunderstood and perverted by less spiritually-minded followers of the great masters, with the result that a countervailing legalism has in practice become a standard feature of popular Christian morality. What is significant though is that in Christian teaching legalism has always been regarded as wrong, and it has frequently been attacked as hypocritical and self-righteous. One has only to compare this with Jewish and Islamic attitudes to religious law to see how very different Christianity is from them on this point. Christians have never looked to law for their salvation, but to a personal relationship with God, established by grace through faith. Its morality comes from a righteousness given by God to those who believe in Christ, not from a set of abstract principles recommending themselves as law and 'justice'.

Morality, or ethics, is in reality a pagan concept, not a Christian one. Aristotle was deeply concerned with it, as of course was Plato. In their wisdom, they looked for behavioural norms by which to live, believing that people could save themselves and their society by adhering to a logical set of legal principles. Modern atheists who argue against the common nineteenth-century belief that religion is a necessary buttress for morality are merely echoing Plato, who saw no need for the gods and their immoral activities, and therefore rejected pagan Greek religion. On the other hand, it is true that the Bible lays down principles which could be called ethical, and the so-called 'moral law' was supposed by the classical Reformed theologians to be one aspect of the old covenant which is still valid today.

It is therefore particularly interesting to note that modern scholarship does not support the traditional division of the Old Testament law into civil, moral and ceremonial categories. These divisions are now generally recognized to have come from a much later theological analysis, which does not fully accord with the evidence of the texts themselves. The Bible teaches that the supreme moral virtue is spiritual obedience to the Word of God, whatever that may entail in material terms. It is not to be identified with 'situation ethics', which lacks an objective, spiritual reference point, but neither is it to be assimilated to a fixed legal code which can never be modified. Once this is understood though, an appeal to moral principles as proof for the existence of God is ruled out, because without him Christian morality would not exist either.

## The aesthetic argument[14]

The last major argument for the existence of God is the one which appeals to quality, or value. The word *value* is nowadays often used in a moral sense, but here it refers to something rather different. In the world as we experience it, some things are considered to be of more value than others. This judgment may be purely arbitrary, as when we decide that gold is more valuable than silver, for example. World literature is full of stories warning us not to be misled by false value systems which put an arbitrary price on things which do not by their nature deserve it. Yet when all is said and done, even that criticism can be made only if it is accepted that there is another value system which has got the right criteria for judging what is good and what is not.

Beauty is another concept which reflects value judgment,

and although it may often be mainly in the eye of the be-
holder, it is not entirely so. Art critics of very different kinds
will be quick to point out that great paintings, symphonies
and plays are thought to be worthwhile not because people
like them, but because they fulfil a number of fairly strict
requirements of composition. Anyone who has tried to produce a work of art will know what a struggle it is to maintain
the values of proportion and harmony which are fundamental to the finished product, and a true genius will never
be swayed by the praise of uncritical admirers.

But where do these artistic values come from? There are
many Christians who have claimed that they are rooted in the
created order, having been put there by a God who wants his
world to reflect something of his glory. The aesthetic appeal
of Christianity has had a powerful influence in the twentieth
century, not only on writers like C. S. Lewis and T. S. Eliot,
but on painters, composers and theologians as well. The
nineteenth-century belief that neo-Gothic architecture was
somehow more expressive of God than any other has given
way to a much more liberal spirit of creativity, but the principle that beauty glorifies God remains the same. It is at least
arguable that aesthetic considerations lay at the heart of the
faith professed by both Karl Barth and Rudolf Bultmann,
and they have provided the dominant theme for the systematic theology of Hans Urs von Balthasar. Aesthetics has
also had a strong influence on the liturgical movement,
though with much more mixed results.

At a humbler level, the aesthetic dimension has always had
a powerful effect on popular devotion, as the veneration
accorded to sacred images and music testifies. Protestants are
often accused of philistinism on this score because of their
distaste for pictorial representations of spiritual beings, but
they make up for this iconoclastic streak by their music and
hymn-writing, as well as by their devotional literature. There
we read of the beauty of the crucified Christ, the magnificent
order of the universe, and the intellectual satisfaction derived
from systematic theology, or even from a good sermon, all of
which bear witness to aesthetic principles at work.

These things can and indeed must be given their due, but
none of them proves conclusively that God exists. Alongside

THE DOCTRINE OF GOD

beauty, Christians also believe that there is a place for ugliness at the heart of their faith, not least in the torn body of the one who died for them (*cf.* Is. 53:2). There is something very repulsive in the cross of Christ, which makes a mockery of this world's standards of beauty. The Bible seems to concur with the human observation that our values are ultimately subjective, and dependent on some deeper reality. For Christians this reality can be only a living relationship with Christ, which can never be reduced to merely an aesthetic principle.

We are therefore forced to conclude that concepts like *good* and *beauty*, while they undoubtedly exist, have a variety of possible meanings which allow for little objective unity. The principles which the great critics have laid down are valid in their context, but like any other form of legalism, if they are elevated to the level of a controlling abstraction, they are more likely to stifle creativity than to promote it. Certainly we are not entitled to deduce from their existence that there is a God who has created all things, which to our eyes may be beautiful or not.

## Summary

Our brief examination of the different arguments which are put forward to prove the existence of God shows that, although they all have a certain plausibility, none can be regarded as constituting proof in the eyes of someone who does not already believe in him. And it is a fact that these arguments have only ever been really successful in reassuring people who are already believers of one kind or another. Sceptics have never had any difficulty in pulling them apart, or in offering alternative explanations for the phenomena which Christians cite as evidence for the existence of God. As evangelistic arguments the proofs have only a limited value, although it can be argued that taken together, rather than considered separately, they add up to a powerful argument in favour of the probability that there is a God whose nature is consistent with that of the God revealed in the Bible. Christian theology does not deny the positive assertions which the classical proofs make, but it is careful to place them within the framework of a system of belief which does not depend on them as evidence for its claims.

## The analogy of God's being

In the course of the exposition of the so-called proofs for the existence of God, we have seen how they presuppose that those who develop the different arguments will already have a specific idea of God in their minds. Scholastic theologians did not start from the natural world alone, but from the premiss that there is a Creator God who can be studied in the things which he has made. To those who deny this assumption the proofs carry little weight, and certainly fail to convince, since alternative explanations of the same phenomena can usually be found without too much difficulty.

It follows from this that the formal proofs for the existence of God would never have taken shape if the philosophers and theologians concerned had not already had some concept of God in their minds. At the popular level, God may have been thought of as a kind of heavenly man, who ruled the universe much as an oriental king governed his empire. More intellectual people poured scorn on ideas of this kind and the Greeks, at least, sought to 'depersonalize' God, but even they could not get away from anthropomorphic imagery completely.[15] Plato, for example, thought of God as a mind which consisted of a non-material substance, bits of which had broken off and fallen into the material world, to become the rational souls of human beings.

The early Christians were keenly aware of this concept, and were accordingly slow to use mind (*nous*) as an analogy of God's being. The word is never used in this sense in the New Testament, and the few references which occur in second-century writers generally have the explicit purpose of explaining the Christian God to pagans in terms that the latter could understand. Even Clement of Alexandria (*c.* AD 200), who made what would later become the standard connection between mind and God the Father, was quite clear that the idea had come from Plato, not from the Bible.[16]

But Clement also knew, as did the Christian apologists who preceded him, that the Scriptures were by no means as hostile to Plato's idea as we might be inclined to think today. It was quite clear, for example, that the God of the Bible was the 'supreme mind' whose thoughts and ways, though they differed from those of mortals, could at least be expounded by those prophets and others to whom God had revealed himself. The very concept of a written law implied that he was a rational being, whose mind could be known, at least to some extent, to human beings.

This basic belief was confirmed by the New Testament, where Jesus Christ, the final revelation of God, is actually referred to as the Reason (*Logos*) who had been with God from the beginning and who could even be identified with him (Jn. 1:1). This seemed to provide the ideal text for claiming that God the Father was the mind (*nous*) which had begotten (or conceived: note the link between mental and physical conception) its reason, which thus became the Son of God.

Clement's rather neat deduction certainly did not go unchallenged, and there were many who doubted whether the Logos could be regarded as an objective being along the same lines as the nous. These doubts were reflected in a number of christological heresies, put about by people who did not understand how the function of the mind could be considered to be the equal of the mind itself. One or two people, like Tertullian for example, realized that the Son of God could not simply be the functioning of the divine mind, since God obviously did not stop being rational after giving birth to the Logos as a distinct person, but they lacked a conceptual framework which could explain the co-existence of the Logos and the rational mind within the one God. Only by adopting an idealist philosophy like Platonism, to which Tertullian was implacably opposed, was it possible to maintain that the mind's conception of its reason produced another concept, equal to the mind itself.

The Platonic mind was non-material, and this aspect was easily assimilated to the biblical concept that God is Spirit (Jn. 4:24). Augustine explained it by saying that the spiritual mind had conceived the spiritual logos which, because it shared the mind's perfect nature, was equal to the mind in every respect (*On the Trinity* IX). But Augustine went on to say that the mind was bound to its self-conception by the power of love, since it was inconceivable that the perfect mind should not love the image of its own perfection. But this love was not to be confused with the self-image, since it was not begotten in the same way. Rather, it was necessary for the self-image to appear first, and then love would proceed naturally from the mind to embrace it.

Augustine identified this love with the Holy Spirit, thereby establishing a connection which eventually developed into a general linking of love and spirit in the being of God (*On the Trinity* XV). This provided mediaeval theology with a very powerful analogy, according to which the mind and its concepts were bound together in mutual love, not only in God but also in human beings, although imperfectly in the latter case. It would not be too much to say that the whole of Western civilization has been built on this picture, in which the spiritual power of love was exalted as binding, constituting and finally even transcending the mind and its thought.

Yet although this intellectual tradition has been very powerful, it is open to question just how much it can be said to reflect the true teaching of Scripture. Augustine himself struggled long and hard before he was finally able to equate spirit with love as two definitions of God's being; like others before and after him, he was aware of the force in the argument that 'God is Spirit' (Jn. 4:24) is ontological in emphasis, whilst 'God is Love' (1 Jn. 4:15) describes the way he acts. Of course the two aspects are not unconnected, but it was probably only the influence of Platonism which finally pushed Augustine into the position of arguing that love was an objective being in its own right. Little did he know that in later times this idea would be so divorced from its biblical roots that even God himself would be judged by some people to be unloving – or at least to be presented as such in the Bible (especially in the Old Testament).

The chief failure of the analogies of God's being is that they do not do justice to the reality they are trying to express. Of course this is true of all analogy to some extent, but in the case of God the implications for our understanding may be very serious indeed. We may certainly want to agree that God has a mind, but to say that he *is* 'mind' leads to a theological outlook which is excessively intellectual. Likewise, God is definitely a spiritual being, but to call him simply 'spirit' is to invite that curious lack of discernment which regards every-thing spiritual as somehow pointing to God, ignoring the very real warnings in the Bible about the power of evil spirits in the world. Then again, to say that God is 'love' expresses a vital truth about the way he acts, but if it is made into a false absolute it will inevitably detract from the majesty of his law and the wrath which is visited on those who transgress it.

Lastly and most seriously, the analogies of God's being have tended to take some aspects of God's nature and identify them with particular persons of the Trinity. Not only does this turn the Trinity into a union of abstract or imper-sonal principles, but it also detracts from the majesty of each individual person. As Tertullian implicitly understood, *each* person of the Godhead shares *all* the characteristics of God in full measure (*cf.* Col. 2:9) and so it is quite wrong to isolate reason, say, and identify it exclusively with the Son. The prologue to John's Gospel does not use logos in the Platonic sense, but in direct continuity with the Old Testament, where the Word of the Lord is the key to God's self-revelation. In our own time this has been recovered by Karl Barth and made the cornerstone of his theology, but for many centuries it was not properly understood. Even now, there is a danger in overreacting against the earlier tendency and reducing the Word (*logos*) to little more than a timebound message from human beings who claim special insight into the ways of God. As with everything else, a balance must be carefully struck here in our understanding of biblical teaching, although one thing at least must be quite clear – we shall never build a satisfactory doctrine of God as long as we persist in believing that each person of the Trinity represents some aspect or other of the divine being.[17]

## The attributes of God's nature

The futility of trying to find analogies of God's being was clearly recognized by the Protestant Reformers. John Calvin, for example, wrote:

Those who propose to enquire what the essence of God is, only delude us with frigid speculations, it being much more our interest to know what kind of being God is, and what things are agreeable to his nature (*Institutes* I, 2, 3).

Calvin went on to explain that Scripture did tell us something of what God was like, and that this information was important as a safeguard against false conceptions of his character which, if wrongly absorbed, might lead us astray in the practice of our Christian calling. Later on, when speaking of the 'immensity' (*i.e.* omnipresence) and the spirituality of God's being, he has this to say:

Although God, in order to keep us within the bounds of soberness, treats sparingly of his essence, still, by the two attributes which I have already mentioned, he at once suppresses all gross imaginations, and checks the audacity of the human mind (*Institutes* I, 13, 1).

This statement expresses very clearly how Calvin understood the already well-developed theological systematization of the properties which by nature were inherent in God's essence, and provides a link not only with the teaching of the Bible, but also with the development of the Christian tradition in pre-Scholastic times. For unlike the so-called proofs for the existence of God, the analysis of his natural properties can be traced back to the Fathers of the early church. The classical summary of their teaching was made by John of Damascus (*c.* 675 – *c.* 749) in his *Exposition of the Orthodox Faith* 1, 8. There John lists no fewer than eighteen distinct attributes of God (only two of which are grammatically positive), and his catalogue, though it has often been reworked, may in essentials be regarded as still definitive today.[18] The attributes which he lists may be further classified according to whether they refer to time (*pote*, when), space (*pou*, where), matter (*ti*, what) or quality (*poion*, like what). The first of these categories can then be subdivided according to whether the attributes in question refer to time's beginning or to its end. The divisions are not specified in the text itself, but the attributes are listed in logical order as follows:

81

| Time (Beginning): | without beginning, uncreated, unbegotten |
| (End): | imperishable, immortal, everlasting |
| Space | : infinite, uncircumscribed, boundless, of infinite power |
| Matter | : simple, uncompound, incorporeal, without flux |
| Quality | : passionless, unchangeable, unalterable, unseen |

As far as the biblical evidence for these attributes goes, there is little difficulty with those whose reference points are temporal and spatial. It is true that theologians argue over the details of what they mean, and philosophers sometimes question their meaningfulness and inner coherence as concepts, but in spite of these difficulties, most people agree that the Bible portrays God in this kind of way. On the other hand, serious disagreements about what the Bible itself is saying occur in discussions about attributes falling into the categories of matter and quality. It is often on biblical grounds alone that God's simplicity is attacked, and many people would want to qualify, if not actually deny, his incorporeality – again on the strength of the biblical evidence. Divine impassibility is nowadays often thought to be incompatible with the teaching of Scripture, and so is his immutability. It is therefore inevitable that we shall direct most of this discussion of the divine attributes to a consideration of these issues, which are the main subjects of current debate, although in doing so we must not overlook the attributes which are less likely to provoke controversy today. Theology, like other disciplines, has its fashions, and what is generally agreed today may quite easily become the subject of heated argument tomorrow.

## Temporal attributes

The temporal attributes listed above are relatively straight-forward. God cannot have a beginning, because that would imply that he had a cause of origin, which is impossible. He is neither created nor begotten, points which seem obvious enough, although their appearance in this list reminds us of longstanding christological controversies which cannot be ignored. The Son of God is begotten according to his personal relationship with the Father, but not according to his participation in the divine essence. This is an important point which was frequently denied in the early church, notably by the arch-heretic Arius (d. 336). Nor is it possible for God to have an ending. He cannot perish or die, as Psalm 102:25–27 (quoted in Heb. 1:10–12) reminds us. There is some question as to whether 'everlasting' (aiōnios) means that God has his being inside time and not, as is usually supposed, outside it, but this is a slightly different matter. In using this word, which by itself could mean simply 'as long as time lasts', neither John nor the Scriptures want to deny the extra-temporal eternity of God; their chief concern is to emphasize only that God does not have an end. For most Christians, then as now, acceptance of that belief automatically implied eternity outside time, since within time, an end to God could always be conceived. It was to make this impossible that the concept of extra-temporal eternity imposed itself, in spite of the difficulties it raises.[19]

The conceivability of eternity is more a philosophical than a strictly theological issue, but its implications are so great that it can hardly be ignored. Agnostics often ridicule the idea of a God who sits outside time, watching the world from a vantage point which makes intervention either impossible or meaningless. Some Christians have felt the force of this argument and advocated the abandonment of eternity as a concept, whilst others have felt obliged to defend it against attack. Still others sit on the fence, prepared, at least in theory, to accept either possibility.

Needless to say, there will always be problems with the concept of eternity, however it is defined. If God is timeless, it will be difficult to establish what his recorded activities within time might mean. For example, how did Jesus manage to be God on earth and the eternal Logos in heaven at the same time? On the other hand, if God is everlasting in a temporal sense, what happens to his omniscience, and what are we to make of biblical statements to the effect that for God a thousand years are like a day, or even a watch of the night

(Ps. 90:4)? Can we say that God has a time which moves at a different speed from ours? Some theologians have been tempted to adopt this hypothesis, but it is liable to create just as many problems for a doctrine of divine intervention in the world as we find in the doctrine of a timeless eternity.

Perhaps the key to the problem of eternity can be found by examining the concept of the 'present'. Most of us believe that time can be divided into three segments – the past, the present and the future. Yet when we look at them more closely, we discover that in fact time consists only of the past and the future: the present does not really exist. This is because no matter how carefully we pinpoint the moment in time which we call 'now', as soon as we have uttered the word, that moment has become past. The present is therefore only a notional concept which we use to separate time which has occurred (the past) from time which has not yet occurred (the future). In fact, when we recognize that time which has not yet occurred does not exist, we are entitled to say that, in a sense, the present is really the end of time – the point which time has now reached.

If we agree about this understanding of the present, we must admit that strictly speaking, it does not belong to the sphere of time at all. The present is in fact more closely related to the eternal, which is also the end of time and not definable in a purely secular context. In speaking of eternity, and in particular of the being of God, the Bible in fact uses the present tense: the God of Israel is the great I AM (Ex. 3:14). The one who dwells outside time is in our experience always present, because the present is the only mode in which we can experience the eternal. Indeed, we may go farther and say that by giving us an indispensable but undefinable notion of the present, God has implanted in us the ability to know the eternal as a dimension outside the flow of time.

If this is true, then it also opens up for us an answer to the problem of how an eternal being can make himself known within the time framework. God can reveal himself to us as present without violating his nature, because the present is the vehicle by which we can apprehend the eternal. But that is not all. When we human beings apprehend the eternal in this way, we enter into an experience which is contrary to our finite and temporal nature. We can do this, because as persons created in the image of God, we have the ability to transcend our nature in our personal relationship with him. But if our personhood gives us the ability to transcend our nature, is not the same also true of God, whose personhood is the archetype of ours?

This understanding of the person lies at the heart of classical christology. According to the orthodox formulation, the person of the Son of God took on human nature (bound by time) which remains completely separate from his divine nature (not bound by time), in order to do his work within the time and space framework. The reconciliation of time and eternity occurred in the ascension which, scientifically speaking, is the greatest mystery in the life of Christ. When he ascended into heaven, Jesus took his manhood into God, thereby making it timeless. (Whether it was also made spaceless is a matter of controversy. Some, like Luther, have argued that it was, because time and space were usually held to be inseparable. Others, like Calvin, argued that it was not, on the ground that such a change would destroy the natural appearance of a human body.[20])

What is accepted in classical christology can surely be extended to the other persons as well, and would tie in nicely, for example, with Calvin's insistence that we know God in his persons, and not in his essence. A solution along these lines would make it possible for the eternal God to be involved in human affairs without compromising either his divine nature or the authenticity of his involvement in the time–space framework. It avoids many of the inconsistencies which result from the attempt to picture eternity-in-time, and allows for the maintenance of important corollary attributes, like immutability and omnipotence, on the same principle of a distinction between person and essence in God.

## Spatial attributes

The spatial attributes are almost as straightforward as the temporal ones, although it is necessary to point out that God's infinity is not a mathematical concept. In mathematics, infinity is merely open-ended finitude, though it may be open-ended in an infinite number of dimensions. Number, for example, is essentially a finite concept, which governs the meaning of both 'countable infinity' (*e.g.* 1, 2, 3, 4, 5 *etc.*) and 'uncountable infinity' (*e.g.* the number of possible decimal places between 0 and 1). God's infinity is qualitatively different from that of mathematics, in that it is boundless as well as endless. The inclusion of infinite power as a spatial category may cause some surprise, until we remember the close association which existed in ancient minds between God's being and his energy. His power was conceived of in terms not dissimilar to what we would now call his omnipresence, since it was thought necessary for him to be everywhere in order to act without restraint.

This idea is well expressed in the phrase 'Never will I leave you; never will I forsake you' (Heb. 13:5), a promise which is typical of the God of the Bible, but incomprehensible unless we recognize that his omnipresence, which this picture presupposes, is the foundation of his power. The only point in saying that God is everywhere lies in implying that he can act anywhere, and not just within particular limits. This was a problem with the pagan gods of antiquity, and it is common in polytheistic systems whose gods are usually limited in space, in function, or in both. Thus for example, Bel and Nebo were gods of Babylon who had no power in Egypt, while Astarte (Aphrodite) was the goddess of love, a concept which, although it gave her authority over every sort of fertility, gave her no control over other things like death. Pagan gods could therefore be thwarted in their desires by other deities, or even by shadowy figures like the fates who, strictly speaking, were not gods at all.

The God of the Bible is thus distinguished from all pagan deities both by his omnipotence and by his omnipresence. It is true that he was the God of a particular people, but even in the Old Testament his lordship was not confined either to them or to the land of Israel, as Jonah discovered to his cost. The only instance in which it seems that such a view of God was tolerated is the curious case of Naaman, who took sacks of Israelite earth back to Damascus, in order to be able to build an altar to God on his own soil (2 Ki. 5:17). It seems that this peculiar extraterritoriality was permitted, however, as a concession to Naaman's pagan background and surroundings; there is no indication that it was ever tolerated among the Jews.

In this connection, it should be stated that the subsequent longing of the Jewish exiles for their ancestral home in Palestine, and their conviction that the covenant sacrifices must be carried out in Jerusalem, are not in themselves evidence that Israel worshipped a territorial God. The land of Canaan was regarded as part of the covenant promise, not as the boundary of God's power. This is quite clear from earliest times, when we observe that God created man in Eden, a location somewhere in Mesopotamia. Later he dispersed the human race over the whole earth, which he flooded in the time of Noah. Eventually he called Abraham from Ur and led him, by way of Harran, to the Promised Land. Yet even there the Hebrews were little more than sojourners, and after only two generations God led Jacob into Egypt, where they remained for several centuries. When God eventually led them back out of Egypt, he did not bring them straight to Canaan, but kept them in the wilderness for a whole generation, during which time he gave the law to Moses. We might say therefore that virtually the whole of the Pentateuch, the foundation document of Israel's religion, is concerned with events which took place outside the covenant territory, not in it, a circumstance which appears to prove decisively that Yahweh was never regarded as simply a local deity.

Later on we find that there was a spiritual awakening in the exile, when Israel once more found itself outside its national home. If Yahweh had been only a local god, he might well have been abandoned during this time, but instead of that, we find that it was during the exile that Israel was finally cleansed of the latent idolatry which had dogged them, not in Egypt or Babylon, but in Canaan. Devotion to Yahweh was strengthened, not weakened by the exile, a fact that does not tie in with the idea that he was just a local Canaanite deity. From the beginning, his glory and power were to be seen in the whole of creation (Ps. 19), and this theme recurs throughout the Bible.

The God of Israel, furthermore, is omnipotent, even in

hell (Ps. 139:7–12). This point is important, because it raises the most frequently debated question about God's power: what connection is there between God and hell? Can God do anything about things which are contrary to his nature? Can he sin, for example, or commit suicide? What does it mean to say that God can do anything? Here there has been a great deal of argument, often to very little purpose. Logical contradictions have been invented, like the question as to whether God can make anything greater than himself, in order to discredit the whole concept of omnipotence. The main answer which is given to this sort of thing today is that such questions exist only as mental gymnastics. The 'problem' is an imaginary invention which does not, and cannot, exist in reality; therefore it can neither be asked nor answered by theology, which is concerned only with what *is*.[21]

There is, however, a traditional response to this sort of question which begins with the statement that God's omnipotence is perfect. This may be done by saying, along with Anselm of Canterbury, that sin (or whatever is contrary to God's nature) is really a kind of imperfection, or impotence. To speak of it as a possibility for God is therefore to deny, rather than to affirm, the plenitude of his power. Anselm's idea may be taken further, as it was by the Scholastics, to say that God's omnipotence is fully realized, *i.e.* that whatever God can do, he actually does. Therefore God cannot sin, or commit suicide, because he does not do so. There is no latent potential in him which is currently unused, since that too would be a sign of imperfection. To the obvious objection that in the future, God will convert people who do not yet exist, the answer is that in eternity that is already done. Salvation is an eternal act of God in himself, not a series of rescue operations performed in the world of time and space. It follows from this fact that what we see as a particular action of God is in reality only the manifestation within our universe of a power which is at work in eternity. It is for this reason, argued the Scholastics, that temporally distinct conversions lead to a common, eternal confession of faith. The Reformers went further and insisted that the work of Christ was completed once for all on the cross, so that present experience is tied to that unique event in eternity. What has happened to me has happened to every Christian, and will continue to happen in the future, even though the temporal circumstances obtaining then may be very different from those obtaining now or in the past.

Linked to God's omnipotence, and in John of Damascus' way of thinking almost certainly a spatial attribute, is God's omniscience. We do not usually picture infinite wisdom as something which extends everywhere, but if we remember that God was thought of as a mind, or to use John's words, as the *phōs noēron* (intelligent light), the idea becomes more understandable. The main point is that God's knowledge is never detached from the reality which it professes to know. The word *detached*, which also reflects the spatial dimension, sums up the main problem which many modern theologians and philosophers have with the concept of omniscience. They isolate it as an attribute, and try to picture a god who knows everything because he sees it from the vantage point of a timeless spectator. It then becomes a problem for them to determine how God can know future events of which he is not the immediate cause. But in the Bible, omniscience cannot be isolated like this. It is closely tied both to omnipresence and to omnipotence, and cannot be understood apart from them. As far as Scripture is concerned, a truly omnipresent and omnipotent God must also be omniscient, since otherwise neither his presence nor his power would have a rational foundation. Yet this combination also makes it clear that an omniscient God cannot be a mere spectator in human affairs. If human knowledge, as we are often reminded, is power, then divine omniscience must logically be tantamount to omnipotence.

## Evil and freedom

This causes problems when we examine questions like the existence of evil in a world governed by God. What meaning can these things have if God actually possesses the attributes which are ascribed to him?[22] Christians are not called to believe in chance, but neither are they expected to be fatalists; God's plan somehow has the existence of evil built into it, without making him responsible for it. But how?

Linked to the problem of evil is the question of human freedom. The Bible tells us that the service of God is perfect freedom (Rom. 6:18) but in spite of that, philosophers have often argued that human freedom is meaningless if it cannot be exercised in a way which differentiates it from the will of God. Yet if human beings exercise their freedom in this way we are inevitably confronted with the problem of sin. Can we say that God ordained the fall of the human race as the ultimate proof of human freedom?

Many people avoid this question by saying that God knew what would happen but did not interfere with it. According to them, the human race fell on its own, but then God intervened to rescue it from the consequences of its error. The danger in this argument is that it runs the risk of making God either immoral or impotent. Human beings did not fall in a vacuum; the Bible tells us that Adam and Eve were tempted by a pre-existent being, whom it calls Satan. Where did he come from? And why did God do nothing to warn or protect humanity against prowlers of this type? Appealing to human freewill at this point merely puts the whole issue back a stage, to the problem of how spiritual evil could arise in heaven even before the creation of the world. Somewhere along the line things have apparently gone wrong with that part of the created order which is most like God himself, and God's omnipotence is inevitably called into question.

To help solve this dilemma, mediaeval theologians invented the concept of the 'happy fault' (*felix culpa*). They pointed out that the created Adam lacked two things – moral awareness and eternal life. The first of these he obtained by his sin in the garden, but the second, though it was denied him for a time, was also ultimately the result of his disobedience. Christ, the tree of life, would never have become available to human beings had Adam not sinned; therefore, so this argument runs, even sin ultimately furthers the purposes of God and is subject to his omniscient power and will.

The *felix culpa* argument was certainly an ingenious solution to a difficult problem, and it contains a good many valuable insights. It fell down in the end, however, because it was believed to make God the author of sin. The Reformers were insistent in their denial of this idea, and shifted their emphasis from the concept of *felix culpa* without affecting the doctrine of divine omnipotence.

Predestination has frequently been attacked on the ground that it is supposed to be a denial of free will, although its defenders point out that in fact it is the very opposite.[23] The real trouble with the concept is that it has been made synonymous with determinism by people who do not distinguish the person from the essence, either in God or in humanity. At the level of being, it is true to say that both the divine and the human are determined by their respective natures, an obvious point which everyone admits. Human beings might do something out of character, but they cannot go against their nature. Freedom is really conceivable only in personal terms, and it is at that level that both free will and predestination operate. God's plan is worked out by the persons of the Trinity, who have created the human race to share in their personal freedom. The essence of this freedom is voluntary obedience and self-sacrifice; it is the freedom to forget oneself and to live for others.

But humanity could always reject this freedom by disobedience, and this eventuality was also foreordained by God. Here there is a mystery which the Bible reveals but does not explain. We are told that the immediate cause of Adam's sin was his surrender to the tempting power of Satan, who had already fallen, presumably because of his pride (*cf.* Ezk. 28:12–19), but exactly why God wanted this to happen is unknown. It may be, as the *felix culpa* argument suggests, that God had in store for his elect a greater destiny than that of Adam, and that in his wisdom he knew that only by the fall could this destiny be realized. It may even be that he wished to reveal depths in his own love which only the sin of his greatest creature could bring out to the full. If we believe that it was on the cross of Christ that God poured out the deepest resources of his love for us, we ought to reflect that this would never have happened had Adam and Eve not surrendered to temptation in the Garden of Eden. Of course, as many theologians and moralists have always objected, none of these considerations is even remotely adequate as an explanation of God's predestinating will. The human mind continues to believe that God need not have done these things in the way in which human history has worked out; that in a world completely controlled by him, the pain and misery we experience could never have occurred. But at the same time, we rebel against the thought that humanity can lead only a robot existence in the hand of God. We want to insist on our freedom as individuals, but at the same time avoid any of the more unpleasant consequences. Divine predestination may be a difficult doctrine to accept, but the preferred alternative contains a built-in contradiction and is based on nothing more than personal desire.

Whatever the final explanation of the mystery of predestination may be, two things are of vital importance for the Christian. First, sin and the fall are realities which God has dealt with according to his wisdom. We may not understand their cause, but we have access to their cure, and it would obviously be silly to reject the latter simply because we cannot fully understand the former. Second, freedom entails responsibility, which puts the blame for sin squarely on us, not on God. In a time when so many people equate freedom with irresponsibility, it is surely the prime duty of the church to remind us that freedom cannot exist without obligations – of which the greatest is our obligation to seek the forgiveness of God.

Another difficult question which predestination raises is the whole question of *election*. Why does God choose some people and not others? If he is omnipotent, surely he must be able to save everyone. Why then, does he not do so? One simple answer, of course, is to abolish the whole issue at a stroke by saying that that is precisely what he has done. This solution, which is called universalism, may seem to be quite logical on the basis of God's omnipotence, but it ignores the fact that God is sovereign even over that attribute. Whether we like it or not, the Bible presents us with the picture of an omnipotent God who has chosen a particular people and, if only by implication, has excluded the rest of humanity. But how can a good omnipotent God act in a way which condemns a sizeable proportion of his creatures to eternal damnation?

Once again we must first accept that the ultimate answer to this question is a mystery which we shall never solve this side of eternity. We can begin to understand it only in terms of God's *economy*, or dispensation, a theological term which is used to describe the way God has chosen to govern his creation. The most important thing about this economy is that it is primarily personal. That God should do some things and not others is the decision of the persons of the Trinity, who together work out their common will. This decision does not curtail God's omnipotence. What it does is *apply* his omnipotence in a particular way. If we accept that there is no unrealized potential in God, then the way in which his omnipotence is used must be absolute and final. If this is so, then the ground is prepared for the immutable divine decrees, according to which some people are saved and others condemned. God's omnipotence cannot overrule his decision to elect some people and not others to salvation, because his decision is a personal act which makes use of his natural omnipotence to guarantee that his will is carried out. We must never fall into the trap of imagining that God is governed by his attributes, rather than the other way round.

We know that election works out in the way it does because it is a personal act of God, but we cannot finally explain it, because personal acts by their very nature are mysterious. We understand this to some extent from our experience of human relationships. Each of us relates to a wide circle of people with a mixture of love, liking, indifference, dislike and hatred. The reasons for each of these feelings may be many and varied, but they are seldom 'logical' in a scientific way. Sometimes we can even stand back from our situation far enough to realize this, and we ask ourselves why we relate to particular people in the way we do. Sometimes we have an explanation, but very often we really have no idea at all. Human logic and a sense of 'fairness' may tell us that we ought to treat everybody alike, but in practice we hardly ever do this. Partly this is because we have inbuilt feelings and prejudices which incline us one way or another, but partly it is because if we succeeded in such an attempt, we would probably find that we had no real relationship with anybody at all. Total equality in this sphere means practical indifference and non-involvement in the lives of others.

Now the Bible makes it quite clear that God *is* involved in the lives of human beings, and that he *does* show partiality – special favour – to his chosen people. That message is conveyed by the fourth commandment and is echoed throughout the Scriptures. It is a partiality rooted in the relationship which we have with him. As far as we are concerned the relationship is not a just one, because we have done nothing to deserve it. On the contrary, as Paul himself reminds us, as Christians we should be conscious of just how totally unworthy we are to receive the grace of God. But God, in his omnipotence, has overruled our unworthiness by sending his Son to die for us on the cross. What human minds regard as unjust, because it is undeserved, the mind of God has made just by his own sovereign will and act. We may wonder at this, but we are hardly in a position to claim that those who have not benefited from the mercy of God have somehow been subjected to an injustice. The grace of God is a very deep mystery, but although we can never hope to plumb its depths, we can at least know that it is only by his omnipotence, applied to us in mercy, that we are saved at all.

We have spent a long time on this question of omnipotence, but although we have examined it from many angles, it cannot be said that we have solved all its problems. Indeed, we have not even mentioned some of them. But enough has been said to make it clear that the difficulties which it raises for theology are not insuperable, as long as the problems are understood in their context, and not isolated from it in a way which is both unhistorical and untenable.

## Material attributes

When we turn to the material attributes of God we enter what is almost another world. God is described by John of Damascus as simple, uncompound, incorporeal and 'without flux', a rather ambiguous term which translates the Greek *arrheustos*, the meaning of which we must examine in due course.

The simplicity of God means that he cannot be analysed or subdivided into parts. He is the basic minimum of divinity as well as the maximum, the ultimate reality in himself. It is true that the term 'simplicity' has sometimes been used in a wider sense, to argue (quite correctly) that God is 'without body, parts or passions', as Article I of the Church of England puts it, although this is an extension of its original meaning and should not be confused with it. Nor does simplicity mean that God is the primordial substance out of which everything else is made. Creation is not an extension or a corruption of God's being, but something else which is quite a different reality. God's simplicity can be understood only in relation to himself.

As a concept, simplicity has played an important historical role which continues to manifest itself in the field of comparative religion. Christianity has always been obliged to explain the Trinity by positing a level of objective reality in God which is not governed by simplicity. This distinction has failed to penetrate Judaism, and it has been decisively rejected by Islam, so that both these religions, and especially the latter, tend to regard Christianity as a form of concealed polytheism. Both cling to the belief that true monotheism means the worship of a God who is a simple being. To this Christians reply that we worship not the essence of God, but his persons. Of course, both Jews and Muslims would say that God is personal, but in their understanding, personhood is really an attribute of the divine essence. Christianity denies this, maintaining that the persons are subsistent realities in their own right. At the level of the person, which is the point at which we enter into relationship with God, Christians insist that there is a plurality in unity, which is not to be confused with the simplicity of God's impersonal essence. The result is that everything which belongs to God's fixed and immutable essence is mediated to us through the relationship which we have with the persons. Our knowledge of God is therefore not codified in law, nor established according to a fatalism which no power in heaven or on earth can alter.

Objections to divine simplicity which are made on biblical grounds usually concentrate on the secondary, or extended meaning of the term. Thus it is not at all obvious that the God of the Bible is without a body, parts or passions, even if these are not the same as their human counterparts. Some process theologians are prepared to argue that the universe itself is God's body, although it is very difficult to see what biblical evidence can be cited in support of this idea. More common is

95

the assertion that God has a spiritual body of some kind, which is not visible nor entirely analogous to the human body.

This opinion is supported by referring to those Old Testament passages which are supposed to mention the different parts of the body. To some, it appears that the ancient Hebrews, although they were forbidden to make graven images of God, nevertheless believed that he had eyes, hands, a mouth and so on. The somewhat curious co-existence of these anthropomorphisms alongside a clearly spiritual monotheism has provided a tempting subject for scholarly debate about the Old Testament conception of the being of God. Traditional liberalism tends to look on such things either as a survival of a more primitive polytheism or as a sign of the corrupting influence of the adjacent paganism. Classical theism, in contrast, has usually argued that they are poetic forms designed to explain the ways of God in terms which can be absorbed by the finite mind.

According to this second line of thinking, to say that Jesus 'sits on the right hand of God' does not mean what it says in literal terms. It has to be transposed to the spiritual level by means of symbolical interpretation. When this is done, we are meant to realize that what is being said here is that Christ shares the Father's kingdom. In his ascension and heavenly session he has taken up the reins of spiritual government, with the result that our Saviour is now also our Lord and our King. The body's right hand has nothing to do with the being of God, and nobody ever supposed that it did. The use of such imagery can be adequately explained by oriental custom, according to which the heir to the throne was frequently installed as co-ruler and seated at the king's right hand, the hand which held the sceptre of government.

Classical theism argues that only the most superficial kind of literalism would ever have imagined otherwise, although more recently a desire to make God seem as human as possible has given a new prominence to the anthropomorphisms. It may now be argued, for example, that the Hebrews *felt* God in this way, so acutely conscious were they of his presence in their midst. This may well have been true of some people in Israel, of course, just as it is true of some people today, but the Old Testament does not give the impression that the majority of the nation was deeply sensitive to God working among them. On the whole therefore, it seems better to stick with the traditional explanation, that the anthropomorphisms are didactic aids to understanding which are not to be taken literally, or linked in any way to the internal composition of God's being, without speculating too much about the religious awareness of the ancient Israelites.

The attributes expressed in the adjectives 'uncompound' (*asynthetos*) and 'incorporeal' (*asōmatos*) need not detain us long. The first is obvious, that God is not made up of different substances or particles, nor even of things which can have no independent existence. Uncompoundness is thus just the negative side of simplicity. Incorporeality too is fairly clear, although we must remember that John is applying it within a spiritual context. An angel might seem to be 'incorporeal' to us, but it was not so to John, or to his mediaeval successors, who believed that spirits could and did occupy a space, since otherwise they would be co-extensive with God himself. This is one reason why the question of how many angels could stand on the head of a pin did not seem as silly to them as it may do to us.

More difficult is the concept of being 'without flux', although here the problem is more to do with the translation than with the thing itself. 'Flux' simply means 'flow'. The Greek term suggests that what is meant here is first, that God is fully consistent in his omnipresence, *i.e.* there are no parts of him which have a greater concentration of divinity than others, and second, that he does not extend himself in space, like a smell or an oilslick. This last observation is very important because of the belief held by process theologians, that God is expanding along with his universe. God cannot expand because he already fills everything in the total consistency of his being.

## Qualitative attributes

It is when we come to the last category of attributes that the most serious difficulties arise. We have chosen to call them the qualitative attributes, in line with the ancient understanding of quality (*poiotēs*, what is it like?). A modern observer might find this concept difficult to understand, and prefer to call them attributes of motion, or even of energy. But this would be incompatible with the Ancients' understanding, since in their view God's being was itself motion (*esse = moveri*), as we have already seen. It is highly probable in fact that a concept of motion is central to these attributes, although John of Damascus would probably not have thought primarily in those terms.

The first of these attributes of quality is also by far the most difficult. God is described as *apathēs*, which may be translated either as 'passionless' (*i.e.* without any suffering in practice) or as 'impassible' (*i.e.* incapable of suffering in principle). The slight difference in meaning between the two English terms is not conveyed by the Greek, where either sense is possible. Today, discussion centres on the question of God's impassibility in principle, a subject which has recently been debated at great length.[24] As it was understood in ancient times, *apatheia* was the state of perfect tranquillity, free from the cares of the world. Philosophers strove to attain it by any number of devices which were geared to produce complete mental and spiritual detachment. The basic attitude which this kind of thinking encouraged can be seen from the way in which we use the word 'apathy' today, and the pejorative meaning which now attaches to it gives us some idea of why many people do not think that *apatheia* is an appropriate description of God's being. The idea that God exists in a state which is perfectly still, and that he has no involvement with the world, obviously goes against the Scriptures, and it is rightly criticized for being unbiblical.

At the same time we must also recognize that this pagan concept was not really what Christians had in mind when they spoke of God's impassibility. *Apatheia*, as John of Damascus understood it, meant the inability to suffer, *i.e.* impassibility in the strict sense. The emphasis was not on tranquillity in a state of indifference, but on the sovereignty of God, whose being could not be attacked or harmed by any outside power. Because human suffering was generally regarded as the result of man's sinfulness, it was thought that the holiness of God demanded a doctrine of divine impassibility to go with it. In modern times, however, even this view has been attacked as unbiblical, most notably by Jürgen Moltmann. Moltmann believes that Christians must have a God who can identify with the depths of human suffering, a crucified God.[25] He attacks classical theism for having distorted the central message of Christianity by emphasizing a philosophical idea of God which he believes is totally at variance with the witness of the Scriptures. In making this assertion, he is in harmony with perhaps the majority of modern theologians, who share his concerns and accept his arguments. As a result, divine impassibility is now a major topic of debate in Christian theological circles.

The essential point which has to be remembered in this argument is the familiar one, that this attribute, like all others mentioned here, belongs to God's essence. As this essence is above and beyond anything else which exists, the early Christians were right to say that it cannot be subjected to an external power which might cause it harm. Any pain which God might suffer would have to be self-inflicted by using an external object like a knife or a gun, and no external object can have any effect on God. We can hardly say that God finds it painful just to live with himself.

Many people will reject this sort of argument as naive, and claim that God's pain is emotional, not physical. God sees our sufferings and is moved by them, a fact which is believed to be a principal motive, even *the* principal motive, in leading him to produce his plan for our salvation. But further reflection will show that it would not help matters very much if we said that God has been driven to redeem us out of sympathy for our suffering. That would imply that there is some virtue in pain, which is the very thing that proponents of this theory are (rightly) determined to deny. In a sense it is rather like having *felix culpa* again, this time by the back door.

The answer surely must lie in saying that the *persons* of the Trinity are indeed moved by our suffering, but that God's *essence* is untouched by it. If this appears to be heartless and cruel, we need only look to the analogy of the doctor and his patients. The great physician must sympathize with his patients' diseases and be able to alleviate their suffering, but

99

he is not called upon to experience it along with them. In fact, we would probably lose confidence in him if he did. A hospital patient does not want to see his doctor lying in the bed next to him, assuring him that he really does know what it feels like to be ill.

Naturally, opponents of the traditional view have appealed to the atonement as evidence that God really did take our place of suffering – not in a hospital bed, but on the cross. They have claimed that the atonement is irrefutable evidence that God is passible, and some may even argue that if he were not, we could never have been saved.[26] Once again the answer must be that on the cross the divine person of the Son of God suffered and died for us in his human nature, which he had assumed in the womb of Mary. The mystery of the incarnation is that the immortal person took on a mortal nature, in order to make it possible for him to suffer and die on our behalf. To claim, as some modern theologians have done, that the *divine* nature died at Calvary is absurd. Not only would it automatically entail the death of the entire Trinity, thereby making a nonsense of the atoning sacrifice offered to the Father, but it would involve God's essence in a logical contradiction. It would suggest that somehow God's essence could become sin, which goes against the entire witness of Scripture to the perfection and goodness of God's being.

The implications which a doctrine of divine passibility has when applied to God's essence are catastrophic. We are left with a God who can be crippled with pain; to be sure it is on our behalf, but that is cold comfort to the sinner who needs a God who is strong to save, not one who is weakened by our infirmities. We cannot afford to be misled on this point by an unthinking sentimentality, or even by an emotional reaction of our own, however noble it might be, towards human suffering. Moltmann's theology has come out of the Nazi concentration camps, in the light of which its main thrust is perfectly understandable, but the fact that God did not reach down from heaven to stop that terrible slaughter does not of itself mean that we must change our view of God. Our lives are shrouded in mysteries which we cannot fathom, but God has a purpose in everything which will one day be revealed to

100

us. Heaven and earth may pass away, but he does not pass away; even in the deepest human suffering he is there to offer a peace which the world can neither give nor understand.

Compared with the problems surrounding impassibility, those which touch on unchangeability and unalterability seem almost trivial. They are interconnected in that suffering is generally supposed to involve change, and this has often been used as an argument in favour of divine impassibility by defenders of classical theism. Nowadays we would group these two attributes together as immutability, although it is possible that John may have been thinking of two different kinds of change – one produced from without, the other from within. In any case, these are both covered by the concept of immutability. There is little need to say much about this, except to make the point once again that God's personal response to his creatures does not mean that his essence is mutable. Relationship is intrinsic to the concept of person, and anything which pertains to that must be regarded as consistent with his being. The biblical statements which suggest that God changes his mind do not refer to God as he is in himself, or even to the character which he has revealed to us, but rather to the relationship which he has with his human creatures. In this relationship God has perfect freedom, but nothing he does should be interpreted as being inconsistent with his nature. Even in a case like this, the only thing which is affected is the dispensation of his mercy; in itself, the quality of his mercy remains quite unchanged.

The last attribute mentioned by John of Damascus is an oddity to our minds, in that we would normally put it first or at least well ahead of some of the others, and might easily think that it belonged more to the spatial attributes than to the qualitative ones. This is invisibility, a concept which, strange though it may seem, John seems to have understood in relation to motion. The Bible itself supports this connection when it says that God is like the wind, which moves but cannot be seen (Jn. 3:8). His movements and his deeds are real, more real in their way than ours are, but they cannot be detected or measured by the senses. Nor can God's essence, the sum of all motion, be seen or depicted in any way

101

(Ex. 20:4 *etc.*). To us this seems a fairly obvious thing to say, although at the time, in a world full of cultic idolatry, its force must have been keenly felt. At the same time, Christians are often guilty of 'seeking a sign', and we must be careful to guard against this. God is too great, too free and too powerful to be contained within the limits of our feeble vision, and we must never try to limit him in this way.

## Understanding the divine nature today

We have now reached the bottom of John's list, where we have discovered, sometimes in unfamiliar garb, most of the attributes which we would normally associate with God's being. We have approached them sympathetically, and tried to show classical theism in the best possible light. Nevertheless we have also discovered that some of these attributes are being sharply attacked today, whilst others have tended to change their meaning, and still others are no longer distinguished as separate concepts. Can we therefore continue to use the traditional list of God's attributes, and maintain that in spite of these things, it is still valid today?

If we want to rearrange the categories here and there, find other words to express what is meant, or conflate two or more words into a single umbrella idea, there is no real problem, since all we are doing is looking at the *form* in which the classical teaching was expressed. Tidying things up in this way is an age-old practice, and in fact it is what John himself thought he was doing. It is only when our thoughts turn to matters of *substance* that real problems arise. The arguments about divine impassibility for example, will not go away merely by reclassifying the attributes, even if a good deal of debate can be avoided by defining what they mean more carefully. The question will still be asked whether it is right to ascribe any kind of impassibility to God, or whether in fact classical theism has succumbed to an alien way of thinking on this point.

Dissatisfaction with the traditional position may be even greater if we ask ourselves what reality these attributes are supposed to have. Is immutability a thing in its own right? Can one imagine it existing in the pure state, without anything else? We have already seen how omnipresence, omnipotence and omniscience imply each other's existence, which presumably means that it is impossible for them to exist independently of each other. But if that is true, what validity is there in the distinctions which classical theism has traditionally made? Are we not really just finding different words to say what amounts in the end to the same thing?

Classical theism has always tried to maintain a balance here between the individual attributes of God and the totality of his essence by saying that each single attribute is equal to the whole of his being. Omnipotence for example, is not a part of God which might theoretically be removed; it is a concept which describes God as he is in his fullness. The other attributes all co-inhere in his omnipotence, and the same can be said equally well of his invisibility (since God is completely invisible), his immutability, his impassibility and so on. Yet it is also true that some of God's attributes are more fundamental than others. Omnipotence entails impassibility and possibly invisibility, but the same could not be said in reverse. God could easily be impassible and invisible without being all-powerful as well. Is there any way in which a hierarchy, or scale of attributes can be established?

As it happens, there is a good reason for regarding omnipotence as God's most fundamental attribute. This is because in the Bible, this attribute is not described as an adjective, or alluded to in some kind of metaphor, but is given to us as a name, which is a title of God. He is *El Shaddai*, *Ho Pantokratōr*, the Almighty. For this reason, a modern restructuring of the divine attributes ought probably to begin with omnipotence, and arrange the rest accordingly, interpreting their meaning in terms of the requirements of God the Almighty. If this were done in a systematic way, it would effect a major realignment in the form and definition of the attributes, although in the end it would probably do little to affect the substance of the classical doctrine. In this connection it must be said, in order to avoid any possible misunderstanding, that a hierarchy of attributes based on omnipotence would not mean that some of them would be less essential than others, or even optional to God's being. The divine simplicity assures us that there is no such thing as

103

a non-essential attribute in God's being, a position which is in no way compromised by logical rearrangement.

By the same token there is no reason to retain the other distinctions which are traditionally used to classify God's being. To argue, as some have, that there is a real opposition in principle between the 'negative' attributes like infinity, and the 'positive' ones like eternity, is to introduce a purely lexical distinction into the substance of God. It is hard to see what practical difference there is between infinity and omnipresence, for example; the one would seem to imply the other. If they are just two different ways of saying the same thing, the fact that infinity is a 'negative' word loses whatever special significance it may originally have had.

It is equally futile to attempt to maintain a distinction between the 'communicable' and the 'incommunicable' attributes of God, at least at the level of the divine essence. There is certainly a real difference here, but it is tied to, and logically dependent on, the prior distinction between the persons and the essence of God. It is because the persons communicate, but the essence does not, that the attributes of the latter are incommunicable. In some cases what appears to be a single attribute may occur in both categories, as for example, eternity. In the context of their personal relationship with God, Christians have the gift of eternal life, without thereby being exempt from death at the natural level. Failure to relate this distinction to the theological principles of person and essence makes the classification of the traditional attributes look arbitrary, and may even lead to serious error, as, for example, when it is said that Christians have a right to be healed from their diseases in their mortal flesh. There is a confusion here between the spiritual and the material which is the direct result of a failure to distinguish between person and essence in God and in human beings.

Of course none of this affects the deeper question posed by the apophatic ('negative') approach to theology, which is whether God's essential attributes are ultimately conceivable at all. When all is said and done, what can we really say about the divine infinity? Does not the very concept imply that we have formed a mental image, an idol in the mind, which cannot correspond in any real sense to the one who is above all thought and beyond all being? There is a long tradition of incompatibility and even antagonism between the Scholastic approach to theology and the mystical one, although curiously enough, both have found inspiration in the writings of John of Damascus. It is evidently possible to read John from either perspective, without sensing any incongruity. This is because John did not state clearly whether he regarded the attributes which he listed as literally negative or not. Quite probably he did, and the Eastern tradition has followed him on that assumption. But the matter is not so clearcut as to preclude the mediaeval Western development, which followed a rather different course. So much so in fact, that eventually it even got to the point of regarding attributes like immutability and incorporeality as real entities in themselves, which could be conceived, and even perceived, by the intellect.

The Reformers were not comfortable with Scholastic intellectualism, although later Protestants were to take it over with little change. As we have seen, Calvin was very reluctant to say anything about God's essence, and concentrated instead on saying that we know God only through his persons. In this he was moving away from mediaeval Western theology towards the more primitive Eastern, or mystical, view. Unfortunately it is not known whether this shift was the fruit of his independent reading of the Bible, or whether it reflected the influence of the ancient Greek Fathers, whom he had also read. Probably there is something of each in his work, though we must remember that Calvin did not embrace apophatic theology in anything like its developed form. In saying that God could not be known in his essence but that he *could* be known in his persons, Calvin allowed that apophatic theology was right as far as the divine essence was concerned, but he did not accept that it could be applied to our experience of the persons as well.

Calvin's position seems to us to be fundamentally sound, both because it makes the right distinction between what is knowable and what is unknowable in God, and because it insists that what is knowable can be understood only in the context of a personal relationship with him. Detached or disinterested knowledge of God is inconceivable. Calvin's

105

position also managed to retain a proper concern for God's unknowable being, something which is in danger of being forgotten today. An overemphasis on knowing God in personal relationship can so easily lead to a semi-conscious denigration of his divinity, and a loss of a sense of his glorious power and majesty. We are faced with this danger today because we have either neglected the attributes of God, or tried to reinterpret them in ways which are foreign to his nature. Process theology has gone further than most by completely reworking its vision of God to make him fit within a temporal and spatial framework. In its more radical forms it is too extreme, and too easily shown to be untenable in certain crucial areas, to be able to be a lasting rival to traditional Christianity. But there are many ways in which it is possible to stop short of a full-blown process theology, yet still do injury to the biblical concept of God's essence. The attitude which sees God exclusively in subjective and functional terms, and denies him a transcendent objectivity, is the first step along the road to the abandonment of orthodox Christianity. It may be true that the forms in which classical theism has been expressed are inadequate in places, and open to revision, but to abandon their substance completely is to abandon the God of the Bible.

## The failure of natural theology

From our brief survey of the traditional arguments for the existence of God, and our examination of the attributes which are customarily ascribed to his nature, we return inevitably to the question which underlies all attempts to study God in this way. What place, if any, can a natural theology have in the modern world? The ontological framework, which classical theism shared with other scientific and cultural disciplines, has now given way to a much more functional approach. We are no longer as concerned as our ancestors were with the problem of pure being; today it is the action and power of God which excite our interest and attention. On the one hand this has led to demands for the revision of classical theism along lines which could accommodate a more 'dynamic' theology, and this explains the rise of movements like that of process theology. On the other hand it has also contributed to the spread of atheism and agnosticism, because a functional approach to God demands evidence that he works in a way which directly affects our lives. If nothing happens to us which can be attributed to God (and to nothing else), then we can live without him, and not be concerned with whether he exists or not.

Not surprisingly, the demands of the modern functional outlook have left natural theology, which has been challenged at every turn by recent scientific theories and discoveries, in disarray. Natural theology built its case very largely on the analogy of being, a procedure which now appears to be discredited by the abandonment of the traditional concept of substance. The picture of a hierarchy of beings extending upwards from the amoeba to human beings to God, which had been worked out at different times over the centuries, has been completely overturned by modern biological theories. Evolution may look like a survival of this idea but of course it is not, as there is no evolution from human beings to God. The evolutionary scale stops with the human race since no other form of life is available for scientific investigation, and natural theology is left without viable support.

This unavailability of God is in fact the greatest argument against natural theology, at least in the forms which it has traditionally taken. God's activity may always be 'read into' the universe, the origins of which may even be attributed to him. But as far as hoping to find him in his creation by scientific means is concerned, natural theology is a complete non-starter. There is simply no way in which God can be measured or his existence made necessary to explain the course of events. In strictly scientific terms, therefore, God's existence is superfluous, because it does not come within the scope of scientific investigation.

Of course it is equally true that science does not prove that God does *not* exist either. Scientific atheism of the type practised until recently in Eastern Europe is just as untenable as natural theology. It depends for its superficial validity on the unwarranted assumption that scientific methods are adequate to explain everything that exists in the real world.

Western opinion has never been committed to that view-point in any dogmatic way, although it has often been accepted by the intelligentsia in the West even more absolutely than it has been in Marxist societies.

One result of this commitment to science can be seen in the widespread urge today to examine what is tellingly called the 'paranormal'. The word is interesting in itself because it reveals a fundamental belief in a scientific norm. The study of the paranormal has in fact never received universal approval in scientific circles, being most staunchly opposed by those who believe that scientific method is the key to all truth. In spite of this, there is now a greater openness to the paranormal, partly because scientific experiments have revealed complexities in the universe which were previously undreamt of, but partly also because confidence in the power of science to resolve every problem has waned considerably. What was once supposed to herald an age of progress for humanity, free from fears rooted in superstition, has turned out instead to be a hidden monster which dangles in front of us a fiery destruction infinitely more terrible than any medi-aeval picture of hell. The modern world once hailed as a liberator the force which now threatens to destroy it, a terrible paradox which has driven many people to look elsewhere for meaning in their lives. Does this mean that traditional Christianity, with or without its natural theology, will experience a widespread revival?

The search for meaning has certainly led some people back to Christianity, although it may be true that at least as many again have been attracted to oriental mysticism, esoteric philosophies and fads of different kinds. In some cases it is probably true that Christianity itself has been perceived in this light, and there are many aspects of current popular devotion which look more like a mystical fad than biblical teaching in action. It certainly cannot be assumed that a widespread abandonment of the God of science will lead automatically to a revival of the Christian faith in its traditional form.

Christianity is not something which human beings have invented or discovered; it is something which God has revealed. Human strivings and natural theology fail because

108

their starting point is too weak to be able to carry them through to the end. Disillusioned people will not be able to rediscover God by looking around them, not even by reading the Bible or by contemplating the figure of Jesus. Of course these things are valuable and necessary, but belief in the existence of God is ultimately dependent not on them, but on a conviction in the heart which only the Holy Spirit can produce. From the beginning Christianity has been a proclamation, not a thesis supported by various logical arguments. The apostles called for commitment to Christ by preaching the gospel of sin, righteousness and judgment (Jn. 16:8–11). When that emphasis has been diluted or abandoned, as it has to a very large extent today, the glory of the Lord has departed, the power of the church has been weakened, and belief in God has faded away.

When that happens, people looking for truth may appeal to the phenomenon of Jesus, but if they lack the Spirit's conviction they are liable to conclude that we can know next to nothing about his life and teaching, since so many scholars disagree about them. Such people may even look for vestiges of the Trinity, either in human beings or in the created order. Traditionalists may resurrect the proofs for the existence of God, modified in order to respond to the arguments raised against them, and in the right climate, they may attract the disillusioned to a form of neo-conservatism. Their attempts to rescue God from oblivion may strike us as courageous, irrelevant or disastrous, according to our point of view, but in terms of results, they are perhaps best described as pathetic. The God of the Bible can be known and experienced only in the way in which he has decreed. At the end of the day, the proofs of God's existence offered by natural theology are unconvincing, except to those who have already surrendered their lives to him who is the way, the truth and the life, and experienced for themselves that peace of God which passes all our natural understanding.

## Summary

At the end of a long and often difficult chapter, let us summarize our findings as follows:

1. God is a being who exists in an objectively conceivable eternity, free of all the limitations of time and space. In his being (or essence) he is completely different from us or from anything else in the created order, and is therefore fundamentally unknowable.

2. The being of God can be described only in terms of its nature, which stands in sharp contrast to everything else of which we have experience. For this reason, most of the words used to describe the divine nature are negative in form, telling us what God is not, rather than what he is. It is therefore wrong to build too much on them, and assume that we can somehow define God's being. The most we can ever hope to do is to exclude certain misunderstandings, even as we accept that any description of his being will have its own logical difficulties.

3. In line with this, the so-called 'proofs' for the existence of God can be used only as supporting evidence for a belief which is already held for other reasons. Natural theology, of which the 'proofs' are a cornerstone, can never take the place of a direct encounter with God, which can occur only at the personal level. So it is that the substance of our knowledge of God lies in the realm of personal experience, which takes us automatically to the second aspect of our theology – the identity and relationship of the three persons who make up the unity of the Godhead. It is with this that the remaining chapters of this book will be mainly concerned.

# 3

## ONE GOD
## IN TRINITY

### Knowing God personally

The big difference between Christian faith and any kind of philosophical theology is that Christians claim to know God, the ultimate reality, personally. The belief that God is a personal being is one which is shared with other monotheistic religions, especially Judaism and Islam, but Christianity is fundamentally different from them in that it claims that the *one* God in whom we all believe is known to us not as one, but as three distinct persons. To a Jew or to a Muslim, this appears to be a denial of monotheism, and it must be admitted that many Christians also find it difficult to hold the Trinity of persons together in the unity of a single divine being. Yet without the Trinity there would be no Christianity. Our belief in the saving work of Christ the Son of God, and in the indwelling presence of God the Holy Spirit demands that we worship God in that way.

In this chapter we shall look briefly at the picture of God given to us in the Old Testament, and then examine how and why Christians were forced to modify this in the light of the revelation given in and by Jesus Christ. As we do this, we shall consider the alternatives to trinitarianism which have emerged, and discuss the reasons why the church rejected them. The chapter concludes with a detailed examination of the New Testament evidence for the trinitarian doctrine of God which the early church eventually elaborated as its definitive interpretation of biblical theology.

## The Old Testament picture of God

There is no doubt that the great monotheistic religions, including Islam, owe their theological understanding primarily to the witness of the biblical texts. What is perhaps less clear is the extent to which the Scriptures really represent a unique way of perceiving reality. As we have already noted, some scholars would argue that the ancient Israelites were henotheistic. According to this theory, Abraham and his descendants specialized in the cult of Yahweh, originally a tribal god of the Semites, and made this cult the badge of their distinctiveness. They were not originally hostile to other deities, although inevitably the exclusiveness of the tribal cult would have made itself felt right across the board. By the time of the Israelite monarchies (c. 1000–586 BC) the existence of rival gods was increasingly being regarded as a threat to national survival. Because of this the Jerusalem establishment, always champions of Yahwism, began to suppress rival cults and to centralize the worship of Yahweh in the temple, where its purity could be controlled. Much later, after the exile (586–539 BC), Yahwism developed a philosophical strain. This was based partly on native traditions of wisdom, and partly on Greek influence, which became very powerful after the time of Alexander the Great (336–323 BC). This strain turned henotheism into monotheism, and paved the way for the exclusivist claims of Christianity.[1]

This rough sketch of the development of Israelite religion has many variations, including the belief that the early Israelites were really polytheists, for whom Yahweh came to have special importance, but there are two things which are common to all its forms. The first is the conviction that one God, Yahweh, is central to the religious identity of Israel; the second is that the Israelites, or gifted individuals among them, were responsible for selecting him as their tribal deity, and for moving him from the primitive stage outlined above to the sophisticated monotheism we know today. To put it another way, these theories maintain that the picture of God given in the Old Testament is the result of human insight and perception, which gradually extended and adapted a strand latent in the early traditions of the Israelites. Needless to say, this view contrasts dramatically with the traditional picture of what is presented in the Bible, and which has been accepted by orthodox Christianity down through the ages. The orthodox tradition says that Yahweh was from the beginning the only true God, who revealed himself in different ways at different times (Heb. 1:1–2). It accepts the fact that human perception of this revelation has always been in some sense inadequate, although whether it is right to say that it has therefore been faulty or distorted, remains a matter for discussion. Even the most Judaistic Christians have always been prepared to admit that the New Testament is a fuller revelation of God than is the Old, but along with the mainstream of Christian tradition they do not accept that this progression involved the correction of earlier mistakes. The God of Abraham, Isaac and Jacob is also the God of Jesus Christ, plainly recognizable as such in all essential particulars. It is a certain strand of modern scholarship, say the adherents of the orthodox tradition, not the text of the Bible, which suggests that Yahweh began his career as a narrow-minded, bloodthirsty tribal tyrant, who was later transformed into the universal God of love and peace.

Those who believe that traditional monotheism was also the most primitive religion of Israel can point out, with some justice, that arguments against their view are largely speculative. Primitive henotheism is a thesis based more on inferences from the silence of the texts than on any specific, positive statements. It is the fact that other gods are not condemned in the patriarchal narratives or elsewhere in the early literature of Israel which gives rise to this supposition, and very little else. It used to be thought that the co-existence of two names for God, El and Yahweh, was an indication of such a primitive stage, but this is no longer generally accepted. In the earliest documents the two names are interchangeable, as well as being used side by side, so that it is impossible to isolate distinct strands at any stage in the known development of Old Testament literature. It is probably true that El is a more general term for deity than Yahweh, but the suggestion that the latter is inferior, dependent or more restricted in scope than the former, cannot be sustained from the evidence.[2]

Another important point is the fact that according to the Old Testament, Yahweh is a God of unlimited power, sufficient to meet every conceivable need of Israel. He can defeat the gods of other nations, bring tangible blessings to his people, and generally do whatever he pleases. There is never any suggestion that a cry for help to Yahweh will not be heard on the ground that the plea in question is beyond his abilities, or outside his sphere of competence. This suggests that for the Israelites other gods were superfluous; and the fact that in the Old Testament Yahweh's claims depend on his ability to act implies that other gods were not thought to exist in the same way as Yahweh. It is possible, as many Christians have in fact believed, that the gods of the heathen were demonic powers, and not just figments of the imagination,[3] but whatever one thinks about this suggestion, there is no question that the pagan gods could ever be regarded as the equals of the God of Israel. There were thus very good reasons for believing that Israelite religion, from its earliest stages, was a practical monotheism, even if it only slowly achieved the articulated, philosophical systematization familiar to us nowadays.

The Christian church adopted the form of Jewish monotheism with which it was familiar, and has always maintained that the God of Israel is the same God that we worship in Jesus Christ. But even a casual observer can see at once that Christian trinitarianism distances its theology from any kind of Judaism. What were the factors which impelled the early Christians to depart from their inherited understanding of God in this way, and why have subsequent attempts to revert to a strict monotheism been rejected? This question is perhaps the most important single issue which Christians have to face, especially if they engage in interfaith dialogue, or in mission to those of another religion. It would be comforting to be able to say that trinitarian theology was as simple and straightforward as any kind of monotheism, although of course it is not, and the steps by which Christians moved away from Judaism were often almost as complex as the doctrines they proclaimed.[4] In this chapter we shall look at each step in turn, and try to demonstrate how and why the church found itself obliged to hold to its own unique form of monotheism.

# Unitarianism?

## Non-Christian forms of unitarianism

For Judaism and Islam, not to mention a number of heretical offshoots of Christianity, the essence of theology is a belief in the absolute oneness of God. This belief is so strong that any compromise of the basic principle is immediately regarded as false, and even blasphemous. Of course Christians agree with Jews and Muslims that there is only one God, but much to the latters' bewilderment, they insist that this one God is also a Trinity of persons. To make matters more complicated, Christians do not believe that the Trinity is formed by cutting God up into three pieces, or by regarding him from three different angles – ideas which, however unacceptable they may be in themselves, would at least preserve a semblance of basic monotheism. Christians insist that each of the persons is fully God in his own right, while remaining at the same time distinct from the others. To Jews or Muslims it might appear that Christians affirm everything they believe about God, and then go on to add two extra persons, whose existence seems to contradict an otherwise common affirmation of monotheism.

These differences between the great monotheistic religions are important, not only for historical reasons but for contemporary religious dialogue as well. Christians need to be aware of other religions and their theology, partly because the generally tolerant climate in which we live tends to be sympathetic to non-Christian beliefs, but also because of the very real challenge which they present to our faith. In interfaith dialogue, Christianity is bound to appear as the odd one out among the great monotheistic systems, and the temptation to

115

reduce Jesus to the level of Moses, Muhammad or the Buddha becomes very great. The traditional orthodox insistence that Jesus was not just a great moral teacher but God incarnate is bound to appear unreasonable and even arrogant in a spiritual climate which, contrary to his teaching, accepts that there is more than one way to God.[5] Because of this, Christians must have a clear understanding of how and why they differ from those whose beliefs at first sight appear to be remarkably similar to theirs. In the case of Islam, there is also the sobering thought that historically it has won innumerable converts from Christianity – far more, in fact, than Christians have ever won from Islam.

To start with, everyone must agree that Judaism stands in a special relationship to Christianity. The Christian church began among the Jews, and it was severed from its parent religion only gradually, and with some difficulty. Moreover, Christians accept the Jewish Scriptures as having been inspired by God, and they have appropriated the spiritual inheritance of ancient Israel. It is certainly true that there has sometimes been a tendency among Christians to downgrade the Old Testament in actual practice, and this has even been justified theologically by saying that its picture of God is fundamentally sub-Christian. This opinion was held by the second-century heretic Marcion (d. *c.* 144), and it can be found today among some of the more liberal theologians and biblical scholars. On the other hand, there has also been a tendency, which was particularly strong in the fifth century, and again after the Reformation, to make Christianity into what Tertullian called a *nova lex* ('new law'), that is to say, a revamped and universalized form of Judaism. Somewhere in the middle stands the mainstream Christian heritage, which canonizes the Old Testament and its teaching, while recognizing that it must be understood differently in the light of the new dispensation.

This is important, because when Christians try to assess Judaism, they are prone to fall into one of two fundamental errors. Either they regard Judaism as basically the same religion as Christianity but without the latter's universal spiritual appeal, or they see it as a once living faith which got stuck in a dead form of legalism, from which Jesus and the

116

early Christians were trying to free it. The trouble with these approaches is not that they are altogether false, but that they concentrate on secondary matters, and fail to get to grips with the basic difference between the two religions, which lies in their understanding of God and their approach to him.

In Jewish eyes, God has made a covenant with Abraham and his descendants, who now form the nation of Israel. This covenant is a personal relationship with Jacob (Israel) in which the nation participates by a kind of corporate extension. How this operates is worked out in the law of Moses, where the role of each member of the society is defined in relation to the covenant, and especially in relation to the atoning sacrifice made each year by the high priest in the temple of Jerusalem. As a cultic official, the high priest is a representative of the people before God, a kind of mediator between him and them. But although his role was unique, he was not necessarily the only intermediary between God and the people, as we can see from the special place given to the prophets, and later to the kings as well. In the classical, Davidic form of Israelite society, the prophets, the priests and the king were all officials through whom God entered into contact with his people.

In later Judaism these offices gradually ceased to function. The kingship was overthrown in 586 BC and was never restored. Prophecy faded out about 400 BC, and religious writings after that date were later excluded from the Hebrew canon. The priesthood though, lasted until AD 70, so that in the time of Jesus it appeared to be the most important office in Israel; but its subsequent demise left the Jews with nothing but the law and the traditions by which it was interpreted. As a result, there followed a development of Jewish legalism which produced the Mishnah and the Talmud, writings which are not accepted by Christians but which today form the real basis of Judaism.

From the Christian point of view, what is striking about these later writings is how little they actually say about God. Even Jewish mysticism, which to some extent is a compensation for the dryness of the legal tradition, does not as a rule speak of that union and communion with God which is the main feature of its Christian counterpart, and when it does –

as in the writings of Martin Buber – the probability is that it has undergone substantial Christian influence. Jewish mysticism tends to be esoteric, almost magical in its use of prayer and material objects, with a strong emphasis on angels and other spiritual beings who stand, but seldom mediate, between God and human beings.

In Judaism God is one and personal, but although these characteristics are fundamental to his being, they are not the most important element in Jewish worship of him. Jews tend to be preoccupied with the holiness of God, and especially of the divine name, an attitude which is inculcated by the covenant law of Israel. The main purpose of this law is to keep Jews clean, pure and undefiled, so as to make them worthy of their calling as God's chosen people. But the restrictive legalism which this has entailed is not regarded by those who uphold it as a fetter on their spiritual liberty. On the contrary, it appears to them to be the main basis of their spiritual assurance and freedom, since only within the narrow confines of the law can Jews be assured that they are living according to God's will. The law, supplemented by the interpretations of later generations, is revered as the voice of God, through which the nation enters into a living experience of its covenant relationship with him.

In principle, Christianity subscribes to the Jewish covenant, and the belief in a holy God which that entails. It accepts the law of Moses as a revelation of God's holiness, but argues that it cannot be used as a means of salvation. In Christian eyes, nobody can keep the law in every respect, because at bottom the problem of human sin is that of a broken relationship with God. Only when that is put right can the spiritual character of the law begin to make sense, and become applicable to us. In putting that broken relationship right, Christians agree with traditional Jews that the atoning sacrifice provided for in the law is fundamental, but they insist that this sacrifice was made once for all by Jesus Christ. He became both the high priest and the victim of the sacrifice, and now he stands in his Father's presence as our mediator and advocate at the judgment. When Christians are asked why they believe this, they reply that Jesus was no ordinary prophet or rabbi, but God himself, who became man in order

118

to put an end to the need for sacrifice and to make permanent the reconciliation between humanity and God.

In the early church, there were probably Jewish-Christian sects which thought that Jesus was an angel, not God himself.[6] Later on there was the famous heretic Arius (d. 336) who believed that Jesus was the highest of the creatures – a divine creature in fact – whose nature bridged the gap between the divine and the human by standing halfway between them but not combining each nature in its fullness with the other. There is no reason to doubt the popularity of such ideas, which for many people would have been much easier to absorb than the uncompromising union of opposites which took place in the God-man Jesus Christ. The significant thing is that they were rejected, despite their attractiveness, because they did not do justice to the Christian claim about God, and how he could be known in Christ.

The difference between Judaism and Christianity was not simply that the latter offered a superhuman mediator between God and humanity, but that it preached the need for, and the possibility of, a new type of relationship with God. To express this as simply as possible, Christianity gave human beings the opportunity to know God from within, on the *inside*, whereas the Jews had only ever known him on the *outside*. In religious terms, this means that the veil which had divided the Holy of Holies in the temple from the people was torn apart, and that all the other partitions which previously had separated male from female, slave from free, Jew from Gentile, came tumbling down (Gal. 3:28). A Christian was one who was seated in '... the heavenly realms in Christ Jesus' (Eph. 2:6), able to stand in the presence of God the Father, through union with Christ, in the power of the Holy Spirit.

The revelation of the Trinity, as opposed to the implied unitarianism of Judaism, can be explained only by the transformation of perspective brought about by Jesus. The Trinity belongs to the inner life of God, and can be known only by those who share in that life. As long as we look at God on the outside, we shall never see beyond his unity; for, as the Cappadocian Fathers and Augustine realized, the external works of the Trinity are undivided (*opera Trinitatis ad extra*

119

*sunt indivisa*).[7] This means that an outside observer will never detect the inner reality of God, and will never enter the communion with him which is promised to us in Christ. Jews may recognize God's existence and know his law, but without Christ they cannot penetrate the mystery of that divine fellowship which Christians call the Holy Trinity.

When we turn from the monotheism of Judaism to that of Islam, we encounter a rather different set of problems. In spite of constant contact and interaction since the time of Muhammad, Christians and Muslims today generally know far less about each other's beliefs and have much less sympathy with each other than Christians and Jews, or even Muslims and Jews. (In this connection we must not forget that Jewish–Muslim hostility is a relatively recent phenomenon, caused by the establishment of a Jewish state on the soil of Arab Palestine, and that for centuries followers of the two religions got on remarkably well.) Christians and Muslims, on the other hand, have seldom been friends and have usually been deadly rivals. With very few exceptions, neither side has seen much common ground with the other, on which mutual understanding could be built. Christians do not feel they share a common heritage with Islam in the way that they do with Judaism, nor do Muslims see any real need to consider the claims of Christianity, which they believe Islam has superseded rather in the same way that Christianity itself superseded Judaism.

Muhammad (*c.* 570–632) is known to have had contact with Jews and with some Christian groups, although the precise identity of the latter is a matter of dispute.[8] It is probable that the Christians he knew confessed a heterodox type of belief which mainstream Christians would not have acknowledged, but the exact nature of their heterodoxy is unknown. Probably they were linked to the Monophysites of Egypt and Syria, who denied that the incarnate Christ had two natures, although Muhammad may also have had contact, as later Muslims certainly did, with Nestorians, who maintained that the two natures of Christ were only juxtaposed, not inseparably linked in a single person. Another problem is that we have no way of knowing how far Muhammad understood the Christianity he encountered, or what made him reject it. In the Qur'ān there are isolated references to various prophets and kings of the Old Testament, as well as to Mary and Jesus, but the understanding of the Bible which these allusions reveal is fragmentary and superficial. Apparently Muhammad accepted the virgin birth of Christ but denied his crucifixion, on the ground that a divine prophet like Jesus cannot have suffered such an injustice at the hand of a merciful God. There are frequent references to Jesus' miracles, but these merely contribute to the general impression gleaned from the Qur'ān that Muhammad thought of him as an extraordinary wonderworker more than anything else.[9]

The general impression of superficiality is strengthened by the designation of both Jews and Christians as 'people of the book', the possession of a sacred scripture evidently being regarded as praiseworthy in itself. There is no appreciation of the covenant, and no sign that Muhammad knew anything about having a personal relationship with God in Christ. Indeed, the general drift of his theology is away from anything personal, even if he retains that category in his description of Allah. Concepts of redemption common to Judaism and Christianity are replaced by the idea of submission (*islam*) to the will of God, and the covenantal predestination of the Bible is reduced to fatalism (*kismet*).

Allah is a holy God, whom Muhammad doubtless intended to be equated with the God of the Bible, but this holiness appears as a remoteness to which no human being can ever hope to attain. Allah is merciful and just, but the Muslim believer is expected to take whatever comes to him as God's will, not to work out his own salvation in fear and trembling (Phil. 2:12). Wrestling with God, that peculiar dignity which Yahweh conferred on Jacob (Gn. 32:22–32) and which lies at the heart of the name Israel, is a concept foreign to Islam, where the notion of God and human beings relating to each other at a level of personal equality is blasphemy. As in Jewish mysticism, Islamic experience of the spiritual is confined to the world of angels and demons (*jinn*), no direct contact with God being possible.

A Christian looking at Islam is almost bound to say that Muhammad misunderstood the central teachings of the Bible, and even that he may have counterfeited them in the construction of his own religion. Some of its features are oddly similar to Mormonism, like the appearance of the prophet, the divine book, the importance of angelology and even the toleration of polygamy. From the theological angle it appears to be a kind of monotheism for beginners, simplified and purged of any doctrinal or cultic complexity. Islam's demands on the individual conscience are slight – very unlike Christianity's – but it makes up for this by the institution of a social order which exerts considerable external pressure, and which it is almost impossible to break out of. The doubting and questioning, not to say the rebellion and soul-searching, so characteristic of the Christian experience of conversion, are completely lacking in Islam, where the importance of the individual is minimized and social coercion is all-pervasive.

When we turn from the avowedly non-Christian religions to heresies which have emerged from a Christian context, we find a complex situation which has points of similarity with Judaism and/or Islam, but which also differs from them in many ways. Heretical Christian unitarianism, as it now exists, can be divided into two main categories which are quite distinct: the intellectual and the popular. The former traces its origins to the work of theologians like Servetus (1511–53) and Socinus (1525–62),[10] who aroused the ire of both Catholics and Protestants at the time of the Reformation. In their zeal to reconstruct the church along lines of primitive simplicity, these men went far beyond the Reformers, and were even prepared to throw overboard the elaborately constructed classical theological tradition, which included the doctrine of the Trinity. They were repudiated by the leading Reformers, and their doctrines made little headway until they were taken up and reinforced by a revival of Platonism in the seventeenth century.

In the climate of religious conformity which then prevailed in Western Europe, philosophy was often the only refuge for the heterodox; and so it was naturally from that source that a new and non-dogmatic deism made its appearance. Deism was a philosophical theory which held that God was 'prime mover', or 'first cause' of the universe, but that once he had set it in motion he did not interfere in its affairs. Miracles were therefore impossible, and prayer was useless. The supreme being was an idea which was thought to be necessary to explain reality as it is, but there was no point in seeking to establish a relationship with it. As in the case of Islam, to which some of the deists felt a superficial attraction, the predestination of orthodox Christianity was reduced to determinism, and belief in an active loving providence was ruled out.[11]

In continental Europe this 'scientific' theory never got beyond the confines of a philosophical élite, which soon moved on to a complete atheism. In England and the American colonies, however, deism caught the mood of some Protestant Dissenters, who transformed the theology of their churches into unitarianism. As an intellectual pastime, unitarianism has never had a popular following, but it continues to exist on the fringe of religious life in Anglo-Saxon countries, where it has occasionally produced distinguished figures of one kind or another. The most famous theologian to have come from its ranks was F. D. Maurice (1805–72), who was converted to trinitarianism and became an Anglican divine, although he did not completely abandon his earlier beliefs, as can be seen for example in his universalistic understanding of atonement and redemption.[12]

Maurice's relatively easy passage from unitarianism to Anglicanism, and the doubts that were later cast on his orthodoxy, are reminders that trinitarian belief was not to be taken for granted in the established churches after the eighteenth century. The Athanasian Creed, in which this belief was spelled out most clearly, was omitted from the American Prayer Book of 1790, and attempts were later made to have it excised from the English Book of Common Prayer as well. These did not succeed, but it would be fair to say that the Athanasian Creed is no longer widely known, and that a latent unitarianism has been present in English theology for many decades now. It is particularly associated with the so-called 'modern churchmen', and has surfaced from time to time in the writings of people like Geoffrey Lampe (1912–80), whose 1976 Bampton Lectures, entitled *God as Spirit*,[13] are a typical exposition of this line of thought.

At the popular level there has been quite a different

development, which is still not taken seriously in academic circles. In the early nineteenth century most Anglo-Saxon Protestantism was broadly Calvinistic in its main emphases. In some places, notably in the United States, this was pushed to extremes, and a strongly-held covenant theology, which almost exalted the Old Testament above the New, was combined with a literalistic biblical fundamentalism. As a result there emerged different sects, like the Seventh Day Adventists and the Mormons, whose Old Testament fundamentalism is clear, in spite of various alien accretions. Mormons are vague and inconsistent about the doctrine of the Trinity, which does not loom very large in their teaching, and the same can be said of the Adventists. This is not true, however, of the Christadelphians, for whom Christ is no more than a man, nor is it true of the Jehovah's Witnesses, for whom unitarianism is a main article of belief.[14]

As their name suggests, Jehovah's Witnesses are Old Testament fundamentalists for whom Jehovah is the Father of Jesus Christ, not the Trinity. They teach that Jesus is not God, but only a divine man, which is reminiscent of the heresy of Arius. In recent years Jehovah's Witnesses have made a surprisingly strong appeal to nominal Roman Catholics and Eastern Orthodox, who have become disenchanted with their own churches. Theirs is a simple, dogmatic creed, ideally suited to uneducated people who wish to appear learned and authoritative without troubling to acquire the necessary credentials. It is probably largely because of this characteristic that it has remained a popular, almost working-class movement, ignoring the academic establishment and being in turn ignored by it. In theological matters, Jehovah's Witnesses generally confine themselves to attacking the orthodox Christian doctrine of the Trinity, often by a rather simplistic exegesis of biblical texts such as John 1:1, where they claim that 'the Word was God' means that the Word was divine, or 'a god'.

Popular unitarianism of the Jehovah's Witness type would undoubtedly be less influential if more Christians were conscious of knowing the Trinity in their own spiritual experience. Sadly, many nominally orthodox Christians are unitarian in all but name. They regard the Father as God,

124

Jesus as divine but somehow inferior to God, and the Holy Spirit as an impersonal force, whom they may quite happily refer to as 'it'. Such people have little to say when they meet Jehovah's Witnesses, or read about the existence of heterodox theologians in the universities. Even many preachers scarcely know what to say about the Trinity, and feel embarrassed when the subject is raised. To them it is an aridly intellectual doctrine without practical application to the life of the church and so they ignore it, probably claiming some justification for their attitude on the rather specious ground that the word does not appear in the Bible. The curious phenomenon of theoretically orthodox people being unitarian in practice is not new, however; it goes back to the earliest stages of Christian theology, where it represents a primitive outlook which the classical theological construction of the fourth and fifth centuries tried to overcome.

## Early Christian forms of unitarianism

To understand why unitarianism is unable to do justice to Christian claims about God, we have to turn to the experience of the early church. The early Christians began with the Jewish picture of God as their theoretical starting-point, but found that it could not fully capture the experience of God which they had in Christ. Gradually they were forced to adjust to a new understanding of God, not merely in their experience but in their theology as well. The process by which a Christian theology distinct from Judaism was developed and articulated was fraught with difficulties and setbacks. There were many theories which though popular at first eventually had to be condemned as heretical, when it was realized that they contained assumptions and implications which were not compatible with authentic Christian witness to Jesus. But unlike modern heresies, which are conscious deviations from a received tradition, these ancient heresies were more like false trails pursued by people who wished to be orthodox, but who lacked the conceptual framework needed to express orthodoxy in the right way. As long as Christians of this type felt obliged to stay as close as possible to the Jewish understanding of God, there were attempts to include the Son and the Spirit within a basically unitarian

125

framework. These attempts, elements of which occasionally resurface in modern heresies or in popular expressions of Christian theology, started with the right intentions, but failed when put to the test. Their failure was important because eventually it forced the church to reject unitarianism of any kind as a valid theological option.

The early church developed two main types of unitarianism, which gave rise to two distinct theological traditions. It is interesting that, in spite of the fact that they were subsequently abandoned, the influence of these early traditions can still be felt today in the assumptions which different branches of the church bring to their theology. The first type equated the one God with the Father of Jesus Christ, and regarded the Son and the Holy Spirit as distinct, and therefore inferior, beings. The second type also identified the Father with the one God, but preferred to think of the Son and the Spirit as latent within his divine nature. The characteristic error of the first tradition was to separate the Trinity into three autonomous units, linked only by the most tenuous ties of association. The characteristic error of the second was to obscure the distinctions to the point where the names of the persons of the Trinity were no more than functional designations of a single divine nature. Within their own context, these different types were obviously thought to be opposed to each other, but given the assumption that God is one in a unitarian sense, the emergence of each is predictable, and the existence of both in competition shows that neither was felt to do justice to the Christian doctrine of God.

The idea that the Son and the Holy Spirit are distinct beings in their own right is characteristic of the type of theology which gained favour in the Greek-speaking world, largely under the influence of Origen (*c.* 185 – *c.* 254). Origen believed that the Father was true God, or God in himself (*autotheos*), and taught that the Son was begotten in his image. This meant that he was like the Father in every respect, except that he had a beginning, or at least a source of some kind, which the Father did not have. The Holy Spirit was in turn made in the image of the Son, divine in every respect except that of 'anarchy' ('unbeginningness'). For Origen the idea that God the Father could reproduce himself in this way was no surprise; it was a belief which he shared with his fellow Platonists, who spoke of emanations from the one. In deriving the Son and (indirectly) the Holy Spirit from the being of the Father, Origen in no way intended to minimize their power or authority. On the contrary, he wanted to accord them the maximum degree of divinity which his system would permit, without sacrificing its fundamental commitment to a unitarian monotheism.

As his solution to the problem, Origen said, in terms which were to become classical, that the Father, Son and Holy Spirit were three *hypostases* of a single *ousia*. In the eyes of later orthodoxy, his formula fell down because he equated *theos* with *ousia*, not with *hypostasis*, and because he said that only the Father was truly *theos*. For him, the identity of the second and third *hypostases* was derived from the first, a pattern which we find even in Basil of Caesarea (*c.* 329–79), who reshaped the theological tradition in a way which distanced it from Origen. Indeed, it is still endemic in Eastern Orthodox theology, in spite of the fact that Origen himself has long since been repudiated.[15]

The crisis which provoked the eventual rejection of Origen's system was caused by Arius, whose views have already been mentioned. Origen, as a Platonist, had believed that an *ousia* which existed in one *hypostasis* could reproduce itself in a second, or even in a third. These reproductions would be the same as the original in every respect, except that they would have a source or cause. The first *hypostasis*, being uncaused, would therefore continue to enjoy a certain superiority over the others. Arius, however, was an Aristotelian who believed that if it was necessary to use a different name to describe an object, that object had to be a different thing (*ousia*). If it was necessary, as all were agreed, to maintain a distinction between the *names* Father, Son and Holy Spirit, then logically there must be some real difference between them as *beings*. To Arius this meant that the three persons could not share equally in the same divine *ousia*, which by definition was unique.[16]

To this basic assumption, Arius added the fact that the Son was begotten (*gennētos*) of the Father, a term which he regarded as being synonymous with being created (*genētos*) by him. In support of his argument he adduced the orthodox theology of the second century, *i.e.* of the period before Origen, which generally maintained that the Father had brought forth his Word (*Logos*) and his Spirit only when he began to create the world. This type of theology is now called 'economic' (*i.e.*, dispensational) trinitarianism, because it regarded the Trinity as existing only in the dispensations, which means only in time, not in eternity. The two 'extra' persons were supposed to have appeared at the beginning of creation, and they would endure until the final consummation of all things, when the Son (and by implication, the Holy Spirit) would render up all things to the Father and be reabsorbed into him (*cf.* 1 Cor. 15:28).

Economic trinitarianism developed because the Christians of the time could not understand how the Son could have been begotten outside time. For them, as for Arius, there had to have been a time when the Son had not existed, an assertion which, if true, immediately called his divinity into question. Economic trinitarians of the second century, like Theophilus of Antioch, had tried to resolve the problem by saying that before the beginning of time the Word (*Logos*) and the Spirit had been latent in the Father's being (*ousia*), from which they had subsequently emerged. But as we saw in the last chapter, this question of whether the Father, as God, was temporarily deprived of his reason (*Logos*) and his Spirit produced an absurdity which demonstrated the weakness of this theory. Arius maintained that the Word and the Spirit were not eternally latent in God but had been created, an assertion which he supported from the Septuagint reading of Proverbs 8:22, which says 'He created me as a beginning for his work'. Arius was eventually defeated by Athanasius (*c.* 296–373) who claimed that 'for his work' meant 'for the Creation'. Because the Son could hardly have created himself, argued Athanasius, the verse could not be interpreted in that way, and the word 'created' would more correctly be interpreted as 'established'. Of course, modern scholars see no christological significance in this verse at all, a conclusion which makes Arius' argument even more untenable.[17]

In the end, Arianism was defeated because it did not do

justice to the New Testament portrait of Jesus. No-one questioned the importance of monotheism, but it was recognized that this had to be held in tension with the belief that Jesus was fully God (cf., e.g., Col. 2:9). Arius' failure to do this, not to mention his quite inadequate understanding of the Holy Spirit as still further away from true divinity than the Son, made his theology ultimately unacceptable. It was condemned at the First Council of Nicaea in 325, which declared that the Son was consubstantial (*homoousios*) with the Father, and again at the First Council of Constantinople in 381, which clearly affirmed the deity of the Holy Spirit.

The second tradition of unitarianism which we mentioned is perhaps older than the first, and it is certainly much more complex. It is usually associated with the Western, or Latin, theological tradition, as this developed from the time of Tertullian (*fl. c.* 196 – *c.* 212) onwards. Its roots obviously lie in economic trinitarianism, which Tertullian and others received and developed in a highly original manner. They accepted the basic premiss of the economic scheme, which was that the Son and the Holy Spirit came out of the Father *in time*, not in eternity, but they tied this to a specific dispensational understanding of history in which the Father too had his role to play.

According to this type of dispensationalism, the Old Testament was the age of the revelation of the Father, the time from the incarnation to the ascension was the age of the revelation of the Son, and the time since Pentecost is the age of the revelation of the Holy Spirit. As Tertullian expounded this, all three persons of the Trinity continue to work in the lives of Christian believers, the present work of the Holy Spirit being merely an extension of the work begun by the Father and the Son. Tertullian explicitly rejected any suggestion that the earlier ages of revelation were no longer valid for the church, which explains why he became a leading opponent of Marcion. On the other hand, he was prepared to accept that the third age of revelation might well have prophets, and produce a written record which would stand in relation to the New Testament as the New Testament stood in relation to the Old. It was for that reason that he was to be so sympathetic to the new prophecy of the Montanists, who

129

claimed to be the apostles of the Spirit, and who foretold the imminent descent of the New Jerusalem.[18]

Tertullian was, however, opposed to another misunderstanding of dispensationalism, which he encountered in the teaching of Praxeas, an unknown heretic whom some have identified as Sabellius, but whose teaching is more like that of Noetus of Smyrna (*fl. c.* 150). Praxeas taught that the distinctions between the persons of the Trinity were not real. The three names of God had some value in explaining the pattern of redemption, but they did not correspond to any real distinction within the Godhead. The name Father emphasized God's role as Creator; the name Son, his role as Redeemer; and the name Holy Spirit, his role as Sanctifier. But in real terms, the agent of all these operations was the one God of the Jewish Scriptures. This God had become incarnate in the man Jesus Christ, had died on the cross, and had risen again from the dead. Tertullian pointed out the absurdity of this scheme by saying that Praxeas 'chased away the Paraclete and crucified the Father'. The latter phrase has stuck, and this heresy is now sometimes called patripassianism, which is the belief that the Father suffered and died on the cross.

Patripassianism was regarded as absurd because God was both impassible and immortal in his nature, but Tertullian was careful to back up that basic argument with numerous scriptural texts in which the Son is clearly portrayed as a distinct being. The theory of Noetus and Praxeas is impossible because it makes a nonsense of the dialogue between Father and Son, which is such an important feature of the gospels, and which culminates in the cries of the crucified Jesus in his final agony. In answer to this rather naive idea, Tertullian developed a more sophisticated trinitarianism than had appeared up to that time. He argued that both the Son and the Spirit were fully divine beings, distinct from the Father yet sharing his essence and bound inextricably to him. The analogies which he drew from nature in an attempt to explain this are now famous – the sun with its light and its rays; the source, the river and the canal, all sharing the same water; the root, the shoot and the fruit, which together constitute a single plant.

In his counterblast to Praxeas, Tertullian came as near as

he could to trinitarianism, without abandoning his fundamentally monotheistic and, to our minds, unitarian position.
The Father always remained God in a way which did not
apply to the other two persons, however much he might
share his power and authority with them. The second and
third persons are described as 'portions' of the first, a word
which is very difficult to interpret in the case of a being who is
by nature immeasurable and indivisible, but which must at
the very least imply that they are somehow inferior to the
fullness of that being, which is the Father. He also explains,
though, that this inferiority is one of *status*, not *gradus*, a word
which apparently refers to a quality (compare a modern
expression like 'high-grade oil'). If this interpretation is correct, Tertullian stumbled on the key which would eventually
overthrow the latent unitarianism of his dispensationalism.[19]

As later writers, not all of them familiar with Tertullian's
work, but all inheritors of a very similar mental outlook,
would point out, equality of *gradus* implied identity of *ousia*
(Latin=*substantia*), and made the argument about portions of
the Godhead meaningless in that context. The difference of
*status* on the other hand, opened the door for the assertion
that the Trinity was a distinction of persons, not of natures or
attributes. In God, the perfect equality of the Father, Son and
Holy Spirit is manifested in a distinction of position not
unlike the distinctions found in an earthly hierarchy, where
people who are equals at the level of nature are inferior or
superior to others by virtue of the dignity attaching to their
persons. Of course, as we shall see, even this subordinationism would later be rejected, but the move away from
distinctions of nature to distinctions of persons, which is
implied by the shift from *gradus* to *status*, marks a decisive
break with the residual unitarianism of the early church.

Before leaving this subject we must consider just why it was
that the early Christians felt compelled to abandon the
unitarian assumptions of their inherited Judaism, without
rejecting its fundamental monotheism. The overriding
reason appears to be that the person of Jesus Christ could not
be accommodated within the Jewish framework. In the New
Testament Jesus' claims are presented in such a way as to
preclude identifying him with a Jewish teacher, or even with

131

an apocalyptic figure like the Messiah, at least as that was understood by Jewish people at the time. It is well known that Jesus fought shy of being labelled in that way, and in his direct confrontations with Jewish leaders like Nicodemus (Jn. chapter 3) we find him making claims which go far beyond anything the Pharisee had thought possible.

Jesus is presented, and according to the gospels he presented himself, as one who possessed the authority of God, whether to forgive sins (Mk. 2:5–12), to fulfil the law of Moses (Mt. 5:17) or, perhaps most important of all, to introduce people to a new relationship with God, as Father (Jn. 5:18). The last point is especially significant, as we can see from the fact that the Aramaic word which Jesus used, *Abba*, is left untranslated in the Greek New Testament, and is specifically mentioned by Paul (Gal. 4:6) as belonging to the very heart of the Christian spiritual experience. It is true, that even in the Old Testament there are occasional references to God as the Father of Israel (*cf.*, *e.g.*, Is. 63:16; Je. 31:9), and some scholars have claimed that there is nothing surprising in Jesus' use of the word to describe his own relationship with God.

That, however, is a view from hindsight which goes against both the witness of the New Testament and the general practice of Judaism, in which a personal relationship with God, even if it is not totally excluded, is not particularly emphasized either. What is never found is the combination of this relationship and the claims which Jesus made for himself. Those who drew near to God in the Old Testament did so in fear and trembling, deeply conscious of their unworthiness to stand in his presence and unable to deal with him face to face. But Jesus appeared to approach the Father as an equal, and it is this which caused the offence. At times, even Christian theologians have tended to emphasize Jesus' subordination to the will of the Father who had sent him, but in the Jewish context what is really surprising is the degree to which Jesus points people to himself as the object of faith. The mere fact that there was some ambiguity and uncertainty about his identity, as in the story of Nicodemus, is evidence in support of claims far beyond the normal range.

When we add to this the confessions of Peter (Mt. 16:16)

and Thomas (Jn. 20:28) and the message of the apostles, who preached belief in Jesus as *Lord*, a word which in the context can mean only Yahweh, the God of Israel, we begin to appreciate the dimensions of the theological problem. For Jesus was not a theophany of the Father, as Noetus of Smyrna would have it, but another person, in constant and intimate relationship with his Father. To account for him adequately, it was necessary to abandon unitarianism and look for ways to include a second person within the one God, that would do justice to the evidence of the New Testament.

## Binitarianism

The central importance of Jesus Christ for Christian faith is obviously beyond dispute. In the New Testament, his exercise of divine authority, and the fact that his name is frequently coupled with that of God the Father, especially in the salutations of the Pauline epistles, suggest that at the very least we must be prepared to accept some kind of duality in God. It can even be argued that the use of the word 'Father' as a name for God presupposes the existence of a Son, or at least of offspring. The need which the early Christians felt to find a place in God for Jesus Christ made it inevitable that sooner or later somebody would propose a theology which provided for a duality in God, in which both the Father and the Son could find their rightful place.

Dualism, as a philosophical or religious belief, found little favour in the ancient Mediterranean world. It might have been thought that the obvious contrasts between light and darkness, good and evil, or odd and even numbers, would have produced dualistic beliefs, yet in spite of the obvious opportunities for such ideas to flourish they did not do so. Judaism maintained that darkness and evil were forces which were ultimately in the hand of God, and this view is stated with greatest power and clarity just at the point where its tenability is most in question, in the sufferings of the righteous Job. There it is made quite plain that Satan can act only within the limits determined by God, who is elsewhere declared to be in sovereign control of the entire universe (Is. 45:7). The refusal to accept that evil powers are independent of God has left

133

THE DOCTRINE OF GOD

Judaism and Christianity with the problem of *theodicy*, or the existence of evil in a world governed by a righteous and omnipotent God. But both Jews and Christians have always preferred to live with that problem rather than accept anything that smacks of dualism.[20]

The same is true, though for different reasons, of the humanistic tradition of classical philosophy. In this tradition there has been a strong tendency to discount evil as non-being, a trap for the ignorant and the unwary, leading to the dissolution of their existence. It has been a constant criticism of this way of thinking that it has failed to take evil with sufficient seriousness; but in spite of this, the tradition as a whole has never been tempted down the path of dualism. The basic belief in the underlying unity and goodness of all things has proved too strong for that, although the concept of opposing forces at work has found a place in the dialectical philosophy of Hegel (1770–1831), which has exercised a great influence on modern thought.

Hegel believed that significant movement occurred when one thing (*thesis*) met its opposite (*antithesis*) and the two entered into conflict with each other. But unlike the classical dualistic system of the East, Hegel did not believe that these forces were in constant stalemate. On the contrary, he thought that the conflict between *thesis* and *antithesis* served to produce a higher *synthesis*, born out of the two conflicting powers but different and superior to them. The obvious natural example of this conflict was the male–female relationship which produced offspring. The offspring then repeated the process by becoming themselves *theses* and *antitheses*, and this movement produced the dynamic which led to further conflict and kept the world in being. Hegel's dialectic was meant to be a universal principle, and as such it has been applied to many things, even to the Trinity. According to the Hegelian dialectic, the Father (*thesis*) and the Son (*antithesis*) combined to produce the Holy Spirit as the *synthesis* of the first two persons, a view which is not unlike that of the great Augustine.[21]

Dualism, when it appeared in the West, came as an import from Persia, where the teachings of Zoroaster, and later of Mani (third century AD) provided the intellectual base for a dualistic religion of opposing forces. Manichaeism had some influence on the young Augustine, although how much is a matter of dispute, and forms of it surfaced at different times during the Middle Ages. The Albigensian Cathars of Languedoc held dualistic views, but they were forcibly suppressed by crusading armies in the thirteenth century. The Paulicians, who were actually deported from the Persian borderlands of the Byzantine Empire and resettled in the Balkans, survived until they were converted to Roman Catholicism in the seventeenth century; and the Bogomils, who were an offshoot of the Paulicians, were a powerful threat to orthodox Christianity in South-Eastern Europe. They are now thought to have been responsible for the spread of catharism, and they did not disappear until the Turks conquered the Balkans and induced them to accept Islam (fifteenth century). Many of these heresies existed mainly at the lower levels of society, however, and had no real influence on Christian doctrine, apart from perhaps aggravating the church's already very negative attitude to dissent.[22]

Dualism of the oriental type has been unknown to most Christians until very recently, although it has now begun to appear on the fringes of church life. The best known system at the present time is that of the Korean heretic Sun Myung Moon, who has tried to graft the Buddhist concept of the yin and the yang onto Christianity. There are important resemblances here to a Hegelian dialectic, which may not be accidental, although Moon has concentrated on erecting a religious system to a degree which Hegel could scarcely have imagined. Whether the Moonies will have any enduring success remains to be seen. It is certainly much too early to say whether Sun Myung Moon is to be ranked with the great binitarian heretics of the past.

Of these, the one who must claim pride of place is Sabellius (third century AD), who has given his name to a way of thinking which some theologians, most of them Eastern Orthodox, believe is characteristic of Western theology in general. Sabellius apparently sympathized with the monotheism of Noetus of Smyrna and of Praxeas, but he saw the weaknesses in their system. He therefore modified it in an attempt to avoid some of its more obvious problems, developing in the process a kind of dualism which came as close as anything can to binitarianism.

Basically what Sabellius said was that the one God contained within himself an eternal double principle, whose two aspects were normally held in tension but which were capable of separation and even opposition. This principle he called the Son-Father (*hyiopatōr*), who became incarnate in Jesus Christ. Separation came on the cross, when the Son cried out: 'My God, my God, why have you forsaken me?' At that moment Father and Son split apart, so that the Son alone was crucified. This was a rather crude way of avoiding patripassianism, and it is easy to see that it cannot be made to work consistently. Apart from anything else, the dialogue between Father and Son is carried on throughout the gospels, where it is clear that the Son has been sent, as a distinct person, by the Father.

Sabellius went on to add that the crucifixion was not the last word. Just before he died, the Son cried out: 'Father, into your hands I commit my spirit', a reminder that the Holy Spirit was to be the power which would reconcile Father and Son in the unity of the divine nature (which was both holy and spirit). As Sabellius expressed it, the theory was crude and unacceptable, but there is an important sense in which his teaching has been reflected in Western thought ever since.[23]

First, there is the tendency to look for the distinctions of the persons within the unity of the divine nature. This procedure reached its highest form of expression in the trinitarian theology of Augustine, through whom it has continued to influence Western theology to this day. Within the basic framework of monotheism, the relationship between the Father and the Son is seen as one of complementary opposites. This way of thinking is closely tied to the names of the persons, which are believed to be fundamental to their identity and to imply each other.

Second, there is a tendency in this way of thinking to demote the Holy Spirit to the status of an impersonal force. The fact that his name is not immediately thought to be a personal one lends weight to this view, and one or two scholars have even relied on the fact that the Greek New

Testament occasionally uses a grammatical neuter (*i.e.* 'it') to refer to the Spirit as evidence in support of this tendency. Of course it is easy to point out that the neuter is employed simply to agree with the Greek noun for spirit, *pneuma*, which happens to be neuter, and that this says nothing about his personhood one way or another. The Hebrew word for spirit, *ruach*, is feminine, as is the Spirit's nurturing activity, but although some ancient Syriac mystics said that the Spirit stands for the female principle in God, theologians have found scant support for this view in Scripture. The Bible does, however, use the name Paraclete, which in Greek is masculine, as a designation of the Spirit (Jn. 16:7), and when the occasion arises he is described in the masculine gender, not in the feminine (or the neuter). Because of this, the orthodox theological tradition has always assumed that the Holy Spirit is a masculine person, just as the Father and the Son are. On the other hand, there has often been a tendency to demote him to a secondary, sub-personal level within the Godhead, and this tendency has been far more important historically than the idea that the Spirit is feminine.

Third, and more positively, there has been a strong tendency to regard the crucifixion and Christ's work of atonement as an act of the triune God. This is an important emphasis which the Eastern tradition, with its latent predisposition to a type of theology which in Western eyes smacks of Arianism, has found very hard to understand. Sabellius certainly got it wrong, but the belief that Father, Son and Holy Spirit all have a part to play in the redemptive work of Christ is one which has always characterized Western theology, and which has reappeared with renewed vigour in recent years.[24]

From all this it can be seen that Sabellianism contained within it a latent trinitarianism; it failed to be stronger because, in his desire to avoid a crude patripassianism, Sabellius did not elaborate a theological framework adequate to contain the person of the Holy Spirit. A similar problem emerged in the fourth century, when a Greek monk by the name of Macedonius elaborated a kind of binitarianism based on the decisions of the First Council of Nicaea. That council had declared that the Son was consubstantial with the

Father, but it had said nothing about the divinity of the Holy Spirit. Macedonius concluded from this silence that the Holy Spirit was an inferior being, and he began to teach binitarianism as the true interpretation of the Nicene faith. For a time he had many sympathizers, among them a number of semi-Arians who were still unhappy at what they regarded as Nicaea's dilution of pure monotheism. Eventually though, Macedonius was defeated by the arguments of the Cappadocian Fathers (notably Basil of Caesarea), which we shall examine in the next chapter.

Apart from periodic revivals by modern scholars, subconsciously supported by the tendency of Western theology to demote the Holy Spirit to the status of an impersonal being, binitarianism has never enjoyed much success either within the church or outside it. Its inherent weakness is dualism, which, as we have seen, runs counter to the strong philosophical and religious current in the Judaeo-Christian tradition in favour of a monotheistic unity. Those who have tried it have invariably discovered that in a dualistic system the position of the Holy Spirit becomes an embarrassment; indeed, it is the doctrine of the Spirit, even more than the doctrine of Christ, which has made the church affirm belief in a Holy Trinity of three, not two, equal persons in God.

## Trinitarianism: the biblical evidence

The first question we must ask in a discussion of the Trinity is whether the term can properly be applied to the God of the Bible at all. This doctrine is frequently singled out by theologians and commentators as a classic case of a concept which has grown out of the evidence of Scripture, but which is not actually contained within its pages. Its development in the creeds may be regarded either as a necessary consequence of the biblical data, or as a possible inference from certain texts, or even as a distortion of the New Testament proclamation.[25] According to many theologians, the classical doctrine contains elements of all three of these possibilities. In practical terms, the basic assumption that the doctrine of the Trinity cannot be found in Scripture has raised the question of whether belief in it should be required for membership of the church. The Reformers obviously believed that it should, as the execution of Servetus made clear. But later generations were less sure, and since the later eighteenth century a kind of practical unitarianism, or occasionally binitarianism, has crept into church life, even in those denominations which theoretically uphold the authority of the ancient creeds. Even the great revival of trinitarian thought which has occurred in the twentieth century, to a large extent as a result of the influence of Karl Barth, does not necessarily mean that this tendency has been effectively countered, as we shall see.

The claim that the doctrine of the Trinity can be found in the Bible has, of course, been made by Christians throughout the history of the church, and sometimes they have used great hermeneutical dexterity to demonstrate their case. More important than this, however, is the fact that conservative orthodox Christianity continues to uphold this claim, even though critical awareness has obliged it to abandon some of the evidence which has been traditionally cited in its support.[26] Moreover, all branches of the church, even those which do not set a high value on tradition, continue to accept that so fundamental a doctrine ought to be as firmly grounded as possible in the biblical evidence.

The evidence which is usually produced in support of a biblical doctrine of the Trinity can be divided into three very unequal parts, as follows:

(1) possible references to a trinity in the Old Testament;
(2) direct (formulaic) references to the Trinity in the New Testament;
(3) indirect references to the Trinity in the New Testament.

In addition we must make a further distinction of two categories which cut across all three of the above. The first category consists of references to the Trinity as such; and the second contains references to the divinity of each of the persons separately. In modern theology the second category of texts is usually treated under the headings of christology and pneumatology, but we must not forget that they are closely tied to the trinitarian question as well.

Such evidence as there may be in the Old Testament for the Christian doctrine of the Trinity has been fully catalogued and discussed by A. W. Wainwright in his book *The Trinity in the New Testament*,[27] which remains the most readily accessible treatment of the biblical evidence as a whole. As far as the Old Testament is concerned, there are basically two considerations in the first category and three in the second which might be used as evidence pointing towards a Trinity of persons. In the first category, there is the plural name of God, Elohim, combined with such phrases as 'let us make man in our image' (Gn. 1:26) and 'The man has now become like one of us' (Gn. 3:22), which suggest that the plural here may be something more than just the so-called 'royal we'. On the other hand, it is not altogether clear whether God is speaking to his angels or to himself; nor does the text say *how many* persons are included in this use of the plural.

Sometimes cited as evidence for a theophany of the Trinity is the incident in Genesis chapter 18 where three strangers appear to Abraham, but the great patriarch addresses them in the singular as 'Lord'. It may of course be that he was speaking directly to the spokesman for the group, but it is interesting to note that Philo of Alexandria, a Jew who was writing quite independently of any Christian prompting, saw in this incident a clue, or desire to prove, that Yahweh could be known in more than one person; his main concern was to show that God was perfect, even in mathematical terms. In the Greek world it was widely believed that three was the perfect number, so to Philo, finding the number three in God was additional proof that he was absolute perfection.[28]

Philo's intriguing exegesis is not mentioned in the New Testament, which is completely silent on this point, but it was taken up by Clement of Alexandria (*fl. c.* AD 200) and rapidly became a stock allegorical proof for the doctrine of the Trinity. But Calvin abandoned it on the ground that it was fanciful, and today it is no longer mentioned, except as a historical curiosity.[29]

In the second category, that of the individual persons, there is evidence in the Old Testament for attaching some kind of divine status to the Word, the Wisdom and the Spirit of God. The issue here is whether these agents are personifications of aspects of God's being, or whether they can be said to appear as persons in their own right. Wainwright argues, and most modern scholars would agree with him, that although the personification of these elements is powerful and striking, it never goes to the point where we can say for certain that they are something more than mere extensions of God's being. In particular, there is no sign of God's independent activity, or of dialogue with the Father, a feature which is so prominent in the New Testament. Nor did the apostles emphasize this kind of evidence in their own teaching, a fact which can mean only that they did not regard the parallels as conclusive.

This may seem disappointing to some, but as we have already seen in our discussion of Judaism, there is a very good theological reason for not accepting Old Testament texts as evidence for the existence of a trinity of persons in God. To admit belief in the Trinity without belief in Christ would be to confuse irretrievably the logic and purpose of revelation. It is not necessary to go as far as Karl Barth did in identifying revelation, including the revelation of the Trinity, with Jesus Christ, to see that the redeeming work of the Son of God is fundamental to the whole pattern of trinitarian faith. It is the Father who sent the Son to be our sacrifice, the Son who satisfied the just demands and appeased the wrath of the Father, the Holy Spirit who comes into our hearts and gives us the faith to cry: 'Abba, Father' as adopted sons and daughters of God (Gal. 4:6). The persons of the Trinity must certainly be distinguished from their work, but in the scheme of revelation they can never be separated from it. To know the Trinity is to know the gospel, to have passed from the old dispensation to the new. It is therefore not surprising that we find no clear evidence for such a doctrine in the Old Testament, and that Philo's speculations are more akin to abstract mathematics than to spiritual reality.

When we turn to the New Testament we discover at least two, and perhaps three, direct references to the Trinity. The doubtful case is 1 John 5:7, where it seems certain that a later hand has glossed in the reference which we find in the Authorized Version of 1611. Only a few later manuscripts contain this addition, and although the context is by no means wholly inappropriate, it would seem best to discount this mention of the Trinity as a spurious addition to the original text.[30]

It is rather different with the other two passages, both of which are well known. The first is Matthew 28:19, 'baptising [all nations] in the name of the Father, and of the Son, and of the Holy Spirit'. There is no doubt that these words belong in the earliest manuscripts, and there is no sign that they are out of place in the 'great commission' of Jesus. The only question is whether these verses reflect something Jesus himself actually said, or whether they represent a later development of his teaching. Those who are reluctant to accept the possibility that Jesus himself taught a doctrine of the Trinity are naturally inclined to be suspicious here; some theologians have even used the appearance of the threefold name as evidence that Jesus could *not* have said these words.

Of itself, there is no doubt that the formula of Matthew 28:19 represents the earliest specific expression of a trinitarian faith, which we know from other sources to have been closely connected with baptism. Baptismal vows were being made in the name of the Father, Son and Holy Spirit long before any Christian worked out a full doctrine of the Trinity, so there is little reason to believe that their appearance here is anachronistic in the context of contemporary church life. The date of Matthew is of course uncertain, but it must have been written sometime before AD 100 at the very latest. Probably it was in existence before AD 70, well within the lifetime of people who had known Jesus in the flesh.[31]

For something as central and important as the rite of Christian initiation, the practice of the church at this stage must have rested on very good authority. There is no sign, even in Matthew 28:19, of the catechetical instruction which rapidly became obligatory *before* baptism; in the gospel, instruction in the faith is mentioned *after* baptism, which reflects the pattern of the earliest period. It is well known that the practice of baptism preceded the coming of Christ, and that Jesus also instructed his disciples to baptize people during the course of his earthly ministry, as a sign of the coming kingdom. The inclusion of baptism in his last charge to his followers is therefore entirely to be expected, as being in keeping with the rest of his ministry. The fact that teaching is mentioned as coming after baptism is further evidence of a very early date for this passage.

Furthermore, how conceivable is it that the first generation of Christians would have mentioned the threefold name of God if Jesus had not explicitly commanded it, and if there had as yet been no theological reflection on the subject? It is highly unlikely that a person of even Matthew's stature could just have invented the phrase; it must have represented some tradition, and struck a chord with church members, most of whom would have been able to recall their own baptism – perhaps even at the hands of one of the apostles. Even as late as AD 100 there would have been some Christians alive who had been baptized before AD 50, and possibly even one or two who had been baptized at, or soon, after, Pentecost.

There is an interesting incident recorded in Acts chapter 8 which supports the belief that trinitarian baptism must go back to the earliest years of the church. The apostles had heard that Samaria had received the gospel, but that many there had been baptized 'only' in the name of the Lord Jesus. When they heard this, they sent Peter and John, the most senior of their number, down to Samaria in order to pray for them to receive the Holy Spirit. This incident must have taken place within five years of Pentecost, yet the defective baptism was perceived immediately, and was rectified only by an emergency visit from the leading apostles. Could such a thing have happened if baptism in the name of Jesus alone was sufficient for salvation? Indeed, it must be a matter of some surprise that such baptism, if it was the normal practice of the church did not include the descent of the Holy Spirit.[32]

It is always possible of course, to argue that this incident was normal practice in the earliest years of evangelistic outreach. If Jesus himself had explicitly commanded otherwise, it is assumed that such a practice could never have begun. Yet against this, we must bear in mind that it was cited as an anomaly that was quickly put right by higher authority, which suggests that there were evangelists who had not been fully instructed, rather than that their practice was the accepted norm. Not many years after this, when factional divisions appeared in the church at Corinth, Paul did not hesitate to appeal to the unity of Christian baptismal practice as the best argument against division, although admittedly he mentions only the name of Christ in that context (*cf.* 1 Cor. 1:13–15). This problem had not arisen in Samaria, but it is at least possible that the unity of the church was high on the apostles' list of priorities, and that their action was partly due to the need to preserve this unity at the level of Christian initiation. The high-level delegation which put matters right indicates both how serious the error was and that it must have been very rare, if not unique to this occasion. The apostles certainly did not spend their time chasing around Palestine to put right matters of this kind.

The theological foundation for the practice of trinitarian baptism is confirmed by the baptism of Jesus, an event recorded in all four gospels (Mt. 3:13–17; Mk. 1:9–11; Lk. 4:21–23; Jn. 1:32–34) in much the same terms. The Spirit, appearing in the form of a dove, alights on Jesus, whom a voice from heaven – unnamed, but clearly that of the Father – proclaims as the beloved Son (of God). Here, more clearly than anywhere in the earthly life of Christ, the heavens are opened to give us a glimpse of the inner life of the Triune God. It was a union which the church did not forget, and which we now find enshrined in the very rite which symbolizes for every believer the beginning of his imitation of Christ.

The other explicitly trinitarian formula is 2 Corinthians 13:14: '. . . the grace of the Lord Jesus Christ, and the love of God, and the fellowship of the Holy Spirit be with you all.' This famous verse is theologically anomalous in that the Lord Jesus Christ comes first in the triad of persons, and there is no mention of God as Father. Many theories have been advanced to explain its appearance in this form, and its relevance to the trinitarianism of the early Christians has been affirmed – as well as denied – by a wide range of scholars. Probably the best explanation is the one which says that the trinitarian shape of this blessing is secondary, perhaps even incidental to its main purpose. Paul adopts a trinitarian framework not in order to teach a doctrine of the Trinity, but in order to express the pattern of God's active involvement with his people. It is because that involvement is trinitarian that this verse has acquired its present shape.[33]

One might go even further than this, and say that the verse's primary emphasis is christological. In ancient literary style, it was customary for the second and third elements in triads of the kind found here to be governed by their first element (*cf.* Origen's triadic arrangement of the *hypostases*). If the principle is applied to this verse as well, the apparent 'inversion' in the order of the persons can be explained by saying that the main emphasis of the verse is christological. This would also make the second and third elements primarily christological, so that 'the love of God' would be a reference to Christ, the manifestation of God's love, and 'the fellowship of the Holy Spirit' would be union and communion with Christ, which it is the Spirit's task to foster. Looked at in this way, the verse is no longer an anomaly, or even an alternative pattern of trinitarianism. Rather, it is above all a practical illustration of how all three persons must inevitably participate in the work of each one – in this case, the work of Christ.

If this interpretation is correct, 2 Corinthians 13:14 ought probably to be understood as a trinitarian reference belonging to the second category rather than to the first. If that is so, it fits quite well with a number of other Pauline passages in which the Trinity is revealed indirectly. In many of these, Christ is mentioned first, and the Father is referred to simply as God, *e.g.*:

> — . . . a minister of *Christ Jesus* to the Gentiles with the priestly duty of proclaiming the gospel of *God*, so that the Gentiles might become an offering acceptable to God, sanctified by the *Holy Spirit* (Rom. 15:16);
> — I urge you, brothers, by our *Lord Jesus Christ* and by the love of the *Spirit*, to join me in my struggle by praying to *God* for me (Rom. 15:30);
> — Now it is *God* who makes both us and you stand firm in *Christ*. He anointed us, set his seal of ownership on us, and put his *Spirit* in our hearts (2 Cor. 1:21–22);

145

— You show that you are a letter from *Christ*, the result of our ministry, written not with ink but with the *Spirit* of the living *God* (2 Cor. 3:3).

Similar to the above but with 'Father' instead of 'God' is the following:

— For through *him* (= *Christ*) we both have access to the *Father* by one *Spirit* (Eph. 2:18). (My italics throughout)

It is noticeable that in these passages there is no consistency in the order of the second and third elements, a pattern which is also common in secular literature. It is also curious that the word 'Father' appears only once, although there is also another instance of this in Ephesians 3:14–16, this time in first place. Lest anyone think though that the use of 'Father' is a peculiarity of Ephesians (and for that reason late, or even non-Pauline, in origin), it should be pointed out that it also occurs in one of the most strikingly trinitarian, as well as one of the earliest Pauline texts, *viz.* Galatians 4:6: 'God sent the *Spirit* of his *Son* into our hearts, the Spirit who calls out *"Abba, Father"'*.

There can be little doubt that Paul's mind was fundamentally trinitarian in cast and that each person occupies the same relative position, in spite of the great variety of combinations in which they appear. Thus in fourteen passages cited by Wainwright as clearly trinitarian, we find the following:

| | | | |
|---|---|---|---|
| God/Father | Christ/Son | (Holy) Spirit | twice |
| God/Father | (Holy) Spirit | Christ/Son | four times |
| Christ/Son | God/Father | (Holy) Spirit | four times |
| Christ/Son | (Holy) Spirit | God/Father | three times |
| (Holy) Spirit | God/Father | Christ/Son | once |
| (Holy) Spirit | Christ/Son | God/Father | – |

It appears that every possible combination except one is represented, but in spite of this, the pattern of personal operation is remarkably stable. God the Father is the person who ordains, establishes, judges and appoints; he is also the

146

person to whom worship is chiefly directed. The Son Jesus Christ appears as the Redeemer, the sacrificial victim and the mediator; he is the guarantor of our salvation and the person in whose likeness we are being moulded. The Holy Spirit is the Sanctifier, the first-fruits of the inheritance of the glory to come. He dwells in our hearts by faith, although not to the exclusion of Christ (*cf.*, *e.g.*, Eph. 3:16) and is responsible both for giving us access to the Father and for producing the image of Christ in us. In these capacities he appears as the servant of the other persons, accomplishing their will for us and bringing their work in and for us to its perfect fulfilment.

This particular task may explain why Paul showed some reluctance to put the Holy Spirit first in a triad, although even that possibility cannot be excluded, as Philippians 3:3 demonstrates. The Spirit also appears first in Jude 20–21, a passage which is much more obviously trinitarian; and if mention of sanctification can be construed as an allusion to the Spirit, the number of instances in which he comes first would multiply substantially. We must therefore be careful to guard against the temptation to say that what is unusual is undesirable, or even impossible, and we must be even more careful not to demote the Holy Spirit to an inferior rung in the divine hierarchy, on the basis of evidence like this.

In the non-Pauline, non-Johannine literature of the New Testament, a specifically triadic pattern occurs only rarely. Apart from the baptism of Christ, already mentioned, and Jude 20–21, the best known instance is 1 Peter 1:2, where we find:

— foreknowledge of *God the Father*;
— sanctification of the *Spirit*;
— sprinkling of the blood of *Jesus Christ*.

Some authorities would add passages like Hebrews 10:29 or Acts 20:28, although here the trinitarian pattern is less obvious, and its existence is open to question. On a broader scale, there are many passages in which the work of all three persons must be taken into account if we are to understand the full meaning of the text, but in these passages we have passed from establishing the existence of the Trinity to examining its operation in the divine economy of salvation.

The Johannine literature is a world of its own, and forms a fitting climax to our discussion of the Trinity in the New Testament. On the one hand, formulaic expressions of the doctrine are rare to non-existent, unless one relies on a passage like Revelation 1:4–5. But it would be a great mistake to conclude from this that the Johannine books are devoid of any reference to the Trinity. That may be true to some extent of the three epistles, two of which are probably too short for any mention of the doctrine, but both the gospel and the apocalypse more than make up for this. Indeed, the fourth gospel is in parts virtually a trinitarian tract. This is most noticeable in chapters 14–16, but the careful reader will soon discover that these chapters are but a more concentrated discussion of a theme which runs through the entire book. From the very first verse, we are introduced to the relationship between the Logos and God, and this theme is developed in the many references throughout the gospel to the intimacy of the relationship between Father and Son. It is a constant subject of Jesus' discussions with the Jews, so much so in fact that classical orthodox christology is in many respects little more than a systematic commentary on the teaching of Jesus about himself, as John has recorded it.[34]

No less obvious, and in recent years fully studied, is the theme of the Spirit, which is one of the gospel's most characteristic traits. The Spirit is fundamental to Jesus' ministry and teaching, not only at his baptism, but in his whole teaching about true religion (cf., e.g., Jn. 3:5–8). More than anything else, it is Jesus' teaching about the work of the Holy Spirit, and the latter's relationship both to himself and to the Father, which provides the occasion for the great trinitarian exposition of chapters 14–16, a passage which for centuries has formed the cornerstone of orthodox doctrine.

In the New Testament context, what is striking about these texts is the way in which they so closely parallel the teaching of Paul. There is a certain tendency among scholars to polarize Paul, the practical teacher with his 'functional' christology, and John, the theorist who moved away from the Jewish roots of Christianity into the world of Greek 'ontological' thought. In recent years some scholars have been working to break down this polarization, so that the primitive Jewish character of the fourth gospel is now increasingly recognized. Yet suspicions remain, especially at the doctrinal level, so it is as well to go over the ground covered in the Pauline epistles once more, and demonstrate the underlying unity of the New Testament picture of God.

In the fourth gospel the Father is always presented as the directing force behind the mission of Jesus, who frequently refers to the Father as 'him who sent me'. As in the Pauline epistles, the Father initiates all action and is the primary object of worship, although John makes the point that he has entrusted all his prerogatives to the Son in order to ensure that the Son receives equal honour (Jn. 5:19–23). The Son is pre-eminently the Redeemer and sacrifice; indeed, no other gospel dwells to such an extent on the events of the last week of Jesus' earthly ministry. His role as mediator, which is such a recurrent theme in Paul, receives a whole chapter to itself (Jn. chapter 17) and is implicit almost everywhere else as well.

Above all, it is in his treatment of the Holy Spirit that John excels, and in chapters 14–16 we find the theological under-pinning of so much of what Paul says elsewhere about the Spirit's work. The meaning of the Spirit's indwelling presence is clearly spelled out in chapter 14, where there is a complex interweaving of the theme into a trinitarian pattern. For the indwelling of the Spirit entails also the indwelling of Christ (Jn. 14:17), and of the Father as well (Jn. 14:23). The Spirit's work is developed in John 16:5–16, where his sanc-tifying and comforting roles are expounded and related both to the sacrifice of Christ on the cross and the demands of the Father's justice. What is assumed or summarized in the rest of the New Testament is here spelled out in detail, so that no Christian might be ignorant of his calling before God.

The fourth gospel is undoubtedly the main biblical source for trinitarian doctrine, and as with christology, the classical formulations are heavily dependent on it. Yet for all that, it is probably true to say that it has one rival, and even superior, in the subtle art of expounding the Trinity as part of the experience of knowing God. This is the Book of Revelation, the great apocalypse which has earned for John, alone among the authors of the New Testament, the epithet 'divine' (*i.e.* theologian). It is in Revelation, more than anywhere else, that the perfect unity of the Trinity is demonstrated, so that while the persons remain fully distinct, it becomes almost impossible to distinguish between them.

A simple example of this, taken from the opening chapters, will show what is meant. In chapter 1, the Father is designated simply as God, the Son as Jesus Christ – a pattern familiar from Paul's writings. In verse 7 John has his great vision of the Son, but in verse 8 it is God who speaks: is this the Father or the Son, or both? There is an ambiguity here, which is increased in verses 12–18. Here we return to the vision of the Son, who describes himself (verses 17–18) in words which parallel those of verse 8 without actually repeating them:

| Revelation 1:8 | Revelation 1:17–18 |
|---|---|
| — I am the Alpha and the Omega | — I am the First and the Last |
| — who is, and who was, and who is to come | — I am the Living One; I was dead, and behold I am alive for ever |
| — the Almighty | — I hold the keys of death and Hades |

The correspondence between these passages is clear, but so too are the differences between them. If verse 8 is the voice of the Father and verses 17–18 are the voice of the Son, we have a living example of how the two persons can share the absolute power of God without losing their identity. In the case of the Holy Spirit, we note not only that it was he who made John's vision possible (verse 10), but that his voice is identical to that of Christ. In the famous letters to the seven churches (Rev. chapters 2–3), it is Christ who speaks, yet each letter concludes with the solemn command: 'He who has an ear, let him hear what the *Spirit* says to the churches'.

The genius of the apocalypse is that all this appears to be so natural. Caught up in the vision of Patmos we are not surprised. Indeed, we are barely aware that we are passing from one person to another. The sense of the presence of God is so overwhelming that we can move among the persons almost without noticing, yet we are always fully conscious of their presence. There is never any confusion in the reader's mind about who is speaking or acting, yet in coldly logical terms, the three cannot be clearly distinguished from the one God. Father, Son and Holy Spirit reveal themselves to John, and so also to us, as one God, living and moving in the fullness of his trinitarian being. The doctrine, culled from the rest of Scripture and laboriously constructed, is here presented to us in all its profound complexity and splendid simplicity. The God whom we cannot explain, we know, the one we cannot picture, we see. The Book of Revelation is first and foremost a revelation of the Trinity, and it is only when we understand this that we will be equipped to interpret its meaning, which is nothing less than the mystical vision of God.[35]

## Summary

We may now summarize our findings as follows:

1. The Christian church accepted the Old Testament as an authentic self-revelation of God, but was forced to go beyond it because of the deeper revelation which it had received in Jesus Christ. It was this revelation, and the new experience of God to which it led, which forced the early church to develop a trinitarian understanding of God.

2. Both unitarian and binitarian models of God have been put forward, sometimes by opponents of the Christian faith, but sometimes also by Christians who were sincerely trying to explain the mystery of their personal encounter with God in Christ. Neither view found acceptance in the church at large, because the consensus among Christians generally was that they did not do justice either to the witness of the New Testament or to their own experience of God.

3. The New Testament is trinitarian in character, even though there is no explicit development of the doctrine of the Trinity in its pages. This means that the theologians of the early church were being faithful to the biblical witness when they embarked upon the difficult task of formulating a coherent trinitarian doctrine.

# 4

## THE PERSONS AND THE NATURE OF GOD

## Introduction

In the last chapter we saw that the New Testament makes it clear that from the beginning Christians felt compelled to worship God along lines which were recognizably trinitarian. What these early Christians lacked was a conceptual framework which would allow them to express their belief that the Father, the Son and the Holy Spirit were all equally God, without sacrificing their commitment to the monotheism of the Old Testament.

But as we have already seen, they experienced great difficulty in trying to escape from a form of monotheism which was essentially unitarian. This was not simply because the first Christians felt some kind of residual loyalty to Judaism; many did not, and Jewish influence declined dramatically after the first generation of Christians died out. By AD 200 there was considerable antipathy between Christians and Jews, although it must be stressed that this did not mean that Christians were prepared to reject the Old Testament. Tertullian, for example, although he blamed the Jews for having started the persecution of Christians, and although he was a leading advocate of pure religious observance, far exceeding the righteousness of the scribes and the Pharisees, came down firmly on the side of the Jewish tradition when he encountered the paganism of his own society, or the teachings of Marcion. In the intellectual struggle between Athens and Jerusalem he unhesitatingly opted for the latter, and orthodox Christians everywhere followed his example, at least in principle.

It must be said, however, that the church's Jewish inheritance was modified by a basic conviction, shared by almost all the early Christians, that God was an object – a thing, with a nature which could be analysed and compared (*i.e.* contrasted) with other natures, especially the nature of human beings. This belief, which reflects a philosophical outlook only superficially modified by an acquaintance with the Bible, put enormous difficulties in the way of trinitarian monotheism. The attributes of God belonged to his nature, which on this understanding constituted his being, and they all pointed in a unitarian direction. Simplicity, omnipotence, omnipresence and the rest presuppose a unity which does not admit of any sharing among equals. The most which can be allowed is that the omnipresent being may have *delegated* his powers to another. This was the approach of virtually all Christian theology before the fourth century, which explains how Christians could believe that the Son and the Holy Spirit acted as God without actually being God in the fullest sense of the word. It was only when Christians realized that God's powers were not delegated by the Father but were inherent in each of the three persons, that the full and essential deity of Christ and the Holy Spirit were properly established.

The problem was complicated by the fact that personhood (a term now generally used in preference to personality), was regarded as no more than an attribute of the divine nature. God was personal in that he had a name and could be described in terms analogous to those used of human beings. But his essence far surpassed all human understanding, so that descriptions of him in personal terms were not strictly accurate. God was described as a person in order to

154

help us understand him, but the reality of his being remained for ever above and beyond what we can experience.

Classical trinitarian theology came into its own when the concept of person was detached from its place as one of the attributes of God, and made into a principle in its own right. The process by which this occurred was a slow one, and was not clearly perceived at first. Those whose achievement it was, never fully understood what they were doing, because their only intention was to re-express the existing tradition in terms which would avoid particular misunderstandings which had arisen. Because of this, their efforts to put trinitarianism on a solid foundation continued to reflect the legacy of Christian unitarianism, a legacy which was overcome only with the greatest difficulty. Even today, trinitarian theology is frequently influenced by assumptions which reflect a more primitive, basically unitarian phase of development.[1]

The transition from a nature-based theology to one in which the persons were recognized as theological principles in their own right, began in the fourth century. First the Arian controversy, and then the disputes about the divinity of the Holy Spirit, provided the occasion for a restatement of Origen's doctrine in a way which excluded his latent subordination of the second and third persons of the Trinity to the first. This theological task was accomplished by the Cappadocian Fathers, Basil of Caesarea (c. 329–79), his friend Gregory of Nazianzus (c. 329–90) and Basil's younger brother, Gregory of Nyssa (c. 330–c. 95). Working together, and complementing each other's gifts, they established a theoretical base for trinitarian thought which continues to exert a powerful influence even today. Their teaching was soon translated into Latin by Hilary of Poitiers (c. 315–c. 368) and moulded into the classical statement of Western trinitarianism by Augustine of Hippo (354–430), whose *On the Trinity* (*De Trinitate*), composed between 399 and 419, remained the standard work on the subject until modern times.

The Cappadocians and Augustine were almost contemporaries, they shared a common concern and they thought in similar categories. The former influenced the latter via

155

Hilary, and we know that Basil was sympathetic to the Latin tradition which Augustine was to inherit from Tertullian. Yet in spite of all this, what strikes us most about their work is how different they were from each other. Calvin perceived this at once, when he came to write his *Institutes* (I, 13,5), and it has long since become an axiom of historical theology. The Cappadocians and Augustine worked from a different base, and used different principles – a fact which was to shape the mental outlook of their respective followers ever after. By the ninth century these differences were beginning to produce conflict, and this eventually erupted into a schism which has lasted to this day.

Recent attempts to heal the breach have had the salutary effect of taking the theological world back to the first principles which governed the development of these rival traditions, thereby revealing for all to see what the underlying structure of Christian trinitarianism is. In this chapter we shall look at each tradition in turn, and then briefly examine a third possibility put forward by theologians in our own time.

## The nature of God: in the person of the Father?

### Exposition

The basic principle of Cappadocian trinitarianism is the belief that the nature of God is personified, or as theologians generally prefer to say, *hypostatized*, in the person of the Father. This was Origen's basic principle, but the Cappadocians modified it in a number of significant ways. Whereas Origen had thought of the Father as the first in a series of three hypostases, the Cappadocians preferred to say that the third person proceeded directly from him (as did the second). The difference between them may be illustrated thus:

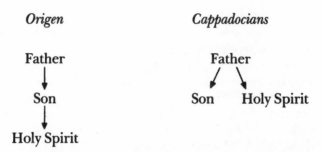

The difficulty with the Cappadocian scheme is that it does not account for the relationship between the Son and the Holy Spirit, although Gregory of Nyssa agreed that the Holy Spirit proceeded from the Father through the Son, and this explanation was later enshrined in the teaching of John of Damascus.[2] Nowadays most Eastern Orthodox theologians go back to the pattern observed at the baptism of Jesus, when the Holy Spirit, *proceeding* from the Father, *rested* on the Son, as follows:

They do not confine this pattern to the earthly life of the incarnate Son, but believe that it is a trinitarian relationship established in eternity. This explanation has not received official sanction but it appears to be gaining in favour, especially among those Orthodox who are most hostile to Western trinitarianism.[3]

A more significant break with earlier tradition was the Cappadocians' insistence that the Trinity could not be imagined as the expansion of one hypostasis into three by a process of emanation. Both the one and the three exist in eternity, and both must be conceived as different levels within the external Godhead. Thus the unity of God is his *ousia* (= essence, being) and the Trinity is found in the hypostases, in each of which the *ousia* is manifested in its fullness. This means that the second and third persons

157

cannot be reproductions of the first person, nor emanations from him, because the *ousia* of God is a simple essence which cannot be reproduced or divided.

In physical terms, one might say that all three persons occupy the same divine 'space'; to see God is to see all three at once, not one after the other in an ascending order of succession. As a doctrine, this belief is called co-inherence (Greek: *perichōrēsis*; Latin: *circuminsessio*) of the persons. Co-inherence, or circumincession, means that each of the hypostases is a complete manifestation of the divine essence, so that it is impossible to say that the Son is God's rationality, or that the Spirit is God's spirituality – as if the Father were somehow irrational and unspiritual. It also means that every divine attribute applies equally to all three hypostases: all are omnipotent, omniscient, eternal and so on. This doctrine avoids the problem of subordinationism, and provides an adequate explanation of Colossians 2:9 ('in Christ all the fulness of the Deity lives in bodily form') without falling into Sabellianism or the patripassianism of Noetus of Smyrna.

The concept of co-inherence was a great advance on the hierarchical model of Origen, but it raised the question of how the hypostases could be distinguished from each other. Here the Cappadocians were less successful. To explain the distinction of hypostases in God, they first developed a distinction between 'being' and 'existence' (*hyparxis*). In contemporary Neoplatonism it was gradually coming to be accepted that 'being' referred to non-temporal, absolute reality, whereas 'existence' referred primarily to the appearance of reality within the time–space framework. This distinction was fundamental to Platonism, but it must be emphasized that even as late as the fourth century AD, the technical terminology needed to describe it adequately had not yet been fixed.[4]

On the other hand, something very like a temporal/non-temporal distinction had governed formulations of the doctrine of the Trinity in the second century. Before the time of Origen, and even to some extent after it, it was generally believed that only the Father had 'being' in the absolute sense; the other two hypostases of the Trinity had something less, corresponding to temporal 'existence'. The Cappadocians broke with this tradition, by asserting the principle that every hypostasis has an eternal mode of existence (*tropos hyparxeōs*). This principle applied also to the first person of the Trinity, who as Father hypostatized the being of God in a special, but no longer unique way. For the first time, the term 'Father', which applied to only one of the Persons, was clearly distinguished from the term 'God', which applied equally to all three.

Because of this equality, the distinctions between the hypostases could no longer be defined in terms of their relationship to absolute being, but only in terms of their relationship to each other, within absolute being. This was fine, and represented a great advance on earlier ways of thinking. The Cappadocians then went on to say, however, that the distinction of hypostases resided in the 'cause' which brought it into being. It is difficult to see what 'cause' can mean when speaking of an eternal person, and all too easy to reflect that the word represents a lingering trace of pre-Nicene subordinationism, which held that there was a time when the Son (and the Spirit) did not exist. But, however difficult it may be to understand, the Cappadocians insisted that 'cause' or the mode of origin, was definitive of the identity of each hypostasis in the Godhead, and this notion remained fundamental to their theology. It must therefore be understood if the differences between their way of thinking and the later Western tradition are to be properly appreciated.

In Cappadocian theology, the three hypostases are characterized by the following distinctions, according to their mode of origin:

— The Father is *unbegotten* (*agennētos*);
— The Son is *begotten* (*gennētos*) of the Father;
— The Holy Spirit *proceeds* (*ekporeuetai*) from the Father.

The language used is scriptural (*cf.* Jn. 1:14; 15:26), although it must be remembered that in the New Testament the term *ekporeuetai* appears in the context of the *temporal mission* of the third person of the Trinity, whereas the Cappadocians used it to describe the *inner relation* of the Holy Spirit to the Father within the Godhead. The assumption which links the inner relation to the temporal mission is the belief that God reveals himself to us as he is in himself. If we claim to know God as he truly is, we have to believe that God dwells in himself in the same way that he reveals himself to us, that is, according to the same pattern of relationships. If this principle is accepted, then it becomes legitimate to transpose the data of temporal mission to the plane of the inner relations, and to suppose that what is true of the one will also be true of the other.

The Cappadocians did not stop there, however. They took up the descriptions of the *process* of origin, and turned them into *attributes* of each hypostasis. Thus the Father, who was unbegotten, was said to possess 'unbegottenness' (*agennēsia*) as an attribute of his existence. In the same way, the Son was said to possess 'begottenness' (*gennēsia*) and the Holy Spirit was said to possess 'procession' (*ekporeusis*), as qualities of their respective hypostases. Furthermore, it was the existence of these attributes which determined the relationship of the hypostases to each other. The primacy of the Father in the Trinity was guaranteed by his unbegottenness; he owed his existence to no-one, and in that respect came closest to representing the divine being (*ousia*) in its attribute of 'anarchy' ('unbeginningness').

The Son, on the other hand, owed his beginning to the Father, who had begotten him in eternity. The Cappadocians did not profess to know how this had happened, nor did they accept the Arian belief that there had once been a time when the Son had not existed. The process of begetting in eternity was a mysterious one, but it had happened, and it determined the eternal relationship of the Son to the Father.

The Holy Spirit in turn proceeded from the Father (*cf.* Jn. 15:26) in a way which was equally mysterious. A very early question, which Gregory of Nazianzus tried to answer, was what the difference was between the generation of the Son and the procession of the Holy Spirit. Gregory could not explain this, and regarded the distinction as a mystery. But he was quite sure that they were not simply different words for the same thing, so that it was wrong to suggest, as some were doing, that the Son and the Spirit were twins. To us, this

160

idea may seem far-fetched, but what it means is that the Holy Spirit cannot be regarded as an alternative to the Son as the mediator between God and human beings. The idea that the Holy Spirit can produce 'anonymous Christians', or bring people to a saving knowledge of God without explicit reference to Christ, is a common theme in the tolerant climate of our own time, but it receives no support from Cappadocian theology.

As we have indicated, the real problem with Cappadocian trinitarianism is its uncertainty about the relationship between the Son and the Holy Spirit. It has sometimes been pointed out that if the incarnation was the work of the Holy Spirit ('conceived by the Holy Spirit'), it ought to be possible to argue that the Son is also in some way dependent on the Spirit as the cause of his hypostatic existence. Yet this apparently logical extension of the principle that temporal mission = inner relation has never been accepted. The work of the Spirit in the womb of Mary has always been held to refer to the virginal conception of Christ's *human* nature, not to the implantation of the Son's divinity. In other words, the Spirit takes the place of a *human* father, and so his participation in the virgin birth cannot be regarded as a reflection of the eternal relationship between him and the Son.

In Christian theology, the only real question has been whether it might be said that the Holy Spirit proceeds from the Son, and not merely *through* him, as Gregory of Nyssa was prepared to admit.[5] On Cappadocian principles, the answer to this question had to be no. For them to say that the Holy Spirit proceeded from *both* the Father *and* the Son would be to say that there were two principles of origin in God, which would be a denial of the distinctive attribute of the Father's hypostasis. Therefore, the Son could not be the cause of the Holy Spirit in the same absolute sense in which the Father was. At most, he could be the cause of the Holy Spirit only in a secondary sense, so that to say that the Spirit 'proceeds from the Son' could mean only that he proceeded from the Father through the Son – the position taken by Gregory of Nyssa.

There the matter might have rested, had the Western church not begun to insist on the double procession of the Holy Spirit, *i.e.* from the Father and the Son. Awareness of this teaching was slow to develop in the East, and it was not until the time of the Patriarch Photius of Constantinople (reigned 864–67 and 880–86) that controversy erupted.[6] Photius reiterated and clarified the principles of Cappadocian theology, adding for good measure that the Holy Spirit proceeds from the Father *alone*. This additional explanation of the credal phrase was generally accepted in the East, and it is now a standard feature of the Eastern Orthodox exposition of Cappadocian trinitarianism, although the word *alone* has never received canonical approval and has not been added to the Nicene Creed.

One last point which must be made is that the Cappadocians believed that the hypostatic distinctions within the Godhead did not affect their external work. When the Trinity did something outside the being of God, *e.g.* created the world, all three persons acted in concert. The Cappadocians did not develop this idea much, and it has remained somewhat dormant in the Eastern tradition; but it was taken over by Augustine, whose mediaeval followers exploited its possibilities to the full.

## Critique

How should we assess the Cappadocian model in the light of centuries of tradition and experience? In its favour, there is the undoubted advance in thinking represented by the doctrine of co-inherence.[7] This was such an important contribution in the struggle against the heresies of the time that it must be described as a stroke of genius. It enabled Christians to maintain that each of the persons was fully divine, without confusing them with each other. Later on, it would allow Calvin to assert that each person necessarily revealed the others in revealing himself, a position which is inherent in the Cappadocian model, although it was not specifically taught by them.

It must also be admitted, that given the limitations of the Origenistic tradition which they had inherited, the Cappadocians did as much as could reasonably be expected to mitigate its consequences, which had manifested themselves in Arianism and in the denial of the full divinity of the Holy Spirit. The Western tradition, following Augustine, developed this doctrine of co-inherence, modified the definition of hypostasis, and built on the idea that the external works of the Trinity are undivided, in a way which the Eastern tradition did not. The Byzantines remained more faithful to the letter of Cappadocian trinitarianism, but even so, they developed the principle of causal relations in a way which the West eventually ceased to understand. The Cappadocians can hardly be blamed for this divergence from a common source, although with hindsight it is possible to see how their silence (reverential though it was) and their hesitations at certain crucial points could give rise to further speculation and lead eventually to controversy.

In fact, if we look carefully at the Cappadocian model of the Trinity, we realize that many features of it are not fully satisfactory. At the conceptual level, they did not develop their understanding of hypostasis in the right way. In their minds the term never reached the full evolution of meaning which we associate with the word 'person'; instead, it remained to a large extent a philosophical abstraction. Signs of this can be seen most clearly in the way in which causation and existence were explained in their theology.

In spite of the fact that they were very careful to remain within the bounds of the biblical testimony, the Cappadocians tended to make abstractions of words like 'begotten' and 'proceeding', thereby revealing a mental outlook basically foreign to that of Scripture. They turned relationships into attributes, and so invented qualities which do not exist. There is no such thing as 'unbegottenness'; it is a category of thought which does not correspond to any observed reality distinct from the eternity which is shared by all three persons alike. By positing abstract notions as the 'cause' of each hypostasis, the Cappadocians effectively said that the relationship between them was an abstraction fixed in their nature, and therefore neither personal nor free. The Son who came to earth to do his Father's will did not come voluntarily; he was sent by his Father, who had the power to impose his will on the Son by virtue of the fact that the latter's hypostasis was dependent on him. To the Western mind, such an absence of freedom in relationship is deeply disturbing, because it seems to reduce the spirit of loving self-sacrifice to the status of a routine obligation. To put it another way, the distinction between sonship and servanthood, so central to our understanding of the Christian life, is blurred if the Son's being is somehow dependent on that of the Father. Christ could not then have freely taken upon himself the form of a servant; he would have been a servant from all eternity.

In opting to describe the 'causes' as modes of existence, the Cappadocians were also betraying a latent tendency to regard the divine *ousia* as more fundamental than the hypostases. However much they may have emphasized co-inherence as a means of maximizing the divinity of each hypostasis, they could not avoid the fact that existence was by definition a lesser concept than being. This inevitably reinforced an already existing tendency to regard the divine essence as ultimately more significant than the Trinity of persons, a position from which the Cappadocians were in other ways trying to break free. The theology which resulted hypostatized the divine *ousia* in the hypostasis of the Father, thereby effectively negating the equality of persons implied by the doctrine of co-inherence.

Cappadocian trinitarianism is probably best understood as a transition from one type of theology to another. Looked at in terms of its own antecedents, it was a breakthrough of significant proportions. It revamped the Origenist position in ways which made a retreat into earlier models of the Trinity difficult, if not impossible. But seen from the vantage point of subsequent developments, it looks unfinished in some important respects. There is an unresolved tension between the co-inherence of the hypostases and the primacy of the Father as the fountainhead of Deity, a tension which would later erupt into controversy and produce schism. In the Eastern churches it was to be the latter emphasis which was to triumph in the end, and this explains how the Cappadocians are now read there, and why. In the West the implications of co-inherence would be examined in much greater depth, contributing eventually to a kind of trinitarianism which claimed the heritage of the Cappadocians, but whose principles they would scarcely have recognized.

### Subsequent developments

Of later developments in Cappadocian thought within the Eastern tradition, little need be said beyond what we have already noted in passing. There was a great deal of writing on the subject of the Trinity during the later Middle Ages, most of which concentrated on denouncing the Western doctrine of the double procession of the Holy Spirit (*filioque*).[8]

Of the few truly original orthodox theologians, mention must be made of the Russian émigré Vladimir Lossky (1903–58). Lossky attacked the Thomist thesis that the persons of the Trinity were relations of opposition (see page 183 below), and he insisted that their personhood was an absolute distinction in each case, and not dependent on the existence of the others. His fierce repudiation of the *filioque* was based on his conviction that Gregory Palamas (1296–1359) had been right to distinguish between the essence and the 'energies' of God. The former was beyond our understanding, whilst the latter have been revealed to us by faith. In advocating the double procession of the Holy Spirit, said Lossky, Western theologians have introduced into God's essence something which is proper to his energies. The Holy Spirit might be said to proceed from the Son *as his energy at work in the world*, but he does not proceed from the Son in the hidden essence of God, because the Son is not the fountainhead of Deity.

Lossky's views have not yet become standard orthodox teaching, but he has inspired a whole generation of younger theologians, and given them a new understanding of Byzantine theology and spirituality. It therefore seems probable that this revived tradition, which in recent years has attracted some highly intellectual converts, will be a major ingredient of the theological scene in the future.[9]

# The nature of God: in the person of the Holy Spirit?

### Exposition

The classical alternative to the type of trinitarianism advocated by the Cappadocian Fathers is the one which finds the nature of God most fully revealed in the person of the Holy Spirit. It was formulated in all essentials by the great Augustine of Hippo (354–430), through whose influence it became the standard form of orthodox trinitarian thought in Western Europe. The great mediaeval theologians and the Reformers were all indebted to him, and even quite recent restatements of the doctrine have usually reflected a way of thinking which Augustine would have understood, even when it goes some way beyond what he actually said.

The influence of this seminal thinker can scarcely be exaggerated, although it must be appreciated that not the least part of his genius was his ability to draw on a wide range of sources and synthesize them in a bigger whole. For many centuries he had no real successors; it appeared to most of his readers that no more needed to be said on the subject, and his work remained unmodified. This situation began to change only in the ninth century, after which time there was a powerful development of trinitarian thought in the Western church. Even so, those who led the way in this were fervent in their professions of loyalty to Augustine, and claimed to be doing no more than expounding his teaching in a way which would make it relevant to contemporary needs. This is especially true of John Calvin, who acknowledged Augustine as the leading authority on the Trinity and quoted from him frequently, while at the same time developing an understanding of the doctrine which was radically different from that of his master.

Of the sources on which Augustine drew, pride of place must go to Tertullian, whose theology we have already discussed at some length. From him, Augustine gained his basic approach to monotheism, and the major part of his theological vocabulary. Tertullian placed great emphasis on the moral holiness of God, as well as on other attributes like his rationality and his spirituality. Augustine was profoundly marked by Tertullian's picture of the divine being, which had a strong influence on his own spiritual development. Although he did not follow Tertullian's dispensational scheme, which by then had already shown itself to be inadequate, he did not hesitate to latch onto the powerful Old Testament emphases found in Tertullian's writings.

In terms of vocabulary, Augustine preferred *essentia* (essence) to *substantia* (substance) as a translation of *ousia*, because *substantia* is the etymological equivalent of *hypostasis*, with the result that Tertullian's use of it to mean *ousia* had caused some confusion. But like Tertullian, Augustine also thought of God primarily as a single being, in whom there were three persons. This primacy of the essence over the persons (or of the one over the three) was to become and remain characteristic of the Western tradition, and is one of the main features distinguishing it from its Eastern counterpart.

Augustine borrowed the word *persona* from Tertullian, but was not altogether happy with it, claiming that the word had established itself in Latin as the standard translation of the Greek *hypostasis*, largely for want of a better equivalent (*On the Trinity V*, 9). Augustine's hesitation on this point was due mainly to his deep awareness of the mystery of the Trinity in God, although some modern critics have seized on it as evidence either that he held to a sub-personal view of the Trinity, or that he regarded divine personhood as fundamentally different from the human. In fact, the word had not yet been defined theologically in a way which would avoid any taint of Sabellianism, nor was it as yet a standard synonym for 'human being'. This further definition came later, but as it occurred shortly after Augustine's death, and has always been regarded as an integral part of the Augustinian tradition, many theologians have mistakenly assumed that it was this later, though now classical, definition of the term which Augustine hesitated to accept.[10]

The second major source on whom Augustine drew was Hilary of Poitiers, the faithful translator of the Cappadocians. Augustine, whose own Greek was rudimentary, is frequently accused of having misunderstood, and therefore misrepresented, Cappadocian thought.[11] There is some evidence to support this assertion, but its importance has been vastly exaggerated. The most significant point is that he did not distinguish the hypostases by their modes of existence in the way that the Cappadocians did. Instead, he defined the persons as modes of *being* within the Godhead, along the lines already laid down by Tertullian. Augustine knew that the

167

Greeks used *hypostasis* to mean what the Latins meant by *persona*, but he also knew that *hypostasis* and *persona* were not synonymous. The Latin equivalent of *hypostasis* was *substantia*, and Augustine could never understand how it differed from *ousia* (= *essentia*) which to him, as to us, was the same thing.

Augustine knew that in Latin *persona* did not have the objective quality associated with *substantia*, which made him uneasy in using it to describe the three persons of the Trinity. He did not want to appear to be giving them a lesser status than that which pertained to the divine essence. It would be only at the Council of Chalcedon in 451, half a generation after Augustine's death, that the church would formally declare that *hypostasis* and *persona* were synonymous, thus opening the way for a definition of the latter which included the objective, absolute character of the former. When Augustine spoke of the persons as 'modes of being', it was precisely this sense of absolute permanence that he was trying to emphasize. We may question his choice of vocabulary, which laid him open to the charge of Sabellianism, but his understanding of the objectivity of both the one and the three was fundamentally identical to that of the Cappadocians, so that he cannot fairly be accused of having misrepresented them.

It is probable that the differences between Augustine and the Cappadocians can be explained, at least in part, by the hypothesis that he drew on a different strand of Neoplatonic thought from the one which most influenced them. The exact nature of Augustine's dependence on Neoplatonism is a highly controversial subject, and undoubtedly he was eclectic in this, as in other matters.[12] Nevertheless it seems most likely that the main influence on him came from Marius Victorinus (d. *c.* 360), a converted philosopher who had been a disciple of Porphyry, the second of the three great Neoplatonists.[13]

The Cappadocians had learned their philosophy from pupils of Iamblichus, the third of the great Neoplatonists, who in many ways reflected the original Neoplatonism of Plotinus (*c.* 204–70). Porphyry, however, had modified Plotinus' teaching in many important respects, some of which are clearly reflected in Augustine's trinitarianism. Like Origen, whom he may have known,[14] Plotinus believed that the Divine was a hierarchy of three hypostases. These can easily be correlated to Origen's Trinity as follows:

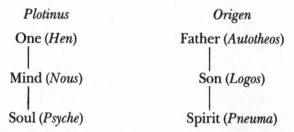

| *Plotinus* | *Origen* |
| --- | --- |
| One (*Hen*) | Father (*Autotheos*) |
| Mind (*Nous*) | Son (*Logos*) |
| Soul (*Psyche*) | Spirit (*Pneuma*) |

Porphyry analysed the Plotinian hierarchy and rejected its usefulness as a working model. On the ground that the One was beyond knowledge and conception, Porphyry argued that nothing could be said about it. Therefore it could not form part of a systematic theology. Apparently he also decided that mind and soul were really a single hypostasis, and so combined them accordingly. This left a rather bleak outlook for any kind of trinitarianism, but Porphyry did not abandon the idea of a three-in-one. He found a triad *within* the single hypostasis of the mind–soul. As understood by Marius Victorinus, this trinity consisted of being (*esse*), living (*vivere*), and knowing (*intelligere*). The use of verbal infinitives, in preference to abstract nouns, is important, because it allowed for the concept of motion. This, as we shall see, was to be a major element in Marius' understanding of God.

It will be realized immediately that Porphyry's idea of a trinity within a single hypostasis corresponds almost exactly to Tertullian's belief that the divine persons existed within the one *substantia*, and so Augustine's appropriation of the model, via Marius, should not be seen merely as the result of Neoplatonic influence. It must also be remembered that Augustine did not take over Porphyry's ideas wholesale; he modified and adapted them to accord with the teaching of the Bible and the existing theological tradition.

Equally important, and foreign to both Porphyry and the Cappadocians, was Marius' notion that *the being of God is movement* (*esse* = *moveri*). This brilliant deduction, which owes its origin to the picture of an active God revealed in the Old Testament, as well as to Christian statements about the origin

169

of the second and third persons of the Trinity, completely overturned the basic assumptions of all previous theology, whether pagan or Christian – the belief that the divine being was static. We have already mentioned this in connection with process theology, which has attacked the classical theological tradition for having started with this presupposition. It is therefore of the utmost importance to grasp that Augustine did *not* believe in a static God, although he would certainly not have recognized himself as the forerunner of process theology either.

By making motion part of God's being, Augustine was able to accommodate the Cappadocian idea that the Father was the hypostasis of the divine *ousia* by saying that it was the special property of the Father eternally to *be*, in the sense of being fully active in, and responsible for, the divine nature. To that extent, the person of the Father retained a certain fundamental primacy in the Godhead, but he could not be perceived as existing by himself. A being (noun) who was fully engaged in being (verb) must also be conscious of that fact, and in a perfect being (noun) such consciousness must necessarily constitute perfect self-knowledge. Thus Augustine modified Marius' teaching by making *esse* = *vivere* (*moveri*) and by putting *intelligere* in second place.

Augustine thought this corresponded very well with the New Testament assertion that the second person of the Trinity was the divine *Logos*. Third place was occupied by another principle, introduced here by Augustine, and fundamental to all his thought. This was the principle of love (*amare*, loving). Love was the essence of God, the bond which united the divine being with its self-awareness. For it was inconceivable that God should not love the self which he knew, since that self was in every way perfect. This 'psychological' image of the Trinity, which Augustine developed, was paralleled in human beings who are made in the image of God, although with the significant difference that sin made it impossible for the human race to know or to love that image as it ought. As St Paul said in Romans chapter 7, human self-awareness was an awareness of sin, which brought only frustration and despair. This could not be removed by any power other than the love of God, manifested to us in Christ, the divine self-awareness who alone could give us a clean conscience by the power of his own self-righteousness.

The link between the Trinity and human salvation is clearer in Augustine than in any other ancient writer, and it has indelibly marked the entire Western tradition. The belief that God is love is now such a commonplace that we seldom realize what a new and powerful idea it was to Augustine. Unfortunately though, Augustine formulated his belief in a way which leaves it open to serious question. As he understood it, the essence of God was both spirit and love. Despite serious hesitations, Augustine eventually argued himself into believing that spirit and love were therefore the same thing, with the result that the Holy Spirit must also be the personification of holy love.

The basis for this equation came from a comparison of John 4:24 ('God is spirit') with 1 John 4:16 ('God is love'). Today we would say that the word 'spirit' refers primarily to the nature of God, whereas love is the way in which God functions. To tie the two together as Augustine eventually did is to unite essence and function in a way which distorts the biblical data. This conjunction later became a standard feature of Western theology, which to this day likes to claim that pure being is the same as pure act. During the centuries when the emphasis was ontological, however, love tended to become a remote abstraction. Now that the emphasis has shifted to the functional, the opposite tendency has asserted itself, and love tends to be regarded mainly as a subjective feeling, which is then somehow identified with the very being of God.

In fairness to Augustine, it must be said that he himself never went anything like as far as that. He did not regard 'Spirit' as the personal name of the third person of the Trinity, but only as a designation of the divine nature. As such, the word could and did refer equally to the Father and the Son. On the other hand, Augustine toyed with this question of finding the personal name of the Holy Spirit, but never really came up with a satisfactory answer. At one point he suggested that it might be 'gift' (*donum*), although that is hardly a personal name in the sense that we would understand it. Later on, he put forward the view that the Spirit's

171

personal name was Holy. This was slightly better than 'gift', but it suffered from the fact that, like Spirit, it was a term which could be applied to the other persons of the Trinity as well.

Augustine's difficulty here is symptomatic of his whole approach, which locates the unity of the Father and the Son in the person of the Holy Spirit. But because the unity of God is expressed at the level of nature, there is an inescapable tendency to think of the Holy Spirit as a personification of the impersonal qualities which constitute the being of God. Admittedly, this tendency is helped to some extent by the impersonal name which is given to the third person, even in the Scriptures, although of course he is also called Comforter (Paraclete). Augustine was aware of this, but neither he nor his successors made much of it when discussing the names of the Trinity in their writings.

Returning to the concept of God as essentially spirit–love, we find that Augustine schematizes the Trinity as follows:

— The Father is the one who loves (Lover);
— The Son is the one who is loved (Beloved);
— The Spirit is love.

If this analysis is accepted, then the existence of a trinity in God becomes *logically necessary*, as well as being a fact of revelation. In the dynamic of love, there must be a lover, but he cannot exist without his beloved. Hence the Father needs the Son if he is to exercise his love, and we cannot imagine his existing without the Son. But two persons in love cannot then go their separate ways. Their activities correspond to and complement each other, coming together in a unity of love which is distinct from both the lover and the beloved, although obviously it proceeds from, and is intimately bound to, both.

According to Augustine, the Father loves the Son, and the Son returns his love to the Father. The Son's love is thus secondary to that of the Father in purely logical terms, though it must be equal to the Father's love if the two are to meet and unite in God. If the Holy Spirit is the unity of the divine love, then it follows that he proceeds first from the

172

Father, but also – and equally – from the Son. This was the basis of Augustine's doctrine of the *double procession* of the Holy Spirit, which became a subject of controversy after the word *filioque* ('and the Son') was added to the Nicene Creed in the sixth century.[15] The double procession of the Holy Spirit is a fundamental assumption of Augustine's theological system, although eventually it became – as it remains – a major stumbling-block in relations between the Western and Eastern churches.

## Critique

Augustine demonstrated by logic that love demands a trinity, but on this model, the position of the Holy Spirit remains unsatisfactory. In human terms, the love between a father and son (or between a husband and wife) does not require a third participant; the love which flows between them remains forever undefined and immaterial (unhypostatized). Such an analogy would leave the Holy Spirit in the same condition, and the question of his personhood has become a major theological issue as a result. In the end, Augustine's model has led to serious doubts about the reality of a trinity of three equal persons in God, which of course is the exact opposite of what he originally intended.

It will be obvious from the above that *relation* is a basic concept in Augustine's trinitarianism. In theory, he subscribed to the Cappadocian idea of causality as the ground of the personal distinctions in God,[16] but his belief that God's being is motion and that the persons are part of this being, changed the way in which he understood this. For Augustine, the generation of the Son and the procession of the Holy Spirit were not so much events, as integral parts of a divine being which could move without changing its nature. It therefore made sense to speak of the persons which resulted from this motion within God as modes of being. These were distinguished from each other not so much by their original causes as by their present relationships. The principle of causality was retained in theory, but its basis was altered in a way which was to have profound consequences for mediaeval theology.

The differences between the Cappadocian and the

Augustinian understanding of the persons of the Trinity may be set out as follows:

| Cappadocians | Augustine |
|---|---|
| — The Father is unbegotten; | — The Father is Father because he has a Son; |
| — The Son is begotten of the Father; | — The Son is Son because he has a Father |
| — The Holy Spirit proceeds from the Father (through the Son). | — The Holy Spirit is the bond of unity between the Father and the Son, and therefore he proceeds from both. |

The difficulty with Augustine's scheme comes when we try to conceptualize what his model of the Trinity *as a whole* actually was. From the Cappadocian picture (A), have we moved to (B) or to (C) in the following diagram?

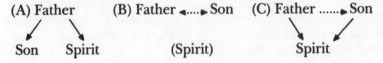

Some things Augustine says suggest that he would have preferred (B), which would leave the personal status of the Holy Spirit open to question. Supporters of (A) have naturally seized upon these statements as evidence that Augustine's theology was defective at its most important point. Western interpreters and followers of Augustine, however, have generally assumed that his understanding of the matter was really close to (C), since they want to retain Augustine's insistence that the Holy Spirit is a person of the Trinity equal in rank to the other two. Yet it cannot be denied that although Western theology has always insisted on this point in theory, in practice it has frequently demoted and even depersonalized the Holy Spirit. Critics of Augustinian theology may well be right when they argue that this aberration is not an accident, and that theoretical protestations to the contrary reflect a dogmatic concern

174

which is contradicted by the inner logic of the Augustinian system.

Closely linked to this is Augustine's lack of an adequate framework in which to distinguish correctly between person and nature, or essence. Like all his predecessors and contemporaries, Augustine thought of the persons as being logically dependent on the divine nature. Because of this, he could not escape from the ambiguities of the word 'Spirit', and was not even able to discern why the Greeks should make a distinction between *hypostasis* and *ousia*.[17] For all his efforts to describe them, Augustine was never able to conceive of the persons of the Trinity as having the same depth of reality which belonged to the one nature of God. For this reason, the accusations of modalism (Sabellianism) which have been made against him cannot be dismissed out of hand, although we may agree that they are an unfair representation of his views.

Another criticism of Augustine which has a long historical pedigree, concerns his doctrine of the double procession of the Holy Spirit. On Augustinian reckoning, the Holy Spirit has two sources, however much they may act together, and however much Augustine himself was willing to accord priority of place to the person of the Father. It is possible to read him in the Cappadocian sense, and say that the procession from the Son is ultimately from the Father, through the Son. Or it may be expressed, as it was at the Council of Florence in 1439, by saying that the Spirit proceeds from each person *according to his particular attributes*. Thus the Spirit may proceed from the Father in the latter's capacity as the unbegotten fountainhead of Deity, and at the same time from the Son, within whatever limits may be imposed by the fact that the Son is begotten of the Father. The difficulty with these interpretations is that the first was almost certainly not what Augustine had in mind, and the second makes little sense, since the anti-Arian thrust of classical christology insists that begottenness implies no limitation at all. Yet the accusation made by Eastern theologians, namely that the double procession splits the Godhead in two by making both the Father and the Son 'sources of Deity', is not what Augustine intended either.

175

During the Middle Ages this problem was recognized as an unsolved element of Augustine's thought. It became the subject of considerable debate, both among the supporters of the double procession doctrine, and among its opponents. The solution adopted by the Western church in 1439 was the formula which said that the Holy Spirit proceeds from both the Father and the Son 'as from one principle and by a single spiration'.[18] In other words, the Father and the Son act together in the matter of the Spirit's procession, which then becomes a single act of God, as follows:

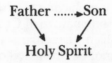

The Eastern churches were not impressed by this. When all was said and done, the Holy Spirit could still be regarded as inferior to the Father and the Son, because he did not participate with them in his own procession. Of course, they are quick to point out that if he had done so, the procession would not have occurred within the Godhead at all. This extraordinary conclusion is based on the assumption that if the external works of the Trinity are undivided, then an undivided work of the Trinity must be external to the being of God. The history of the church has shown that disagreement over the procession of the Holy Spirit cannot be resolved by a compromise between Augustinian and Cappadocian principles. If the dispute is ever to be resolved, either one must give way to the other, or both must be transcended in a new and superior understanding of trinitarian relations.

One last criticism of the Augustinian model of the Trinity must be mentioned, although in strictly theological terms it may well be the most serious of all. This is that Augustine, who started with the high monotheism of the Latin tradition, found the unity of God in the consummation of the trinitarian movement, not in its origin. For him, two complementary opposites made up the supreme unity, which is the expression of their complementarity (love). But in that case, how can the unity of God be logically prior to the Trinity?

The answer is that it cannot be. Without fully realizing or being able to express it, Augustine was moving away from the concept of a single, personal God to that of a single God who was at the same time three eternal and equal persons.

## Subsequent developments

Augustinian trinitarianism has remained the fundamental pattern in Western theology up to our own time, but unlike the Cappadocian tradition in the East, it has developed significantly from its original roots. The Middle Ages in particular witnessed a flowering of trinitarian thought which tied together some of the loose ends in Augustine and gave the theological enterprise a new interpretation and direction.

The first development of importance was the definition of the word 'person'. This came about mainly as a result of the christological controversies which were disrupting the Eastern church. At the Council of Chalcedon in 451 it was agreed, in line with the theology of Leo of Rome, that the incarnate Christ is one divine person, manifested in two natures – one divine and the other human. The controversy which this decision provoked led to a complete reworking of the theological vocabulary. Whatever one said of the incarnate Christ, it was clear that his unity was more fundamental than his diversity. The two natures were obviously necessary to do justice to the concept that the Son of God became a man without thereby ceasing to be God. But instead of saying, as the Monophysites did, that the human nature of Christ had been absorbed into the divine, or as the Nestorians did, that the two natures had come together in external conjunction, which to an outside observer appeared to be the single person of Christ, Chalcedon and its defenders maintained that the person of Christ is a principle in its own right, which constitutes the unity of the two separate natures.

Orthodox christology after Chalcedon was therefore obliged to develop the novel idea that the concept of nature was logically dependent on the person. This involved a complete reversal of the traditional view that person is an aspect or a manifestation of being. Once this new concept was established in christology, it could not fail to make its presence felt in trinitarian theology as well. What was in danger of emerging immediately after Chalcedon was a theology in which this integration had not taken place, as follows:

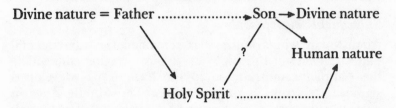

In this system we find that the Father, as the hypostasis of the divine nature, begets the Son and issues the Holy Spirit, with or without the co-operation of the Son. Meanwhile, the Son takes on a second nature – not, as the Monophysites said, by absorbing this nature into the existing divine one, but by attaching it directly to his person. The person of the Son therefore governs the second nature as he governs the first, and the Holy Spirit comes to sanctify this second nature in the baptism of Jesus. The problem is that the Son cannot control a nature on which he is ultimately dependent. If the logic of Chalcedon is to be maintained therefore, the diagram has to be changed to the following:

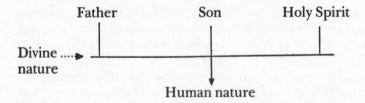

In this diagram the question of the double procession of the Holy Spirit remains unresolved, but he can no longer be subordinated to the first two persons, or confused with the divine nature, which, as the diagram shows, is the common possession of all three persons. It is also impossible, on this model, to follow the Monophysites in saying that the divine nature of the Son absorbed a human nature. As the common possession of all three persons, such an action on the part of the divine nature would mean an incarnation of the entire

Trinity. Instead of this, the logic of this theology is to say that the person of the Son, acting in his capacity as a free divine agent, possessing the divine nature but not bound by it, took on a second nature in the man Jesus Christ, who as a person is the Son of God.

The term 'person' has therefore to be understood as a *substantial reality* in its own right, not merely as an aspect or mode of the divine being. This was actually said by the Roman philosopher Boethius (*c.* 480–526), who defined a person as 'the individual substance of a rational nature'.[19] But if Chalcedonian christology was to prevail in systematic theological thought, it also has to be said that a person is in control of his or her nature. When three equal persons are involved, there is inevitably a danger of tritheism, because it is difficult to see how three persons can be equally in control of a single nature. This heresy occasionally surfaced when the autonomy of each person was emphasized at the expense of the compensating doctrine of the co-inherence of the persons in the unity of a single divine nature.

Which attributes belonged to the nature(s) and which to the person(s) was a problem largely worked out in the context of christology. After long debate, the Third Council of Constantinople (680–81) ruled, on the basis of Jesus' words in the Garden of Gethsemane (Mt. 26:39), that the incarnate Christ had two wills, one divine and the other human. The will therefore belongs to the nature, so that the divine will is common to all three persons of the Trinity. Unfortunately, this conciliar decision was not always applied to the systematization of trinitarian doctrine, and mediaeval Western theology is full of examples where the will of God is hypostatized as the Son – an Augustinian image, rooted in human psychology, which was then mistakenly applied to God.

In the ninth century it was suggested that 'person' was equivalent to 'spirit', so that the names Father, Son and Holy Spirit would indicate the existence of three spirits in God. The third person, in whom the word Spirit became a proper name, would therefore be the fullest revelation of the divine nature as it actually is. To avoid the inevitable danger of tritheism, the Frankish monk Gottschalk proposed making a distinction between the deity of the persons and the 'divinity'

179

of the divine nature, but this was rejected by Hincmar of Reims, who thought it was merely playing with words, and Gottschalk was condemned at the Council of Soissons in 853. This council reaffirmed the co-inherence of the three persons as possessors of a single divine Spirit, thereby rejecting the idea that 'person' and 'spirit' are synonymous.[20]

Later in the Middle Ages, Gilbert de la Porrée (d. 1154) tried to reinstate a meaningful distinction between the divinity and the deity of God, by saying that the former was the ground and cause of the latter. According to him, divinity was the essence, or quality of which the threefold deity was composed. Like Gottschalk, he was also condemned for tritheism, although it seems that his error was one of terminology rather than substance. He was trying to find a way to do justice to the ontological realities of person and essence in God, but he lacked an adequate conceptual framework for tying the two together in a systematic whole. In reviving Gottschalk's discredited distinction he was merely bringing trouble on himself, and confusing an issue which by his day was quite different.[21]

The problem of defining 'person' was taken up again by Anselm of Canterbury (c. 1033–1109),[22] who attempted to reconcile the existence of unity and plurality in God by arguing that unity does not lose its consistency (consequentia) as long as there is no opposition of relation to interrupt it. Because Anselm's understanding of the matter was later sanctioned by the Council of Florence, which tried to harmonize Western and Eastern approaches to the Trinity, we must examine it carefully.

For Anselm, there are no distinctions in God except when the Father, the Son and the Holy Spirit present us with opposing relations of origin. The Son cannot be the Father, because he proceeds from the Father. Nor can the Holy Spirit be the Father, because he too proceeds from the Father. But if both the Son and the Holy Spirit proceed from the Father, is there any difference between them? Only if one proceeds from the other, argued Anselm. The Son clearly does not proceed from the Holy Spirit; therefore the Holy Spirit must proceed from the Son. We are back to the Augustinian doctrine of the double procession, although without the notion of causality which is latent in Augustine. Even more important, the relationship of the Father and the Son is so close that it guarantees that the procession of the Holy Spirit from both is only a single action.

In fairness to Anselm, it should be said that his argument for the double procession was based on a number of biblical texts which the polemicists of the Eastern church were inclined to ignore. In particular, Anselm argued that John 14:26 must be read together with John 15:26, which describes the sending of the Spirit in a different way:

John 14:26: . . . whom the Father will send in my name.
John 15:26: . . . whom I will send to you from the Father.

The Eastern church has always relied on another part of John 15:26 ('who goes out from the Father') to prove its case, but Anselm insisted that the two verses, if taken together, show that each person sends the Spirit on behalf of the other. On the principle that the temporal missions of the Trinity reflect the eternal relations of the Godhead, Anselm concluded that the double procession of the Holy Spirit was a doctrine taught in the New Testament. In answer to this argument, Eastern theologians have had to posit a difference between the temporal missions of the Spirit and the inner relations of the Trinity, thereby going against one of the most basic principles of divine self-disclosure. In the most recent discussions of the problem, Jürgen Moltmann has reminded theologians of the importance of this principle which, if it is accepted, would almost certainly lead to Anselm's position, although Moltmann does not actually draw that conclusion.

It was to be Anselm's philosophical argument, however, which had the greatest influence in mediaeval times, with results which were sometimes unfortunate. It will be noticed that he subsumed the generation of the Son under the general heading of 'procession', as if it were analogous to the procession of the Holy Spirit. We have already seen that Gregory of Nazianzus did not know how generation could be distinguished from procession, but it is almost certain that he

181

believed that there was a distinction, if only in the mind of God. Anselm's schematization here is too simplistic, ignoring the evidence of both Scripture and tradition, and giving the term 'procession' what amounts to a double meaning. Nevertheless, his basic procedure was taken up and developed by Thomas Aquinas (1226–74), who made it part of classical Western theism.[23]

Aquinas began his teaching on the Trinity by saying that natural reason can tell us what belongs to the unity of the divine essence (*ousia*), but not what belongs to the distinctions of the divine persons. For this, we must rely on the data of revelation. Nevertheless, the divine processions must be consistent with the intellectual nature of God, which rather limits the use which may be made of the principle of revelation. The God we know by reason can act in only two ways, by understanding and by willing. For this reason, argued Aquinas, no other divine procession is possible but the processions of the Word and of love.

Aquinas' debts to Augustine and Anselm are obvious, but he was determined to go beyond them and establish a clear distinction between the two divine 'processions', generation and procession (in the classical sense). 'Generation' was defined by Aquinas as an (intellectual) act of conception which produced its like, *i.e.* the Father reproduced his own likeness in the Son. 'Procession' he defined as an impulse of the divine will, which brings forth something other than a straightforward reproduction of itself. When this impulse is perfect, as it must be within the Godhead, the resulting product will also be fully God. Hence there is a real difference between the Son and the Holy Spirit, both of whom are fully God, although once again the Spirit fits only somewhat uncomfortably into what is basically an Augustinian model of the Trinity.

Not content to stop there, Aquinas used the terms 'paternity', 'filiation' and 'procession' to describe the divine relations. He distinguished them from the essence of God by saying that the former are *relative*, while the latter is *absolute*. His abstractions differ from those of the Cappadocians, for whom unbegottenness, begottenness and procession were the absolute distinctions of the hypostases. But like them, he has succumbed to a tendency towards philosophical abstraction which is very different from the spirit of the New Testament. The full effect can be seen in Thomas' definition of the word 'person'. As far as he was concerned, *person was an aspect of a nature which signified what was distinct in that nature*. Because distinction in God is only by relations of origin, a divine person is defined by Aquinas as a *subsistent relation*[24] in the being of God. In other words, 'person' and 'relation' are synonymous, which means that one might easily dispose of the unphilosophical term 'person' and speak only of (Aristotelian) relations in God.

The trinitarianism of Anselm and Aquinas can rightly be criticized for being too philosophical, too abstract, and even reactionary, in the sense that it is dependent on the primacy of nature over person – almost inevitable in any philosophical theology, but directly counter to the spirit of Chalcedonian christology. Unfortunately, christology and trinitarian theology tended to go their separate ways during the high Middle Ages, and they are still not always closely linked even today.

The influence of Thomism on theology was so great that it is often supposed that it was the only theological tradition in evidence in mediaeval times. But to say that would be to ignore the contribution of Richard of St Victor (d. *c.* 1173)[25], and of Aquinas' contemporary Bonaventure (d. 1274)[26], both of whom developed a different strand in Augustine's thought, that of the so-called 'psychological' Trinity.

Richard began by disputing Boethius' definition of 'person', which he replaced with his own improvization. For Richard, a divine person was an incommunicable existence of the divine nature, which sounds odd until we realize that he used the word 'existence' in a way which differs from the Platonic tradition. For Richard, who was unaware of the Greek *hyparxis*, 'existence' means what it says – ex-sistence. 'Sistence', according to him, was synonymous with 'essence', and so 'ex-sistence' was the way in which the sistence (= essence) manifested itself with a distinctive property (characteristic). In the Trinity, there were three realities which shared the same sistence, but each had a different property by which it could be distinguished. In this way, said Richard, the persons of the Godhead were one according to their mode of being, but three according to their mode of existing.

One very important aspect of this way of thinking is that it preserves the dynamic of personal action, which tends to be submerged in the idea of subsistent relations, Richard put this to good use, because he regarded God as the supreme expression of perfect love. This is obviously an Augustinian theme, but whereas Augustine saw the persons as different aspects of love, Richard believed that they created love in the context of their personal relationships. Love cannot exist without someone to love, but – and here there is a notable difference between Richard's and Augustine's outlook – a lover and his beloved must also have a third person to love. Why? Because, according to Richard, the most excellent form of love is to wish that someone else should be loved as much as oneself is loved, and by the same lover. Both the Father and the Son desire to share the love which they receive from each other with a third person, and their mutual wish is fulfilled in the common (= double) procession of the Holy Spirit. Because of this, the Holy Spirit represents the fullness of deity, a conclusion which reminds us to what extent Richard was still dependent on Augustine.

Richard, and later Bonaventure, went to great lengths to prove that there could be *only* three persons in the Trinity, not more, although it cannot be said that their arguments are very convincing. Like the rest of the mediaeval scholastic tradition to which they belonged, they were inclined to prefer ingenious rational arguments to the evidence of Scripture, even though the former were always intended to buttress the latter. But, however attractive their arguments might be, there was always a certain dimension lacking. To the student of the Bible it is obvious, though perhaps not so easy to articulate. For all the subtlety and precision of the mediaeval arguments, there is a curious lack of personal involvement on the part of these theologians in their analyses of the persons and the nature of God. What we see strikes us as being more like detached speculation, not living faith, though doubtless that is a judgment from hindsight which is not entirely fair. What really separates our perception from theirs is the Reformation, and the great sea change which that brought to our understanding of God.

## Modern views

Before we consider the theology of the Reformers, we must record that the Augustinian – Thomist system is by no means dead even now. The Reformation upset it in the Protestant churches and paralysed it among continuing Catholics, so that for many centuries it scarcely developed at all. But in the nineteenth century the situation began to change, and new developments started to emerge. In the twentieth century the pre-Reformation Western tradition has enjoyed a considerable revival among Protestants, as well as among Roman Catholics.

The first stirrings of this revival occurred among Protestants, who had been deeply affected by the rationalistic unitarianism of the eighteenth-century Deists. The most important contributor was Hegel, whose philosophy we have already discussed. Like a good Augustinian, Hegel saw the Father ('*thesis*') react with the Son ('*antithesis*') to produce the Holy Spirit ('*synthesis*') as the supreme expression of the God of love. Unlike Augustine, however, Hegel regarded this movement as the fruit of conflict, rather than of harmony. He also inclined to the view that the emergence of a synthesis made the thesis and the antithesis redundant. Why bother with them once a higher form of life had emerged?

The logical result of this was a theology in which the 'spirit of love' became God, a form of unitarianism (in effect) which is still prevalent among liberal theologians today. Love, as an abstract concept, has taken the place of a personal, triune God, thereby virtually abolishing the dialectic of judgment and redemption which together were the special province of the Father and the Son. Hegel's originality is that he made the Trinity a stepping-stone to a unitarianism of spiritual love, represented as the fulfilment of conflict between opposites. The framework of his thought is clearly Augustinian, but the dynamic is completely different. In Hegel's system the integrity of the relations has been compromised, and the concept of a society of free Persons, united by the bond of love, has been lost. What remains is a monolithic, totalitarian and essentially impersonal love, whose inner nature impels it to seek its opposite in order to begin another conflict in search of a still higher form of life. It is interesting to note here that Buddhism, which is historically unrelated to Christianity, has begun to exert some influence on those most deeply affected by Hegelianism. In the Buddhist universe every opposite tendency, even that between love and hate, is finally dissolved in the eternal nothingness of Nirvana. Here the Christian vision is eclipsed, because the only salvation lies in annihilation, which is the very opposite of the gospel of Christ.

Less radical, but also less influential, is the trinitarianism which has grown out of the revival of Thomism in the Roman Catholic Church. Perhaps the most original representative of this movement is the Jesuit philosopher Bernard Lonergan (1904–84).[27] Lonergan has revived the Thomist teaching about the processions within God, which he understands in the same abstract way that Aquinas did. He integrates Augustine's psychological model of the Trinity into his philosophy, however, by saying that the traditional formulation of three persons in one substance (*ousia*) should be understood to mean that in God there are three subjects of a single *consciousness*. He then says that the two processions in God produce three persons but *four* relations, an assertion which breaks the traditional Thomist equation of 'person' with 'relation', and adds a psychological dimension to the classical Thomist doctrine.

Lonergan understands the four relations as follows:

(A) Two relations of the first procession (generation):

— understanding forming conception;
— conception formed (*i.e.* recognizing its begetter).

(B) Two relations of the second procession (procession):

— understanding evincing love in accordance with conception;
— love evinced (*i.e.* responding to its source/s).

Here we are taken back to Augustine's analogy of God as a mind, which cannot but love the thing which it conceives. The additional element is that the conception and the love thus formed 'have a mind of their own' and are able to respond to the mind's initiative. Lonergan's restatement of Thomism in psychological terms is obviously necessary if it is to retain its appeal in an age enthralled by psychology, but it does little to avoid the dangers of abstraction inherent in the earlier system. On the contrary, it would appear to increase them, and leave the reader wondering whether Lonergan has retained any real link at all with the God of the Bible.

An independent Roman Catholic voice, generally opposed to the dryness of neo-Thomism, is that of Karl Rahner (1904–84),[28] who has come to be recognized as the leading modern Roman Catholic theologian. Rahner's contribution to trinitarian thought reflects the influence of Richard of St Victor, but it also goes back to the primitive theology of the early church. According to him, it is the Father who expresses himself in truth (*Logos*) and love (Spirit). Rahner does not like the term 'person' because it suggests to him that there are three independent subjects in God who dwell together in mutual love. He rejects this picture on the ground that it creates plurality and distinction within the simple being of God. At most, he is prepared to admit that the persons symbolize three different functions of the Godhead, which cannot be confused with one another.

One difficulty with this is that it opens up a gap between the immanent and the economic Trinity. It seems that Rahner is prepared to insist on the existence of a personal relationship between God and *humanity*, but not within the Godhead. This viewpoint is not new of course, but it has always been rejected in orthodox theology because it suggests that God requires a being outside himself in order to manifest his love, and that therefore he is not perfect in himself. It is most unlikely therefore, that his trinitarianism will survive long, since in so many ways it seems to be little more than a return to earlier positions which have long since been superseded.

Finally, we may mention the work of Hans Urs von Balthasar (1905–88),[29] an original thinker deeply imbued with a Platonic sense of God's beauty, which he shares with much of the Eastern tradition. Von Balthasar recognizes that the mutual relation of the Father and the Son is a coincidence of opposites, in which opposition (conflict) is replaced by self-determination in love (Spirit). It is the Son, in particular, who represents the eternal reconciliation which extends beyond the Godhead, and is symbolized above all in the crucified manhood of Christ, which he has united to himself. More than any other modern Roman Catholic theologian, von Balthasar has seen the importance of christology for a doctrine of the Trinity, and has tried to integrate the atonement into his picture of the divine love.

Especially noteworthy is the fact that he has made the Son the instrument of reconciliation, thereby abandoning the Augustinian tradition in which the Holy Spirit fulfils that role. Von Balthasar does not ignore the Spirit, but sees him as the messenger of the reconciliation achieved in the work of the other two persons – a view which is closer to the Reformed, rather than to the Thomist, position.

The contribution which these theologians will eventually make to the historical development of the Augustinian–Thomist tradition cannot as yet be assessed. What is certain, though, is that they have demonstrated, by their ingenuity and concern for the doctrine's place in Christian thought, that the Trinity remains at the centre of any true theologian's preoccupations.

Among modern Protestants, the philosophical tradition in theology has been less prominent, but the work of Eberhard Jüngel (1934–)[30] deserves a mention. Jüngel has revived the idea that God's being is in motion, but he interprets motion in the linear sense of 'becoming'. He therefore posits a development in the Godhead which the Augustinian theory did not accommodate, and which makes Augustinian trinitarianism appear 'static'. Jüngel does not explain how the Trinity originated, beyond saying that it was God's 'primal decision' to be three in one. He does, however, say that from all eternity the persons of the Godhead are constantly drawing closer together in love. By doing this, they are constantly discovering the true depths of their own identity, which thus paradoxically makes them more distinct from each other at the same time. God's 'primal decision' is supposed to have included the decision to become the Son of Man as well as the

Son of God, and so the work of Christ on the cross becomes an essential part of the divine self-discovery. For Jüngel, both the creation and the redemption are acts of God's self-giving which have helped him grow in love – another example of how a basically philosphical trinitarianism has been able to integrate a meaningful psychological dimension.

Jüngel's work is still incomplete, and it is too early to know for sure what impact it will have. But there is every indication that his theories, modified and enriched by the theological tradition, will provide an important addition to the long and fascinating history of philosophical trinitarianism.

# The nature of God: in the person of the Son?

## Exposition

The two great traditions of classical trinitarian thought have emphasized the unity of God in the person of either the Father or of the Holy Spirit. But what of the Son? Is it not conceivable that a trinitarianism might be expounded in which he would be the supreme expression of the Godhead?

In this connection it is well to remember that in the New Testament we are told that it is in Christ that 'the fullness of the Godhead dwelt bodily'. It is he who comes to us as the full and final self-revelation of God, he in whom we see the Father, and he from whom we receive the Holy Spirit. Would it not therefore be natural, for a theology wanting to be truly biblical, if its trinitarianism were to be rooted and grounded in christology?

The question acquires greater urgency when we reflect on the importance of Chalcedon for our understanding of the relationship between the concepts of 'person' and 'nature', or 'essence'. As we have already seen, there was a considerable amount of discussion surrounding the meaning and relative importance of these terms in the centuries after 451, but the application of the results to trinitarian doctrine was not always carried through. When it is, though, is the result not inevitably going to be a christologically-based doctrine of the Trinity?

One might also say that the lack of a christological dimen-sion is largely responsible for the abstract philosophizing

189

which characterizes so much classical trinitarianism. It is much easier, and more obviously in tune with the New Testament, if we can conceive of having a relationship with the crucified, risen and ascended Christ, than if we have to imagine ourselves sharing in the second relation of the first procession of the Godhead. Popular preaching has certainly reflected this over the centuries, by stressing the figure of Jesus almost to the point where the Trinity as such disappears from view altogether.

The problem has reared its head with greater urgency in the last two centuries, as Western civilization has generally abandoned a basic belief in a transcendent God, and theologians have not infrequently responded by advocating a religion of ethical norms which would follow the teaching of Jesus of Nazareth without accepting the 'mythological' claims made for him. In the nineteenth century there was a real danger that Christian theology would be reduced to the moral insights of a first-century Jewish rabbi, modified to suit the needs of an industrial society. This reduced Christianity became almost the only branch of 'theological' inquiry, precisely because it was the only branch which could be pursued without reference to the supernatural.

A reaction to this kind of reductionism was led by Karl Barth (1886–1968),[31] who reinstated God, in all his divine otherness, as the chief concern of theology. But Barth did not simply abandon the liberal heritage of nineteenth-century thought and revert to an earlier model. He agreed with his teachers, who said that christology was the heart of Christianity, and in that respect he worked within the same framework as they did. Where he differed from them was in his conviction that Jesus was not just a gifted Jew, but the revelation of God to humanity. This belief remained the cornerstone of his theology, and everything else was interpreted accordingly.

But if Jesus was indeed the revelation of the triune God to humanity, he was also, inevitably, the revelation of the Trinity. Barth therefore maintained that it is only in Christ that we can have any knowledge of the Father or any experience of the Holy Spirit. In other words, he devised a form of trinitarianism in which, for the first time, the second

190

person of the Trinity occupied the central position and gave unity to the whole.

This christocentric approach is worked out theoretically in Barth's system by saying that the unity of the Trinity must be sought not in a divine essence, which by definition remains for ever inaccessible, but in the concept of revelation, beyond which we cannot inquire. Working from this assumption, the persons of the Trinity appear as follows:

— The Father is the revealer (*revelans*);
— The Son is the revealed (*revelatum*);
— The Holy Spirit is the revelation (*revelatio*).

From the appearance of this scheme it is obviously possible to interpret Barth in a way which is entirely consistent with classical Augustinianism, just as it is possible to interpret Augustine in a way which would agree completely with the Cappadocians. He shows his affinity with the Augustinian tradition in any number of ways, not least in his strong defence of the double procession of the Holy Spirit. But to read Barth this way would be to miss the fact that it is in the designation of the Son as 'revealed' or as the 'act of revelation' that we come closest to his understanding of the essence of theology. Although he was undoubtedly deeply concerned with the ontological basis of Christian theology, there is no doubt that Barth demonstrated this largely by giving the dynamic, subjective and functional aspects of christology an eternal status within the Godhead. For instance, Barth claims that when God reveals himself as Son, he is also revealing himself as Lord, since the essence of true lordship is the freedom to submit, to become 'God for us' without losing dignity or status. In Barth's theology, the love of God is nowhere more vitally apparent than in this profound spirit of humility which stamps the whole of revelation.

## Critique

Barth's theological system has an originality and a depth which places him without doubt, among the theological giants of all time. His ability to open up an entirely new dimension in the Trinity, after centuries of tradition and decades of neglect, is an indication of how great his genius was. He has certainly been criticized, especially by Neo-Thomists, who deplore his rejection of philosophical and natural theology, but his influence has spawned a whole new generation of theologians who, like him, are concerned to root their christology in a doctrine of the triune God.

We must agree with Barth that it is impossible to develop a satisfactory doctrine of the Trinity without a strong christological component, and a biblically-based trinitarian system is bound to concern itself heavily with the New Testament revelation of the second person of the Godhead. After all, this is the emphasis found in the creeds, and in varying degrees in both mediaeval and Reformed theology as well. Much of Augustine's *On the Trinity* is taken up with what we would call christological questions, and Barth was deeply influenced by Anselm of Canterbury, whose *Cur Deus Homo?* set out to explain why the second person of the Trinity became man. Anselm understood, in a way that many of his predecessors had not, that Christ's work of atonement on the cross was a work of God *within the Trinity*. It was the Son who offered himself as a sacrifice to the Father, and it is the Holy Spirit who now makes that sacrifice effective in the life of the Christian. In the incarnate life of the Son we see God as he truly is, in the fullness of his divine wisdom, power and love.

Barth's christocentric approach is therefore vitally important, particularly for a powerful preaching ministry. It also has real antecedents in the theological tradition, although these have been underemphasized in the more philosophical approaches to the doctrine of the Trinity. Nevertheless, more caution must be exercised, for the very reasons that Barth himself gave for promoting a christocentric trinitarianism.

Our first hesitation concerns the content of the *biblical evidence*. It is true that Jesus pointed people to himself, as God's self-revelation, but he also pointed the same people to the Father. It is not enough to say that we can know the Father only as he has been revealed to us in and through the Son; Jesus clearly expects us to enjoy a relationship to the Father as a distinct person – a relationship which is analogous to his own, though not identical with it. Christians are called to become sons and daughters of God by adoption, so that when we pray it is to our Father that we are taught to direct our petitions. We cannot be content with the information about him which Jesus supplied during his earthly ministry; we must discover him for ourselves in the way that Jesus intended we should. We must also be careful not to subordinate the Holy Spirit to Christ in a way which is not biblical. As the 'other Comforter', the Holy Spirit has a distinct role to play in the life of the Christian. He is not merely a leftover from the earthly ministry of Jesus, whom we can afford to ignore most of the time. There can be an extreme type of christocentricity which almost dispenses with the Holy Spirit completely, and Barthian theology is certainly not free from that tendency, even though Barth himself would never have advocated it.

The second hesitation concerns some of the *theological consequences* of Barth's christocentrism. If God is exclusively revealed in Christ, then everything which is said of Christ must logically apply to God. Barth did not develop this reasoning to its full extent, but some of his followers have, with the result that the crucifixion has been understood as nothing less than the death of God. Such an idea is clearly unacceptable, but it follows logically if the person of the Son is made to bear the weight of the hypostatization of the divine nature.

## Subsequent developments

The influence of Barth's christocentric trinitarianism can be seen most strongly in the work of Jürgen Moltmann (1926–), who has spearheaded a widespread revival of interest in the question of God's impassibility.[32] Moltmann is not entirely happy with the classical understanding of this divine attribute, but he has moved the discussion onto another plane altogether. What for the ancients was an attribute of God's nature has become for Moltmann an attribute of the divine persons, and it is in this sense that he cannot accept the traditional doctrine.

Moltmann believes that the ancients made a mistake in recognizing only an essential incapacity for suffering on the one hand, or a fateful subjection to suffering on the other. He proposes a third possibility, which is the voluntary submission of one person to another, to a point where that person is intimately affected by the other. This is the emotional suffering of love, which Moltmann believes is a necessary part of any deep relationship. It can always be argued that although such suffering is common among human beings, it has no place in a relationship which is perfect, but it is important to realize that Moltmann and those who think like him would argue just the opposite. Moltmann's christological approach ties his speculation on this subject to the crucifixion, in which the Son of God actually suffered and died for the human race.

Yet the Son was not alone in this, for in the crucifixion the Father and the Holy Spirit also suffered. How could it be otherwise, if their relationship with the Son has any real meaning? If a human father suffers when his son is hurt, how much more must this be the case with God the Father? A God who could not share in his Son's suffering, says Moltmann, could never enter into a relationship with us in anything more than a superficial way. Here Moltmann's emphasis is significant, in that he brings our picture of God closer to the everyday reality of suffering which we all have to face. It is also an important aid to understanding what the Bible says about the way in which God is said to react to the sins and suffering of his people. The classical theological tradition has never found it easy to explain God's anger, or the sorrow he feels when his people turn away from him, and it must be conceded that Moltmann's exploration of this theme has opened up some very interesting possibilities.

What must be guarded against, though, is a theology which is so wrapped up in the crucifixion that it leaves no room either for the divine transcendence or for the victory which Christ has won over sin and death. His sufferings, and the relationship of the Father and the Holy Spirit to them, are not to be seen as ends in themselves. They were made necessary by that divine love which reaches out to save those who have brought suffering on themselves. In a very real sense, therefore, suffering is an experience of the Trinity *ad extra*, in the relationship between God and humanity, rather than in the relationship between Father and Son. It is for this reason that the classical tradition, which Moltmann and others are now disputing, insisted that the Son of God suffered in his human nature, not in his divinity. In the work of atonement, the divine relations did not suffer (as Sabellius supposed), but were reaffirmed and manifested in their true perfection. The true locus of divine suffering is not to be found either in the nature or in the persons of the Trinity, but in the work which they have come to do in the world.

## Conclusion

Our investigations thus far have taken us through the two major traditions of trinitarian thought, and looked at the emergence in our own time of a third way, in which the divine nature might be revealed to us more especially in a single person of the Trinity. Each trinitarian system has its own inner logic, with corresponding strengths and weaknesses. The concentration of the divine essence in the person of the Father allows the theologian to tie the Old and the New Testament together with relative ease, and to explain why 'God' can be used to mean 'God the Father' in early Christian documents. On the other hand, it is exposed to the danger of subordinationism, especially when a strong monotheistic emphasis is introduced.

The concentration of the divine essence in the person of the Holy Spirit has the merit of giving a clearly definable role to the often neglected third person of the Trinity, it puts the Father and the Son on an equal footing, and it seeks to do justice to the revealed name of the Holy Spirit, which refers to the character and substance of God's being. On the other hand, it has a curiously depersonalizing effect on the Holy Spirit, which has led to abstract philosophizing about the Trinity. It has also developed a tendency to equate the Holy Spirit with God as love, and to psychologize the other persons away. Proponents of this view have often been unhappy with the term 'person', and as a result the threeness of God has generally been underemphasized.

The concentration of the divine essence in the person of the Son is a more recent development, although it has the merit of giving a properly biblical and traditional importance to christology. Its chief defect is that in a secular age it tends to over-humanize God, and to press the psychological images of the Trinity beyond what the evidence will bear. One suspects that it will endure only as long as the modern emphasis on the humanity of Jesus holds sway in theological circles; when the pendulum swings back to an emphasis on transcendence, it seems probable that there will be a corresponding return to one or other of the earlier models.

All this prompts the inevitable question: is it really possible to concentrate the divine nature of the Trinity in a single person? The Bible seems to indicate that the essence of God belongs equally to all three persons, and this of course is a basic tenet of *all* the positions outlined above, although each one finds it hard to maintain in practice. May we not therefore abandon the attempt to discover the essential being of God in one of the persons, and look at the Trinity in a completely different way? To do so will of course demand an understanding of God's unity which is not dependent on the traditional concept of his essence (*ousia*). How such a theology may be developed is the theme of the next chapter, in which we examine the distinctive trinitarianism of the Protestant Reformation.

# 5

## THE PRIMACY
## OF THE PERSONS IN GOD

### Reformation theology: a change of perception

The traditions of trinitarian thought which we examined in the last chapter differ from each other in any number of important ways, but this can largely be explained by their different approaches to the one principle which they have in common. This is the belief that the nature of God is most clearly manifested in one particular person of the Trinity, who thus provides the reference point for integrating the other two persons into the overall system. This is true even of Karl Barth, who based his theology on the essentially abstract principle of revelation, which he located in the person of the Son, Jesus Christ.

It therefore comes as something of a surprise to discover that the Protestant Reformers, in spite of their links with the Augustinian tradition, and notwithstanding Karl Barth's claim that he was walking in their footsteps, had a vision of God which was fundamentally different from anything which had gone before, or which has appeared since. The great issues of Reformation theology – justification by faith, election, assurance of salvation – can be properly understood only against the background of a trinitarian theology which gave these matters their peculiar importance and ensured that Protestantism, instead of becoming just another schism produced by a revolt against abuses in the mediaeval church, developed instead into a new type of Christianity.

The radically different character of Protestantism, and especially of Calvinism, has often been recognized by secular historians, but its theological origins have seldom been discerned. Partly this is because theology is a difficult and unpopular subject, which many scholars in other disciplines refuse to take seriously, preferring to treat theological statements as mythical conceptualizations of what are really socio-economic problems.

Partly too, it is the result of theologians' failure, or sheer inability, to perceive the uniqueness of what the Reformers taught about God. It is often assumed that the Reformers accepted their ancient inheritance without quarrel, and had nothing original to contribute to it. Many people assume that Calvin's defence of the Trinity, for example, was intended mainly as a refutation of heretics like Servetus, and offers little that could be termed new.

Recent ecumenical discussions have tended to confirm this impression. Today both Roman Catholic and Protestant theologians are inclined to stress the superficial causes of the Reformation, like the abuse of clerical power, and play down the underlying theological differences. One is sometimes left with the impression that the Reformation succeeded largely for non-theological reasons, like political convenience, personal rivalries between theologians, and so on. Such reductionism is obviously unable to explain the emergence of a new theological perspective which, in spite of its variant forms and internal divisions, continues to present a unified front over against Roman Catholicism. The great pillars of Reformation doctrine are not Scholastic shibboleths perpetuating an artificial divide in Western Christendom, but claims about the being of God which are of such vital importance that those who rejected them felt that they were no longer in spiritual fellowship with people who insisted on making them the heart of their religion.

Far from being more or less the same as its Catholic counterpart, Reformation theology is distinguished from it by a number of characteristics, of which the following are the most significant. First, the Reformers believed that *the essence of God is of secondary importance in Christian theology*. They did not deny that God has an essence, or reject the type of description found in John of Damascus or the mediaeval Scholastics. They certainly did not speculate that God is a dipolar source of energy, in the manner of process theology. They said only that God speaks sparingly of his essence, because he wants us to focus our attention and our worship elsewhere (Calvin, *Institutes*, I, 13,1).

Up to a point, this relegation of the divine essence to the realm of things not revealed in Scripture takes us back to the world of mystical theology, in which the nature of God is hidden in the cloud of unknowing. There is a very important link between this tradition and the theology of the Reformers, which modern research is only beginning to explore.[1] Mystical devotion was increasingly popular in the later Middle Ages, and it flowered in the sixteenth century, although its most famous exponents were among the more ardent defenders of the Roman Church.[2] Luther's early spiritual experiences could be called mystical, and certainly the religion of the heart which the Reformers preached had strong mystical associations. We know that in its later stages, the Reformation produced new types of mysticism, notably Quakerism and Pietism, which claimed to be upholding the teaching of the first Reformers, in opposition to the dead orthodoxy of their official descendants.

This all points in favour of the view that the Reformers reacted against Scholasticism from a mystical, or semi-mystical background, the details of which are still only imperfectly understood. But although there is a good deal of truth in this assumption, one very important qualification has to be made. Unlike the mystics, the Reformers did not preach a transcendent union of the soul with God by way of ecstatic experience(s). They believed that the limits of God's self-revelation in Scripture were sufficient for the spiritual life of the Christian, and criticized the mystics for going beyond

199

the bounds of Scripture in their quest for union with God.[3]

The second point which distinguishes the theology of the Reformers is their belief that *the persons of the Trinity are equal to one another in every respect.* This belief was already deeply rooted in earlier tradition, as we can see from the Athanasian Creed, which says of the persons that 'in this Trinity none is afore, or after other: none is greater or less than another'.[4]

But in the mediaeval tradition, this credal assertion was qualified theologically in two important ways. First, the Father was recognized as the source of divinity in a way that the other two persons were not, and second, the Holy Spirit was regarded as the bond of unity between the Father and the Son, bringing his own personhood into question. Once again, the Reformers did not deny either of these qualifications, but insisted that they must not be understood in a way which would effectively elevate one of the persons of the Trinity above the others. This was the real burden of Calvin's opposition to Servetus and to those who thought along lines similar to his. When we examine what Calvin says about them, we find that Servetus and his followers appear to have taught an odd mixture of two ancient heresies – Sabellianism and Arianism. Servetus was Sabellian because, as Calvin says, he believed that 'a threefold Deity is introduced whenever three Persons are said to exist in his Essence, and that this Triad was imaginary, inasmuch as it was inconsistent with the unity of God' (*Institutes*, I, 13,2). But Servetus was also Arian, because as Calvin goes on to say of his teaching, 'no other Divinity is left to Christ than is implied by his having been ordained a Son by God's eternal decree'.

Calvin himself identified these heresies in Servetus' teaching, and noted the fact that they were mixed together in a new synthesis of error. What Calvin did not explain, perhaps because he did not fully realize it himself, is why Servetus should have come up with such a strange combination of beliefs, or why he, Calvin, should have perceived it as such a threat to his own position.

From the purely historical point of view, it is worth remembering that Servetus was a Spaniard and may therefore have been heir to forms of Arianism which had been current in Spain for many centuries and which may well have received some encouragement from the long Muslim occupation of much of that country, the effects of which were still being felt in Servetus' time. But Servetus' teachings are more than simply Arianism or Islam in disguise. His particular heresy reflects a kind of Sabellianism, which was the traditional trap of theologians in the Western tradition, where the Augustinian model of the Trinity could easily lend itself to such an interpretation in the hands of the unskilled. Arianism, by comparison, may be regarded as the typical heresy of the Eastern tradition, with its strong emphasis on the Father as the source of the Godhead.

What is peculiar about Servetus is not that he should have professed these heresies in a new guise, but that he should have *combined* them in an attempted theological synthesis which, as ordinary logic should have shown him, was impossible. What is even stranger is that Calvin should have thought that such a mish-mash of ideas was worthy of refutation at a time when there were so many other dangers lurking about. It seems that the explanation for this must be that Calvin saw in Servetus' doctrine the very opposite of what he himself was teaching. In other words, Calvin was attempting to synthesize Eastern and Western trinitarian models in a new and better framework, where they could be absorbed into a more profound harmony, and he thought that Servetus was attempting the same thing. The difference is that while Servetus produced a collage of heresies, Calvin found the key to a more deeply orthodox trinitarianism.

This key was explained by B. B. Warfield (1851–1921) as the teaching that in the Trinity, each of the persons is *autotheos*, that is to say, God in his own right, and not merely divine by appointment.[5] This assertion struck at the heart of the Origenist teaching, which Calvin recognized under the contemporary form of semi-Servetanism (*Institutes*, I, 13,23–29) and which he refuted more thoroughly than the errors of Servetus himself. By claiming that the Son, and by extension the Holy Spirit also, are God in the fullest sense of the word, Calvin not only attacked all forms of Origenism, but also the Sabellianism latent in the Western tradition. It is true that Sabellianism allowed that the persons were equal to each other, but only because none of them was equal to the divine essence itself. Calvin held to a doctrine which said that the three persons were *co-equal in their divinity* and united with each other, not by sharing an impersonal essence, but by their mutual fellowship and co-inherence – the Cappadocian doctrine of *perichōrēsis* in God, applied at the level of person, not essence.

This assertion leads us directly to the third principle of Reformation theology, which is that *knowledge of one of the persons involves knowledge of the other two at the same time*. Calvin does not hesitate to adopt most of the traditionally christological exegesis of the various Old Testament theophanies (*Institutes*, I, 13,9–10), but he does so in the conviction that the people of the old dispensation were unable to distinguish the persons who appeared to them as Jehovah (Yahweh). This was because at that time God revealed himself *among* his people but not *within* them, as he does in the new dispensation. As long as God's presence was external to the worshipper, the latter would see his acts of creation, redemption and sanctification only in the undivided unity of the will common to all three persons.

It was only with the sending of the Holy Spirit at Pentecost that God began to dwell in the heart of every believer, revealing to him the secret of his own internal relations. Thus it is now possible for Christians to think in terms of the person and work of the Father, the person and work of the Son, and the person and work of the Holy Spirit, although in doing so, they will be careful not only to link each member of the Godhead to the others, but more importantly, to see the person and work of the others when examining each member of the Trinity singly.

It was on this principle that Calvin and the other Reformers rejected the conventional division of labour within the Godhead, according to which the Father is the Creator, the Son is the Redeemer and the Holy Spirit is the Sanctifier of the people of God. This very ancient pattern, which has been anachronistically revived in many modern baptismal liturgies, was held to be wrong because it entailed the apportioning of a distinctive element in the divine essence to the dispensing agency of one of the persons. In other words, it was semi-Sabellian, because it treated the persons as channels for the threefold activity of God.

In opposition to this, the Reformers insisted that the Trinity as a whole, not each of the persons separately, was the Creator, Redeemer and Sanctifier, and they attributed a specific function to the Father, Son and Holy Spirit in each of the great works of God. Calvin explains this distinction by saying:

> ... to the Father is attributed the beginning of action, the fountain and source of all things; to the Son, wisdom, counsel, and arrangement in action, while the energy and efficacy of action is assigned to the Spirit (*Institutes*, I, 13,18).

Viewed in relation to action, the three persons of the Trinity can be distinguished as follows:

Father : beginning
Son    : arrangement
Spirit : efficacy

This scheme preserves the priority of the Father, which from ancient times has been expressed by the term 'source of the Godhead' (Greek: *pēgē tēs Theotētos*; Latin: *fons Deitatis*) without the ontological implications which such a statement is bound to have in the context of an Origenist theology. It also preserves the Augustinian emphasis on the Holy Spirit as the one who makes the work of the other two persons real in our lives, without derogating in any way from his own person-hood. Calvin in fact reintroduces the personhood of the Holy Spirit by seeing in his work a type of activity which requires just as much personal initiative from him as from the Father and/or the Son.

Furthermore, by saying that each person of the Trinity is *autotheos*, Calvin has ensured that the relations between them must be voluntary, since no one person can claim the authority to impose his will on the others. But this freedom can never imply contradiction or lead to anarchy, because in God there is but a single will, which is governed by the operation of his perfect love. God's freedom therefore goes beyond what is merely voluntary, so that his unity is compelled by the spiritual love which binds the three persons together in the co-inherence of the one God. Because of this, it is impossible to fall into any form of tritheism or to suppose, as Sabellius had done, that God could separate into his component parts. Neither of these things could happen without automatically bringing God's existence to an end, something which is inconceivable.

The freedom of personal relationships in the Godhead obviously means that any hint of causality latent in the terms 'generation' and 'procession' must be carefully avoided. Mediaeval Western theology had been moving away from the classical position in this respect, but in Calvin the break with earlier tradition becomes complete. It is true that he admits that the person of the Son has his beginning in God (*Institutes*, I, 13,25), but his words are carefully chosen so as to avoid any hint of causality in this expression. What he means is that everything the Son is and does must be understood with reference to the Father, because that is the way the Son understands himself – not because he is ontologically dependent on the Father as the only true *autotheos*.

Finally, Calvin's reference to the single action of God must not be misunderstood as a reference to the Scholastic teaching, inherited from Aristotle, that pure being = act. This equation, which even Karl Barth accepted, cannot be attributed to Calvin, for whom the word 'action' refers to specific events in which the power of God is made manifest. Calvin certainly did not believe that God is essentially static, but that discussion is irrelevant in this context. Here Calvin is referring only to the functions of the different persons, something which in no way determines the nature of their common essence.

The fourth distinguishing feature of the Reformers' theology is their belief that *human creation in the image and likeness of God cannot be understood either as the image of the Trinity or as the image of Christ*. The former of these views was that of Augustine, the latter was the one common to the Greek Fathers, and to the Latin church before Augustine's time. Commenting on this, Calvin was quite ready to criticize the Fathers of the church for their misuse of this expression, even though they were doing so as part of their struggle against

Arius (*Commentary on Genesis* 1:26). On the other hand, he was less able to provide a satisfactory definition of the image of God in man. The closest he comes to that is in his *Institutes* where he claims that the image 'extends to everything in which the nature of man surpasses that of all other species of animals' (I, 15,3–4). In practice, Calvin interpreted this to mean the faculties of the soul (reason and will), the soul being the part of a human being which appeared to him to be most like God.[6]

Calvin's concept of the soul is no longer tenable today, since modern medicine and psychology have demonstrated that much of what he attributed to the 'soul' belongs in reality to the sphere of flesh and blood.[7] But even when that is taken into account, it remains true that the fellowship with God which was given to Adam at creation and restored to us by the Holy Spirit lies at the heart of the concept of the image of God in human beings. As Calvin says, the fruits of this relationship are already visible in the elect, but its full glory will be revealed only in heaven. If we want a word to describe it, we can do no better than adopt the theological term 'person', which is that aspect of human beings which enables them to enjoy communion with God. Augustine may have been wrong to link the image of God in us with the Trinity, but he was right to suspect that the image has something to do with the plurality of persons in God.

Calvin's refusal to say that human beings were created in the image of the person of Jesus Christ alone gave him the freedom to develop an understanding of Christian experience which was fully trinitarian, without sacrificing anything necessary to do justice to the New Testament's teaching about our relationship with the Saviour. It also enabled him to discourse at some length on the importance of our adoption as sons and daughters of God (which is the true meaning of the term 'image of Christ'), without falling into the mediaeval trap of proclaiming that there was a consequent change in human nature, something which would have been inevitable had the image of human redemption been too readily confused with the image of human creation. This enabled him to do justice to the biblical doctrine of grace, by saying that we are partakers of the divine nature (*cf.* 2 Pet. 1:4) by imputation, not by infusion.[8]

205

But the most significant point about the image of God in human beings is the doctrine of election which it entails. Later Calvinism would display a strong tendency to remove this doctrine from its proper sphere and apply it to a philosophical theology in which the divine decrees, predestinating human beings either to salvation or to damnation, would take precedence over almost every other Christian doctrine. Predestination in this sense met with considerable opposition in the seventeenth and eighteenth centuries, not least by John Wesley, and this so-called 'hyper-Calvinistic' caricature of Calvin's teaching has been widely denounced ever since.[9]

The difficulty with hyper-Calvinism is that it replaced the Christian understanding of salvation through fellowship with God by a teaching which is scarcely distinguishable from the fatalism of Islam. Hyper-Calvinism had enormous influence, not only by provoking the growth of heretical sects like Unitarianism, the Jehovah's Witnesses and so on, but also by helping to pave the way for the development of secular ideologies like Marxism, which reflect a similar kind of determinism, though on a different theoretical basis.

Orthodox Christians protest against determinism in the name of human freedom, although too often they tend to overreact and throw out the concept of election and predestination altogether. This is a great pity because, as Article 17 of the Church of England puts it, these great mysteries are:

> ... full of sweet, pleasant and unspeakable comfort
> to godly persons, and such as feel in themselves the
> working of the Spirit of Christ, mortifying the works
> of the flesh, and their earthly members, and draw-
> ing up their mind to high and heavenly things ...

It is always essential when considering predestination, to realize that Calvin placed it firmly in the context of the saving work of Christ. Election is God's choice of some people to share in his trinitarian life by being adopted as sons (in the image of Christ) through the indwelling power of the Holy Spirit. Such an adoption cannot occur except by God's grace, by which he implants the gift of faith in the heart of the sinner. Why this gift should be given to some and not to

206

others is a mystery, hidden in the depths of God's will.

The problem of the will of God, which the doctrine of election naturally raises, has to be set against the backdrop of trinitarian theology as a whole – and not least of its christology. In ancient times this question of the will arose in connection with the incarnation of Christ. The emperor Heraclius I (610–41) had attempted to reconcile the Monophysites of the East to the Chalcedonian definition of the two natures of Christ by a compromise which said that, although the incarnate Christ had two natures, he had but a single will, which of course was divine. This compromise, which went under the name of Monotheletism, was fiercely opposed by church leaders at Constantinople and Rome and it was finally condemned at the Third Council of Constantinople (680–81).

The doctrine which this council approved was based on the words of Jesus in the Garden of Gethsemane: 'not as I will, but as you will' (Mt. 26:39; Mk. 14:36; Lk. 22:42). This was taken to mean that at Gethsemane the human will of Jesus was being submitted to the divine will, although this was also the will of Jesus, because Jesus was God. Because of this apparent conflict of wills in Christ, the will was said to belong to the natures of both God and human beings, not to their persons.

Calvin never discussed this point, although his commentary on the relevant texts shows that he accepted the dyothelete (two-wills) doctrine, his only concern being to show that Christ's human dissent from God's will was not sinful. But the acceptance of dyotheletism is of crucial importance for the doctrine of election, especially once the persons of the Godhead are perceived as having priority over the divine nature. The will of God, as part of his nature, is then seen to be subject to divine sovereignty ('monarchy'), which as the Western tradition from the time of Tertullian has always maintained, can be shared by more than one person.

If this is so, it follows that the persons of the Godhead are free to shape and dispose of their own will as part of the exercise of their joint sovereignty. To suppose that they are subject to their common will, and therefore in themselves merely agents of its execution, is to retreat into a theology in which the divine essence takes priority over the persons – the crudest form of Sabellianism. God's will naturally shares the other attributes of his nature – immutability and eternity in particular – but it is not to be regarded as a kind of fixed law, like the law of the Medes and the Persians, over which the king has no control.

The importance of all this for human election becomes apparent when we realize that it is in the person of the Holy Spirit that God comes to us, pointing us to the person of the Son as our Mediator before the judgment seat of (the person of) the Father. As Christians we enjoy a personal relationship with God, which means that we are not prisoners of his immutable will (any more than we are still slaves to the will of our own nature) but co-workers with him in the kingdom of heaven. In other words, we are called to share with God in the disposition of his will, to become by this means partakers of the divine nature (*Institutes*, I, 13,14), which is the only way we can escape from the evil desires (*i.e.* will) of the flesh.

Now if all this is true, it is of the greatest importance for intercessory prayer, which for many people is either the great casualty of, or the great stumbling block to, a doctrine of divine election. Few of us stop to consider that if we did not have a personal relationship with God we would have no access to the Father, and prayer of any sort would be useless. It is precisely because the Spirit dwells in our hearts that we are enabled and taught how to pray (Rom. 8:15; Gal. 4:6). It is Christ who gives us the access we need to the Father, and who shares his mind with us (1 Cor. 2:16), making it possible for us to pray in harmony with the will of God. In other words, by being elected ourselves, we become active participants in the election of others – which is why petitionary prayer lies at the heart of all effective evangelism.

The one remaining difficulty, and the one which is hardest to resolve satisfactorily, is the problem of limited election, or predestination to damnation. Why is it that not all our prayers for the conversion of the world are answered? Of course, one important strand of hyper-Calvinism says that they are – divine election, whether by God's independent choice or as a result of the prayers of the saints, will

208

eventually embrace everybody, whether they have known Christ as Lord and Saviour or not. This doctrine, which is called universalism, has a parallel of sorts in the cosmic re-creation (*apocatastasis*) doctrine of Gregory of Nyssa and Maximus the Confessor, but its influence has operated within what are usually termed liberal Protestant circles, where it is best understood as a form of positive determinism.

It is not always recognized, although its logic is plain enough, that universalism is a complete denial of human free will, since on its premises everyone will be saved whether they want to be or not. It takes its scriptural justification from 2 Peter 3:9, which says that it is not God's will that any should perish, but that all should come to eternal life, and applies the doctrine of election accordingly. It is one of the great ironies of Christian theology that many people who decry hyper-Calvinism because of its 'inflexible' doctrine of predes-tination subscribe instead to a teaching which is even more rigid, since it prescribes one and the same destiny for all people without distinction.

Calvin's reply to this sort of logic was to say that God's will has two aspects, one revealed to us and the other concealed from us. According to Calvin, God has revealed the universal extent of his love for perishing humanity, to the extent of saying that no-one is excluded in advance from the possibility of responding to the gospel; but in the secret counsel of his own heart, God has already determined who will respond positively and who will not.

Later Calvinists felt that this answer was unsatisfactory because it seemed to drive a wedge between our knowledge of God and God as he is in himself, making it look as if his revelation somehow contradicted his inner being. They pre-ferred to stress the hidden will of God, in line with Calvin's own usual practice, and virtually discounted 2 Peter 3:9, thereby developing a doctrine of atonement which eventually led to hyper-Calvinism.[10] Others, however, sought to resolve the dichotomy by stressing the revealed will of God, and this led eventually to universalism. Still others, and these would include the majority of conservative evangelicals today, have tried to retain Calvin's paradox – even though many would be surprised to hear that it comes from him – and live with

209

the problems it creates for theological systematization.

It would be foolish to suppose that such a thorny question can be resolved in a few sentences, and it may well be that here we have been brought face to face with a divine mystery which we can never hope to penetrate fully. On the other hand, systematic theology has been confronted with seemingly insoluble paradoxes before, and Christians have wrestled with God until an answer was given to them from Scripture. This happened, for example, in the long arguments about the difference between the generation of the Son and the procession of the Holy Spirit, which remained unfathomable until the discussion was freed from the constraints of natural causation and transferred to the level of personal relations in the Trinity.

Is it possible to apply the same procedure here, with similar results? If we recognize that the will belongs to the natures of God and human beings, and accept that God does not deal with us at that level, then it follows that neither his will nor ours is the primary, or even decisive, factor in our redemption. This has always been accepted (by Calvinists, at least) as far as human will is concerned, and the testimonies of great saints like Paul, Augustine, Luther or C. S. Lewis are uniform in their assertion that they were converted *against* their will, not because they had made a voluntary decision for Christ. It was only after they had met God face to face that their will to resist was broken and they gave in, although, as Paul reminds us, the conversion of the will is by no means the end of the spiritual struggle (Rom. 7:18–21).

The decisive factor in conversion is not the submission of the will, which follows as a consequence of regeneration, and has to be worked out in the trials of everyday living, but the meeting with God, in whose presence no unjust person can live. It is this personal encounter which makes the ultimate difference, and which reveals whether or not we are truly God's elect. But the essence of this encounter is that people are free not to embrace God's will but to spurn it as Satan spurned it; for we must surely remember that Adam's rebellion was not self-willed, but came in response to a personal temptation from the devil.

If we can work out the implications of personal encounter

for the role of the human will, is it not possible to do the same for the role of God's will as well? In other words, can we not say that in the face of personal rejection by men and women, God does not invoke his will any more than he calls on his omnipotence, to reverse this decision? If we say this, we can avoid the dangers of universalism without denying that God wants everyone to be saved. Moreover, it would be possible to reaffirm the Calvinist view of election and predestination, since God's saving grace is not dependent on his will but flows from the mutual encounter of persons in the Godhead, and is freely extended to the elect by the work of the Son and the Holy Spirit.

How this operates in practice brings us to the fifth and last of the distinctive points of Calvin's theology. This is that *the persons possess distinctive attributes of personhood which they share with elect human persons.* In the more traditional language of Reformed theology, God possesses communicable attributes (*i.e.* those of his persons) alongside and in addition to his incommunicable attributes, which are those of his essence. This distinction of attributes is a commonplace of later Calvinism, although its origins can be traced back to the *Institutes.* In defining the term 'person' Calvin adopted the usual terminology of mediaeval Scholasticism, describing it as 'a subsistence in the divine Essence which is distinguished by incommunicable properties'. He also appears to follow this tradition when he adds that 'revelation is distinctly expressed' by the properties which are peculiar to each of the persons (*Institutes*, I, 13,6).

But although the language and concepts have a familiar ring about them, we must not be misled into interpreting them in the traditional manner. For the scholastic synthesis of Thomas Aquinas had *identified* the distinguishing marks of the persons with their relations, to the point where Thomas could say that they were really one and the same thing. Calvin recoiled from that extreme, and followed instead the ancient tradition of the church, particularly strong in the East, which maintained that in God there is an absolute distinction of persons. In ancient theology, of course, these persons were bound to one another by ties of spiritual kinship, since both the Son and the Holy Spirit were believed to have derived

211

their personhood from the Father. But Calvin's teaching that each person is *autotheos* means that their mutual relationship is one that had been freely agreed on the basis of mutual respect for the complementary properties of each person within the Godhead.

By moving in that direction Calvin made it possible to say that a divine person can have properties (attributes) which are not necessarily common to the essence of God. In that these properties are used to establish relations within the Godhead, the persons are seen to be in control of them and not, as in Scholasticism, determined by them. From there it is but a short step to say that by entering into relationships, the persons of the Trinity can communicate those properties which are common to all three because they are shared attributes of their divine personhood, not characteristics inherent in the essence of God.

## The attributes of personhood

It may seem obvious that the persons of the Trinity have attributes of personhood, but this concept has proved surprisingly hard for theologians to grasp. Partly, no doubt, this is because so much of the language of theology is philosophical terminology which was originally applied to the divine essence, and the transfer to personal categories is one which philosophers have found equally difficult. A good example of the sort of confusion which can occur is found in the writings of Louis Berkhof (1873–1957), a well-known conservative Reformed systematician. Berkhof writes that the communicable attributes of God are those which belong to his 'personal nature', even though in classical theism, 'nature' is a word used primarily of the divine essence.[11] Berkhof may be technically correct, but it is better to find another word to refer to the properties of the divine persons, in order to avoid this particular misunderstanding. For our purposes, the best word available seems to be 'character', and it is that term which we shall use to describe what Berkhof means by 'personal nature'.

Calvin mentions several personal attributes of God, but does not gather them together in one place or give them a systematic treatment. Later Reformed theologians have attempted to do this, though with somewhat mixed results. Today the generally accepted consensus is that of Herman Bavinck (1854–1921),[12] which Berkhof repeats. It is a complex scheme, with five main headings and several subheadings, which may be set out like this:

(1) Spirituality;
(2) Intellectual attributes: omniscience, wisdom,
          veracity;
(3) Moral attributes:
 (A) goodness, love, grace, mercy, patience;
 (B) holiness;
 (C) righteousness;
(4) Attributes of sovereignty: freedom,
        omnipotence;
(5) Attributes of majesty: perfection, blessedness,
       glory.

If we compare this list with that of John of Damascus, we are struck immediately by the number of attributes which are common to both lists. We may also notice that some of the attributes listed by Bavinck can be subsumed under others, while still others are not really attributes at all, but only words which recall the great gulf between God and his creatures. If we rearrange Bavinck's list according to these observations, we get something like this:

(1) Incommunicable attributes of the divine essence:
     spirituality,
     omniscience,
     omnipotence

(2) Descriptions of God which are not really attributes:
     perfection
     veracity
     freedom
     blessedness
     goodness
     glory

213

(3) Communicable attributes of God's personal character:
                wisdom
                righteousness
                love*
                holiness
                sovereignty

*including grace, mercy and patience

Before we proceed any further, it should be said that the above rearrangement is far from definitive, and makes no attempt to deny the validity of Bavinck's statements. Instead it attempts to explain Bavinck's position in a way which is consistent with an earlier tradition of Christian theology. The 'spirituality' of God, for example, is not mentioned by John of Damascus (although it is obviously implied by such attributes as invisibility and omnipresence), and the belief that 'spirit' is equivalent to 'person' was condemned at the Council of Soissons in 853. It is therefore somewhat strange to find 'spirituality' listed as one of the personal attributes of God, when it so clearly belongs to the divine essence.

As we have already seen, the case for considering omnipotence as a personal attribute of God is stronger, in that the biblical term 'almighty' is a title of God which the early Christians frequently coupled with 'Lord' and 'God'. The concept of omnipotence is really part of the divine sovereignty, as Bavinck classified it, although its status as a 'communicable' attribute must obviously be called into question.

More difficult are the descriptions of God which Bavinck classified as attributes, but which would seem to be somewhat different. 'Veracity', for example, is meaningful only in terms of our understanding, since whatever God says or does is bound to be 'true'. The same goes for goodness and perfection. Freedom would seem to be implicit in God's sovereignty, and the same can probably be said of blessedness and glory, though quite how one is supposed to define those is a bit of a mystery. Furthermore, it is not altogether clear whether they should be regarded as communicable or incommunicable. It seems that to the extent that they are communicable to creatures, it is only as we are called to share in the fullness of the divine life; in other words, only in heaven do we come to experience them. In this respect they differ markedly from the communicable attributes, which are meant to be enjoyed, however partially and imperfectly, in this life.

We are thus left with five personal, communicable attributes of God, which we shall examine in turn.

### Holiness and righteousness

Of these attributes, the most fundamental is that of *holiness*. The term itself means 'separateness', but it is not easy to understand, although it appears in both Testaments as the most fundamental characteristic of God. That it is a personal attribute can be seen from the way in which it is applied to the divine name. The Fathers of the early church recognized this by interpreting Isaiah 6:3 as a reference to the Trinity, and by repeating that the Christian's most important task is to be holy, just as God is holy (1 Pet. 1:15–16).[13] Augustine even claimed that 'Holy' was the personal name of the Spirit, equivalent to the names Father and Son, although he was obliged to admit that the term could be applied equally well to them also.

An important point to notice about this attribute is the close link between it and the covenant. The word 'holy' does not appear in Scripture until God speaks to Moses at the burning bush (Ex. 3:5), the point at which he revealed his covenant name to Israel. From then on, the word is in frequent use, but always with reference to some aspect of the law and its attendant sacrifices and rituals. In the Pentateuch, it is applied to things at least as often as to people, but this has to be understood in the context of the old dispensation of the covenant, when things were called holy because they were pledges and indications of the coming of the Messiah. It was the mistake of later Judaism to treat these objects as holy in themselves, and a similar mistake is common in the different types of Catholicism. According to the teaching of the New Testament, however, it is only Christ and those who belong to him who are called 'holy', so that the personal character of holiness stands clearly revealed.

As a communicable attribute, holiness is given to the Christian as part of his profession of faith. It is for this purpose that the Holy Spirit is bestowed on us, to the extent that our bodies are his temple (1 Cor. 3:16–17). This is a matter of the greatest importance, because it means that we are called to share in the most fundamental personal attribute of God. Everything else in our relationship with him depends on this, as any number of biblical passages testify. Before anything else, we must be holy people if we are to be God's servants here on earth.

But what exactly *is* holiness? The first mistake is to imagine that it is a substance, part of the essence of God. This error has been very common in the history of the church, and the Reformers protested vigorously against it. Luther's famous assertion that the Christian is a justified sinner (*simul iustus et peccator*) is aimed directly against the idea that being holy involves an ontological change in us. For Luther and the Protestant tradition generally, true holiness is found in our relationship with God, which we enjoy on the basis of faith, not achievement. It is true that many Protestants have been unable to maintain Luther's position, and have tried to introduce schemes for becoming holy, which have little or nothing to do with the teaching of Scripture, but the identification of holiness with a particular type of puritanical morality is a perversion of the gospel and must be recognized as such.[14]

Sadly, we have to admit that a well-meaning but essentially mistaken spirituality, which identified 'holiness' with such things as abstinence from alcohol and strict Sabbath observance, has given the word a bad name, and made it even more difficult for us to appreciate what it really means. In abandoning the legalism of the past, we are liable to adopt a kind of permissiveness which may be justified in the name of 'love', but which is really every bit as far removed from the gospel as the earlier error was. Legalism is not the answer, but we must not forget that there is a close link between holiness and *righteousness*, which implies that we are called to maintain a certian standard of moral conduct.

We need to remember that the apostle Paul did not reject the law as such; what he opposed was the human tendency to seek salvation by keeping the law, which is impossible. Sinners that we are, we shall either reduce the law's demands to something which we can live with, as the Pharisees did (*cf.* Mk. 7:11–13), or we shall relapse into a sense of hopelessness

216

when we realize that such an undertaking is beyond our powers. The freedom of the gospel which Paul proclaimed was a freedom from hypocrisy and despair – the twin agents of the power of sin within us. He said that the demands of the law had been fulfilled in Christ, who has made it possible for our righteousness to exceed that of the scribes and Pharisees, not by increased effort on our part, but by starting from a different basis. Even in the Old Testament, Jeremiah said that the new covenant would be written on the heart, not on tablets of stone (31:31–34), and the New Testament echoes this theme (Heb. 8:8–12). The indwelling presence of the Holy Spirit is nothing other than the indwelling presence of the law of God, and their function is the same (*cf.* Jn. 16:8–11).

To be holy is therefore to be righteous according to God's standard of judgment, which is manifested in the inner relations of the Trinity. Here we see the perfect outworking of the principle that God is faithful, even when all human beings are liars (Rom. 3:4). His justice is expressed in his consistent willingness to fulfil his promises (1 Jn. 1:9) and this in turn is based on the perfect communion which exists between the Father and the Son. It was this which enabled the Son to take on the burden of human sin in the certain knowledge that he would be justified by the resurrection from the dead. Likewise, we have the assurance that God will honour the work of his Spirit in us, because the Father and the Son are present with him in it (Jn. 14:15–20).

Loyalty, commitment and perseverance in personal relationships, of which the most fundamental are our relationships with the persons of the Trinity, are the biblical mark of true holiness – an attitude of mind which is beautifully expressed in the imagery which links spiritual life to human marriage. There is no conflict between the divine and the human, since the former gives meaning to the latter, and raises it to fellowship with the inner being of God. Paul even goes to the point of saying that a Christian must remain faithful to an unbelieving spouse, since in that way the entire family will be made holy (1 Cor. 7:10–16).[15] The bonds of marriage and the family are directly dependent on the bonds between God and human beings, which in turn depend on the bonds which express the relationship of the persons of the Trinity to each other (*cf.* Gal. 4:6).

## Sovereignty

The third personal attribute of God is his sovereignty. We have already noted this in our discussion of election and predestination, but we must not forget that it has a wider application to what the Bible calls the kingdom of God (or kingdom of heaven). Jesus says that the Father has committed everything to him (Jn. 3:35), a theme which runs right through the New Testament. The Holy Spirit too, although he is less obviously associated with the kingly rule of God, is called the Lord (2 Cor. 3:17) and entrusted by both the Father and the Son (Jn. 14:26; 15:26) with the task of fulfilling their work of building the kingdom.

But how are we to understand the outworking of divine sovereignty in practice? The first thing we have to take into account is its intensely personal character. God does not work through ideas or structures, important though these may be, but in and through people. This is a vital truth which is in danger of being obscured whenever there is talk of a 'social gospel'. We must never lose sight of the fact that in Scripture evil is a personal power which is exercised by angels and human beings who have rebelled against God. In direct contrast to this we are told that the kingdom of God is within us, if we are obedient to him, so that it too is a personal concept. Just as the servants of Satan do his bidding and exercise his authority, so also the sons of God do his will and share in his glorious power. It is this shared activity and responsibility which constitutes the very basis of the Christian life. Sharing in the sovereignty of God is a liberation which no other power can provide, because it gives us access to the depths of God's wisdom, holiness and power. It is because of this that Paul tells us that we shall judge even the angels (1 Cor. 6:3), although by nature they are superior to us (Heb. 2:7, 9).

It is when we consider this point that we can discern a difference between God's sovereignty and his omnipotence. His sovereignty can be shared with us, but his omnipotence cannot. An analogy with secular authority may help to explain this more clearly. A government official may exercise

218

state sovereignty within his appointed sphere, but he is not omnipotent, and may not even be able to punish those who fail to submit to his authority. The situation of the believing Christian is similar to this, in that our power to act in God's name is circumscribed by our lack of omnipotence. We cannot take revenge on those who fail to obey God (*cf.* Rom. 12:19), nor can we do anything apart from the power of Christ which is at work within us (Gal. 2:20). But none of this detracts from our share in his sovereignty, for we are called to reign with him in his glory (2 Tim. 2:12), as kings and priests of God.

We can thus see that sovereignty and omnipotence are separable. The former belongs to the divine persons, the latter to the divine essence. The title Almighty therefore refers primarily to God's sovereignty as the Lord of all things. It is because God's sovereignty is coupled with omnipotence that he will certainly prevail in the cosmic struggle for power, and which ensures that his authority can never be overthrown by spiritual forces opposed to him.

## Wisdom

The fourth personal attribute of God is his wisdom. Divine wisdom must be distinguished from the mind of God, which is part of the divine essence, as is his will. Wisdom is more than just intelligence, because it includes the ability to control and direct that mind. We all know of bright people who have failed to develop their potential to the full because they are unwise in the use of their gifts, just as we know of people who have caused enormous trouble by tying their will to their intelligence without the discernment which wisdom provides. With God, however, these aberrations are impossible. He is in perfect control of his being, because his wisdom is shared equally by all three persons of the Trinity. This is an important truth, because it reinforces the fundamental equality of the Son and the Father, and reminds us that both participate equally in the divine plan of salvation. It is also a reminder to us that in the wisdom of the Holy Spirit dwelling within us, we have the mind of Christ and are empowered to order our lives according to the pattern of God's will.

The importance of wisdom is reinforced by the so-called 'wisdom literature' in the Old Testament. Many people find

219

Proverbs, Ecclesiastes and the Song of Songs rather puzzling parts of Scripture, because they seem to be so 'unscriptual'. Proverbs offers a lot of good advice on matters of everyday life. Ecclesiastes reads like the confession of a disillusioned humanist, and the Song of Songs appears to be no more than an oriental love poem, in which the name of God is not even mentioned. Reductionist interpretations of this kind have largely silenced these books in the church, much to the detriment of our understanding of God's wisdom.

The wisdom of God is thorough and co-extensive with his plan and creation. There is nothing which escapes his attention, and our lives are entirely in his hands (Mt. 6:25–29; Rom. 8:28). As believers who are privileged to share in God's wisdom, it is our duty to understand how it applies to every aspect of our lives, not just to the so-called 'spiritual' aspects. Christians are frequently in danger of forgetting that commonsense is a divine gift, which needs to be used to the glory of God as much as the more spectacular gifts. Failure to do this often produces a lack of realism in Christian circles which may even prompt believers to rely on 'prayer' as an escape from serious responsibility. The fact that this abdication of our sonship is cloaked in piety does not make it better – rather the reverse. Christians need to learn again that the wisdom of God is shared with his people for our benefit. Without becoming merely rationalistic or calculating in our thinking, we must learn to deploy this resource to the furtherance of the kingdom of God.

### Love

We come finally to the last, and in many respects the greatest, of God's personal attributes – *love*. We have already seen what a strong place love has traditionally occupied in the theology of the Western church, a position which it attained largely as a result of Augustine's doctrine of the Trinity. But we also saw that Augustine, albeit after much struggle, linked God's love with his being as Spirit, by a false equation of John 4:24 with 1 John 4:16. Because of this, the concept of love became subtly depersonalized. This had · serious consequences for the doctrine of the Holy Spirit, whom Augustine portrayed as the bond of unity between the Father

220

and the Son, and ever since, many people have found it easier to think of the Holy Spirit as a force than as a person.

But as Augustine also saw, love is a personal attribute of God, which he shares with his creatures. It is probably best to disregard his rather tortuous linking of 'love' with 'spirit' and emphasize, as the Reformers did, that the Holy Spirit, as the bond of love in the Trinity, not only sets the seal on the union of the Father with the Son, but also imparts their mutual love to us, so that we may share in it also.

In the Scriptures the love of God comes to us above all as the promise and assurance of salvation. Because of its personal character, it is a mistake to equate God's love with material blessings, just as it is a mistake to tie his holiness to consecrated objects or places. Indeed, we are warned in both Testaments that God actually punishes and disciplines those whom he loves, in order to bring them to maturity (Pr. 3:12; Heb. 12:6).

The close link between the love of God and punishment is important when we come to examine the thorny problem of divine wrath. In modern times the idea of God's wrath has been very unpopular, and many scholars and theologians have tried to discount it altogether. Once again, part of the blame for this must be laid at the door of hyper-Calvinism, which at times stressed the wrath of God against unrepentant sinners to the point that it almost ousted belief in his mercy and forgiveness. The reaction against this exaggerated picture of an angry God occasionally went so far that Mary Baker Eddy, the founder of Christian Science, was able to persuade some people that wrath, pain and even matter itself simply do not exist.[16] Even without going to that extreme, it would be fair to say that few orthodox preachers today put much emphasis on this aspect of God, and tend to recoil from what they see as old-fashioned and unattractive 'hellfire and brimstone' preaching.

The result of this softness has been disastrous for the church, whose members often have little awareness of the seriousness of their own sinfulness. A lopsided view of God's love, as something which excludes the notion of wrath, has prevailed against the clear biblical testimony. In the Scriptures there are at least a dozen words which may be translated 'wrath' or 'retribution', and they occur with sufficient frequency to make it impossible for us to ignore them.

Sometimes it is said that God hates sin (impersonal) but loves the sinner (personal), but this attempt to mitigate the wrath of God is not really faithful to the biblical witness. Wrongdoing in the Bible is never dissociated from the wrong-doers, who are fully responsible for their actions. Retribution cannot be shifted to an impersonal level without ceasing to be what it says it is. We cannot imagine a judge excusing a murderer who says he is sorry and offers to clean up the mess, as if the crime were all that mattered. However sincere his repentance might be, the murderer would still be held responsible for his sin, just as we are held responsible for our sins before God.

But curiously, there are many people who for some reason fail to make this equation. Although they might agree in the case of the murderer, they do not accept that this principle can be applied directly to sins against God. By a process of reasoning sometimes disparagingly referred to as 'cheap grace', they believe that verbal repentance is enough to take away sin, and that if they confess to wrongdoing God will not exact any penalty from them. This procedure appears to be automatic and painless, causing the minimum of upset and inconvenience to the normal flow of everyday life. The truth, though, is that people who think like that have never really encountered the depths of the love of God in Christ. If they had, they would have recognized that there is a heavy penalty to be paid for their sin – a penalty which Christ bore for us on the cross. Unless we understand that we are fully deserving of God's wrath, which he will certainly inflict on those who do evil (*cf.* Rom. 1:18–32), we shall never even begin to understand the depth of the love which has rescued us from our misery and from our just desserts. It is impossible to have any understanding of the love of God apart from the message of the atoning power of the cross of Christ, not only because this is the only way in which we can come to experience his love, but because this was the way God chose to demonstrate that love, even within the Godhead. This is the great truth discovered by Anselm of Canterbury, when he wrote that the sacrifice and death of the Son was above all a sacrifice made to the Father, on behalf of sinful human beings. Christ is our representative, or Mediator, at the judgment seat of God, where his sacrifice remains as our plea for forgiveness. Without the love of the Son for the Father, which impelled him to make the sacrifice in the first place, without the corresponding love of the Father for the Son, by which he accepted the Son's work and pronounced the word of forgiveness for us, our salvation could not have occurred. Furthermore, without the love of the Holy Spirit for both the Father and the Son, by which he brings this message to us and sounds the very depths of our hearts, Christ's work of love would have no practical meaning in our lives. The inner love of the persons of the Trinity is the very ground of our redemption, and at the heart of this love we meet both the wrath and the mercy of God.

## The persons and the essence of God

We come now to the final question which the co-inherence of the three persons raises. This is the problem of how we are to regard the divine essence, which in Protestant theology does not generally occupy the high position which it has in other forms of Christianity.

At one time there was felt to be a danger that the essence of God would be regarded as a fourth hypostasis in the divine being. This is an odd conclusion to come to, but it makes sense if the essence can be perceived by the intellect as distinct from any one of the persons. Calvin was accused of holding this view, and he refuted it vehemently (*Institutes*, I, 13,25). He argued that the persons are not separable from the essence, because they reside in it. We may go further and say that the heart of Calvin's teaching was that the essence of God is *not* perceivable as such, but can be discerned only as the predicate of each of the three persons. In this, Calvin followed the Cappadocian tradition, except that he argued that not only the Father, but also the Son and the Holy Spirit, manifest this essence in its fullness and must therefore be regarded as *autotheos*.

More recently, the reality of the essence of God has been challenged by the theology of Karl Barth, who claimed that as

223

it is completely different from anything known to human beings, it cannot be known at all. In other words, the essence of God is a philosophical abstraction which describes the attributes common to the three persons of the Trinity, but is not a separate entity in its own right.

In taking this position Barth was clearly reacting against a philosophical theology which had constructed a supreme being out of the data of the natural world, and then identified this abstraction with the Christian God. His reaction in favour of the Trinity of Revelation was healthy and necessary, but it may be argued that it went too far in the opposite direction. Barth does not really do justice to the Cappadocian principle of the co-inherence of the persons, according to which each person manifests the fullness of God, which means that each person must manifest the other two persons as well. It seems that Barth accepts this principle only in the case of the incarnate Son, which is one reason why his theology has been accused of Christomonism, *i.e.* centring exclusively on Christ.

True co-inherence must apply to all three persons, so that their shared essential attributes are not merely the result of generic affinity (as human attributes are) but the substance of numerical identity, since God is one. Each person of the Godhead must possess all the attributes of God's essence, as well as the particular attributes which define their personhood. The attributes of the divine essence are incommunicable, and belong to each of the persons fully – a definition which supports Barth's assertion that God is the wholly other, but which does not lapse into his radical repudiation of all philosophical theology.

The true heritage of the Reformation, and especially of Calvin, may therefore be defined as a theology of the divine persons, whose attributes express both their distinctiveness and their unity. The incommunicable attributes constitute the absolute, divine essence, which is his unity: the communicable attributes come together in the pattern of divine relations by which we see the model of the divine society, and experience, by our adoption as sons and daughters of God in the image of Christ, the reality of fellowship in the inner life of the Holy Trinity.

# 6

## CONSTRUCTING AN EVANGELICAL THEOLOGY TODAY

We have now surveyed the main trends and schools of thought which have dominated Christianity since biblical times. In spite of the great diversity which exists among theologians of different periods and traditions, there is one vital thread which is common to them all. This is that all true theologians, past and present, have tried to give a coherent account in their writings of what it means to know and experience the presence of God. Without this undercurrent of living faith flowing up to water the field of theological discourse, academic systems can only wither and die. This principle holds good whether we are university professors, desert monks or just ordinary people seeking to find Christ in the midst of everyday life. Furthermore, it is one of the more encouraging features of modern times that this principle is once again being clearly enunciated and proclaimed. Today there are very few people who would deny that it is necessary to have a personal experience of God if one wishes to claim the name of Christian, and even in the Roman Catholic Church the old 'father knows best' approach is now very much in decline.

To say this does not mean, of course, that everyone agrees about the exact type of experience required for true Christian faith. Still less does it mean that most people have chosen more or less the same categories of thought in which to express it. On the contrary, it is often at this level that the ship of the church has struck its rock of offence, and the sailors are by no means agreed as to how best to rescue the foundering vessel. Among the many tendencies in modern theological thought, and dwelling in uneasy co-existence with most of them, is Protestant evangelicalism. The term itself is a controversial one, because in one sense it is claimed by all those who follow the Reformation principle of *sola Scriptura* in debates about authority in the church. More liberal Protestants prefer to talk about conservative evangelicalism, or even fundamentalism, which is now more properly a term of abuse for a kind of naive literalism which no responsible evangelical theologian holds.[1] On the other hand, those who cling to the label most uncompromisingly do not accept such qualifications, and appropriate to themselves a term of wider meaning, just as (Roman) Catholics and (Eastern) Orthodox do with their respective labels. As this usage is now standard among those who are most directly concerned, and is gaining recognition elsewhere, it is the practice we shall follow here.

The commitment to a historical revelation from God is common to all evangelicals, who nevertheless differ among themselves as to how this revelation should be handled today. At one extreme are those who reject any form of systematic theology or interpretation beyond that which is self-evident. This is a true 'fundamentalism' (which must not be confused with the naive literalism of certain 'fundamentalist' sects), but it is seriously deficient in a number of important ways. First, and most obviously, it contradicts itself by being a non-historical approach to history. The Bible clearly contains some kind of progression in the revelation of God, but with no framework in which to interpret this, the reader is liable to concentrate only on those parts which appear to be immediately applicable to his own situation. This may include the less historical parts of the Old Testament (*e.g.* the Psalms) and the epistles of the New Testament, which are historical only in a secondary sense. It probably also accounts for the extraordinary interest in eschatology which is found among such groups, since what was future to the biblical writers may come to appear as present, or even as past, to us. In practice, 'fundamentalist' eschatology almost always seems to connect biblical prophecy to the present or to the immediate future, so that the imminent end of the world becomes a major preoccupation, and even the main content of preaching and 'theology', in such circles.

The non-systematic approach to revelation is also deficient because it leads to misunderstandings and contradictions. The Bible is a difficult book because many of its presuppositions are hidden beneath the surface of what is said. This comes out most clearly in the Pauline epistles, where Paul often refers to his teaching without actually explaining it in any detail. The reader is expected to know it already, and Paul's main concern is usually to correct errors and/or provide supplementary details. It is the job of the systematic theologian to reveal these underlying principles and show how they interconnect in a coherent way throughout the Scriptures. When this theological task is denied or underrated, one of two things is liable to happen. Either readers will be caught up with details which stand out in their minds because of their apparent oddity (genealogies, laws, types of baptism, *etc.*) or they will construct their own sub-system, perhaps unconsciously, and interpret particular passages accordingly. This sub-system is often eschatological, and it may rely heavily on allegory. If it is not, it may be susceptible to the most radical type of liberalism, because of the latter's claim to be relevant to the needs of this generation. It seems that most evangelicals who have passed into the liberal camp have done so because they have started with a non-systematic approach of this type.

The third and most important difficulty of the non-systematic approach is that it loses sight of God. The Bible is first and foremost a revelation, not just *from* God but also *of* God. Behind its apparent diversity there lies this fundamental unity which must be perceived and understood if we are to say that we really know the God of Scripture. Because our theology is nothing more than the expression of our beliefs about the God whom we meet in the Bible, it is clearly a necessary preliminary to any valid profession of faith. Because God is one logical and coherent being, our theology must also be systematic, containing within a single framework all the rich diversity of the textual witness. For this reason more than for any other, the 'fundamentalist' approach to the principle of *sola Scriptura* is neither valid in itself nor viable as an option for Christians today.

What is needed in our time is a new theological confession which will stand squarely in the historical tradition which the evangelical understanding of revelation imposes on us, but at the same time respond to the needs of our own age, seeking perhaps to probe still further the meaning of the theology which underlies and unites the books of the Bible. The main elements underpinning such a confessional theology must be the following:

1. *It must at all times be rooted and grounded in living faith.* This emphasis not only does justice to the legitimate pietist protest against the sterility of Protestant orthodoxy, but it unites evangelicals to the mainstream of the Christian church, the *theologia perennis* which makes us one with the saints of every age. Of course, living faith has to be discerned. It does not follow that because the theologian must be first and foremost a man or woman of prayer, any sort of devotional practice is an acceptable ingredient of theology. Living faith is authentic only when it is submitted to the authority of Scripture, which must at all times judge the validity of its content.

2. *It must accept that the historical Scriptures are a theological unity, and interpret them accordingly.* This means that it is impossible for an evangelical theology to discard parts of the Bible (*e.g.* the Old Testament) or interpret them in a way which falsifies their obvious meaning. It does not destroy the usefulness of typology, which is found in the New Testament, provided that it can be justified theologically. Furthermore, whilst it means taking history with the utmost seriousness, it does not mean that history can be abstracted and employed as a controlling factor in theological confession. In plain English, no evangelical can dismiss the teaching of Scripture (*e.g.* about the role of women in the church) on the ground

that it is now out-of-date. Social and cultural patterns may vary, but it is theological principle and not historical circumstance which must be the ultimate judge of how we interpret and apply the Scriptures.

3. *It must challenge the modern world in the light of the Bible, not adapt the Bible to the thinking of the modern world.* This principle follows logically from the former, and strikes at the root of most liberal thinking today, which tells us to adapt or die. Evangelicals need to challenge the view that they are survivals from an earlier stage of religious evolution, not by abandoning their principles or even seeking to restate them in a visibly contemporary guise, but by using them to challenge the assumptions of our own age. Nothing could be more fatal to a truly evangelical theology than an uncritical acceptance of current fashion. The gospel is a prophetic call from another world which demands what the Bible calls *metanoia*: repentance and conversion. If this is lost, then so are we, and the church will become no more than a social club promoting good works and blessed thoughts.

4. *It must put God at the centre of its concerns.* Whatever else it may be, theology is first and foremost the Christian doctrine of God, and this fact must be made to impinge on every aspect of our systematics. It is for this reason that these reflections are included in this book. The philosophical questions posed by the existence of God must be turned on their head. The real issue is not how we can accommodate the traditional doctrine of God within certain philosophical assumptions, but how we can accept a particular philosophy, given the traditional doctrine of God. It is God who must judge philosophy, not the other way round. Likewise, the doctrine of the Trinity must form the basis of our proclamation *and* of our pastoral practice. This is an issue of life and death for the church, and must be taken with the utmost seriousness. Translated into the thought patterns of our time, these principles strike home at two vital points: the understanding of time and the need to preserve the primacy of the person. We shall look briefly at each of these.

229

## Understanding time

Although it is by no means always recognized as such, the problem of time lies at the heart of most contemporary theological discussion. Nor should this surprise us, because in this respect, as in others, the theological world is merely conforming to its usual habit of being a couple of generations behind the broader currents of Western culture. Time was the major theme of the great literature of the early part of the twentieth century, as a glance at Eliot, Proust, Kafka, Hemingway or Orwell will confirm. The problem of time has occupied philosophers, artists, musicians and scientists, all in their different ways, and theologians have been only catching up with the general trend.

At a deeper level, it was inevitable that in a secular age the problem of time would emerge as the greatest single intellectual question, and Christians should be glad that it is so. For as we saw in our discussion of the names for God, it is a question which penetrates right to the heart of all religion. The Christian church is uncomfortable in a secular society because it worships a God who is neither bound by time nor identical with it. The great breakthrough represented by the biblical revelation is precisely this, that human beings must not worship a being restricted by the limitations imposed by time. Instead they must relativize time, even confound it with the logically nonsensical phrase *hoi aiōnes tōn aiōnōn* (blandly and inaccurately rendered in English as 'for ever and ever'; more accurately 'the ages of ages'). They must worship a God who speaks in time but who dwells beyond it even when circumstances compel us to go on living within it. Here there is a paradox which has always puzzled the greatest minds of our culture, and with which we continue to wrestle.

The primary difficulty which confronts us is that of *revelation*. It is remarkable how insistent the Bible is on the fact that God's revelation comes to us by means of *sound* rather than *sight*, which is often associated with idolatry and unbelief (*cf.* especially Jn. 20:29). Sight is a sense which is primarily spatial in conception, and it is surprising how little difficulty we seem to have with it. We are not disturbed, for example, by images which are greater or less than life-size, even though they are a real distortion of their subject, nor does it seem to bother us that there are things which can be in more than one place at once, like air, for example, or even the image on a television screen.

Sound, on the other hand, is a temporal sense, and time is a more absolute dimension than space. We cannot conceive of sound spreading naturally through time, or disobeying temporal laws. Even a whistle or a bell which rings more than momentarily impresses us by its extension within time, not by its triumph over it; and if we remark on it at all, it is to comment on the length of time which it lasted. We might, of course say the same thing about something which is visible – an ancient painting or rock-formation, for example – but the temporal dimension remains secondary, not primary, as it is with sound.

Revelation in sound automatically implies time, since otherwise it could not occur.

If we say that God speaks to people today, what we really mean is that God has spoken to someone in the recent past and is expected to do so again in the near future. If someone says 'God is speaking to me now' we would raise our eyebrows, since one might reasonably assume that the person concerned ought to be listening to God and not chatting to somebody else. But even so, God's precise words will be either past or future to the speaker's perception, not 'present' in the strict sense. It follows from this that the only revelation of which we can speak must have taken place in the past. We need not rule out the possibility of future revelation, but this will have to bear some recognizable relationship to past revelation if it is to be accepted as the same thing. The Bible is quite clear about this; as the writer to the Hebrews put it, God spoke in different ways in times past but now, in the last days, he has spoken to us in his Son (Heb. 1:1–2). Here all the revelation is past, relative to the time of the writer. But interestingly enough, the writer regards his own time as the end – the 'future' is condensed, like the 'present', into an event which is already past. This can mean only that the normal human time sequence has ceased to have any importance, although it may continue to function in its own sphere. The writer to the Hebrews, like the church, has passed – thanks to the fulfilment of God's revelation – from the dimension of time to the dimension of eternity.

Eternity today is widely regarded as a problem, even as a meaningless concept, because it is supposed to be beyond our experience. Even some Christian thinkers have questioned whether God is really beyond time, because such a concept seems to them to be indigestible. Yet it is precisely this which the Bible claims. Furthermore, and this is what is most interesting to us, the barrier between time and eternity, which has been broken in the past by God, who spoke his Word and sent his Son into the world, will in future be broken also by human beings, who will be seated in heavenly places in Christ Jesus, enjoying here and now the first fruits of eternal life. The question of eternity, therefore, is not confined to problems of revelation or incarnation; it is directly relevant to our own spiritual experience.

In arguing for a certain understanding of time, we have pointed out that the present does not really exist. Yet there can be no doubt that the present is alive and well in the minds of every one of us. It is the fixed standpoint from which we view and evaluate both the past and the future. It is the dimension in which we wish to authenticate our knowledge and enjoy our experiences. In many ways it represents the boundary of our reality, the 'horizon' within which we freely choose to exist. Yet in terms of time, it is not even there. It thus follows that a purely secular outlook, one which is bound by the dimension of time, does not correspond to the way we normally think. Indeed, it is a very real question whether secularism makes any sense at all, since if we really were subject to time we would not perceive it or pass judgment on it in the way we do.

Our concept of the present does not bind us to the secular sphere; it sets us apart from it. As we have already seen, the only way in which we can experience the present within time is by stopping time altogether, by turning life into a frozen snapshot of reality. Naturally this is impossible, and so we are forced to look elsewhere. The Christian explanation is that the present is not part of the past-future sequence, but a foretaste of eternity. To conceive of it is therefore to be aware of an eternal dimension which goes beyond the world of time; to want to dwell in it is a sign that human beings are made for eternity and will not be fulfilled until they attain to a knowledge and experience of it.

The problem of whether or not God can speak within time thus becomes the problem of the present, and of our awareness of a dimension other than that of time. If we who live in time can conceive of the present, then there is no logical reason why we cannot also experience the eternal, which is what the biblical writers claim for their own experience of the Word of God. When we ask what relevance their experience has for us, we are really facing a different set of problems from the ones we have been considering so far, even though they are related. We may accept that if it is possible for us to experience the eternal God in our 'present', then it must have been possible for people in ancient times to have known God in their 'present' too. Furthermore, we may agree that the experience of eternity must be recognizably the same in each case, so that at that level there is a real communion of the saints of every age.

Problems arise not at that level, but at the level of communication from one age to the others, *i.e.* within time. This communication can proceed in only one direction, from the past to the future. We are sometimes tempted to speak in terms of 'dialogue with the past', but what this means is something different from what it suggests. We cannot converse with the past, any more than we can converse with the future. We can only listen to the past, just as the future will be able only to listen to us. In this context, talk of dialogue is really a refusal to listen, and the past ceases to function as a living reality in our pattern of thought.

It must be recognized that in dealing with the past we are sometimes confronted with problems of listening which overwhelm us. In some cases, we have languages which are undeciphered, and therefore beyond our powers of hearing. In other cases, we can read the message but its contents are of no great interest to us. We read a text or an inscription for its historical interest, but do not feel any unity of spirit with whoever originally wrote it. But there are writings, and the Bible would certainly have to be included among them, whose message from the past still speaks today. To this category belongs all the world's great literature; if it were not so, it would have died long ago. Even if they have survived physically, most 'penny novels' of the Victorian era can hardly be said to form part of our living culture in the way the works of Shakespeare do, for instance.

The power of the Bible as literature is universally acknowledged, but Christians insist that it is something more than that: it is the Word of God. Likewise, almost everyone agrees that Jesus was a great moral teacher, but Christians insist that he is something more: he too is the Word of God. In other words, while Christians recognize that the revelation of God in the Bible and in Christ is historically past, they also insist that it is eternally present. To understand its message, we cannot ignore the historical past, but neither can we neglect the eternal present, which is the true dimension in which we experience the integration of our own mind and thought with that of the Bible.

It will be obvious that with such a perspective we cannot give too much importance to concepts like 'cultural conditioning' or the 'horizon of perception' to which our time supposedly binds us.[2] In intellectual and cultural terms, the human being lives in the present and is not bound by time in the way that such theories suppose. If it is true that our outlook today is different from what it was in biblical times, then we must ask just *how* it is different, and to what extent these differences modify our perception of reality. It soon becomes apparent that the main differences are technological, political and economic, and that these are not very important at the moral or spiritual level. Such changes as there have been in these areas have occurred at least partly under the influence of the biblical revelation, and cannot be treated independently of it. Some would even go so far as to say that the appearance of the biblical revelation and its general acceptance in Western culture totally changed the framework in which such things were discussed, so that our secular age is in revolt against the Bible in particular, and not necessarily against the concept of eternity in general. This revolt has often taken the form of saying that technological and economic developments must compel moral and spiritual change, and this assumption has been used to explain and justify the decline of traditional religion in our society. But Christians cannot agree with this, because for them the moral and spiritual realm is rooted in the dimension of eternity, whereas technology and economics are not.

The result of this is that if a past revelation from God is authentic, it must still be valid for Christians today, because ours is the same God and the principles by which we know him remain unchanged. The only real question left is whether the *phenomena* which are recorded in the Bible as applications of the revelation are still normative for us today. Within the Bible itself, we recognize that the culture formed around the Mosaic law is no longer applicable, even though the law is still the Word of God. On the other hand, the law was not the fulfilment of the revelation in the way that Jesus Christ is. The Son of God did not come to replace the law, but to fulfil it by a deeper revelation of its inner meaning and importance.

Has anything comparable happened since New Testament times? Muslims, Mormons and members of other cults believe that it has, and may even maintain that their special revelation is a fulfilment of the New Testament, just as the New Testament is a fulfilment of the Old. Roman Catholics do not go that far, but they are nevertheless prepared to accept that the living voice of the Holy Spirit, speaking through the church, has the power to 'develop' the revelation in ways which effectively supplement the teaching of the Bible. Protestants, on the other hand, reject this, and say that revelation is both full and final in Scripture.

This is fine as far as it goes, but it does not account for developments in the centuries between the Bible and us. Some evangelicals ignore them completely; for them the eternal dimension is enough, and they effectively detemporalize the revelation. Others recognize that to be consistent one must take history and historical tradition seriously, but few have bothered to develop a positive understanding of Christian tradition. A notable exception to this is the American Lutheran scholar Jaroslav Pelikan (1923–), who has made the study of Christian tradition the main work of his life.[3] Pelikan recognizes, as too few evangelicals do, that we have been formed in *two* dimensions, the eternal and the temporal, and that each must be given its proper weight. Fellowship with the saints in heaven includes acceptance of their legacy on earth because they were in living contact with the eternal God during the time of their earthly life, just as we are now. It does not mean that every aspect of this heritage is of equal value, nor will it all be of equal relevance to us. The New Testament itself tells us that our works will be tested by fire, and that in some cases they will be destroyed (1 Cor. 3:10–15). Tradition therefore cannot be regarded as infallible or as authoritative in the way that the Bible is. But neither can it be ignored or discounted, since it is on that foundation that we are called to continue the process of building.

A proper understanding of time among evangelicals must therefore come to terms with the past in the context of the eternal present. The same is also true of the future; the current widespread and basically secular eschatology can hardly be expected to survive a really serious discussion of these matters in the light of the past and of the eternal present. A solid, constructive evangelical theology will inevitably move away from much of what currently goes under that name in evangelical circles, but if it remains true to its calling, it will be doing no more than listening once again to the eternal Word of God, revealed to us in time past.

## Preserving the person

Perhaps the most astonishing thing about the Word of God is that its supreme manifestation is the *Logos*, the second person of the Trinity who became incarnate in the man Jesus Christ. That the Word became flesh and dwelt among us (Jn. 1:14) has always been one of the basic themes of the Christian gospel, but even today the implications of this stupendous fact are far from having been fully explored. One of the stock tactics of liberal theology is to divorce the person of Jesus Christ from the Bible as the written Word of God, on the ground that as Christians we put our faith in a person, not in propositions. Not surprisingly, those who take this line often push it one step further and deny that Jesus was the Word made flesh. This second step is not a necessary one, and there have been many theologians who have refused to take it, but

236

its logic is not difficult to follow. The person of Jesus Christ cannot be divorced from the written Word of God, and if the latter goes there are few grounds for maintaining the divinity of the former. The abandonment of the authority of the Bible is not only the abandonment of Jesus' relationship to Scripture, it is the abandonment of the Word altogether. Jacques Ellul has put the case very succinctly:

> The Word of God is the very person of God incarnate. There is no contradiction in the fact that the word is spoken by God and also incarnate in Jesus, since this word is what reveals God, and God has effectively revealed himself only in the Incarnation of the Son. The incarnate Word is in reality the Word fully given to humankind, so that an individual can finally be enlightened about God's decision concerning him, and about love and justice.
>
> The personality of the Word of God cannot contradict its literalness and intellectuality. The word spoken in ancient times by the Prophets becomes fully the Word of God because it refers to the incarnate Word. And the word newly spoken by witnesses becomes in turn this Word when and because it refers to Jesus Christ.[4]

The personhood of the Word must therefore be seen as the culmination of a development which has reached its fruition in Christ, not as a new departure which has no real relevance to the written text. But there are two important aspects of the modern use of the word 'person' which make it difficult for us to appreciate what the Bible and the Christian tradition mean by the term.[5] It is a commonplace of modern theology that classical theism uses the word 'person' in a sense quite different from that of modern thought. This is a bold claim to make, and often it is simply asserted without being justified by the evidence. In actual fact, the word 'person' is used today in a wide variety of contexts without much concern for precise definition. The theological use of the word was a specialization from the more general uses, but one which was felt to be feasible because the word could be made to express the reality of the Father, Son and Holy Spirit without losing contact with its meaning in other contexts, particularly in Roman law.

In modern times the word has re-entered the common language, but now its basic meaning contains an integrated theological element which was not present in ancient times. To the Romans a *persona* was basically a mask (*cf.* Greek: *prosōpon*), but to us a 'person' is basically a rational individual – quite a different matter. Modern thought has tended to reduce the word's meaning to one of these basic assumptions, and it is because of this that the language of theology is so difficult to grasp nowadays. It may even be the case that the modern reduction of the term's meaning has really been a possibly subconscious attempt to empty it of theological significance, an effort which has met with limited but still significant success.

In effect, the word 'person' has become synonymous with 'individual'. This definition has a certain *a priori* plausibility because whatever else a person may be, he or she is clearly singular and distinct. But to stop at this point is to miss the very important difference which exists between the under-lying dynamic of the two words. In the former case, the unit is established in relation to other similar units; in the latter, the unit is distinguished and set apart from them. To put this another way, 'individual' emphasizes the separateness of the person, whereas 'person' emphasizes the capacity and need of the individual to find expression in relationship.

Once this is understood, a number of common misconceptions begin to appear in a different light. Evangelicals who stress the need for a personal relationship with God appear far less individualistic, without losing their concern for the individual. A personal relationship with God can never be individualistic, if only because God is not an individual person, but three persons in an individual substance. It must never be forgotten that singularity in God is expressed at the level of his essence, which by definition is inaccessible to us. At the level of personhood, which is where we meet him, God is three. By entering into a personal relationship with God we are entering into a divine society, into which we are progressively integrated as we grow in spiritual maturity. Furthermore, we are brought into relationship with all who participate in this same divine society. The church, as this society is called, is therefore not an added extra, but a vital ingredient in our living contact with God. At the same time it must always be stressed that the church is not a human institution which can control access to fellowship with God. Rather it is a divine creation in which we discover our human solidarity because together and individually we have already entered into a saving relationship with Christ. Without that relationship there can be no church, which is why an orthodox confession in the power of the Holy Spirit is the *sine qua non* of authentic membership of the people of God.

Also typical of the modern approach is the emphasis placed on the mind and the will as constitutive of the 'person', which relegates the term to the psychological level. This error may be able to contain, and even insist on, the relational character of personhood which the concept of the individual underrates, but it is still a serious distortion in its own right. Psychology, as we understand it today, is a rational science which seeks to explain, even to the point of controlling or correcting, those aspects of the human being which were once thought to be 'irrational'. Dreams, for example, which had been laughed at by the rationalist philosophers of the eighteenth century, became for the pioneers of psychology like Freud, elements of key importance in understanding the hidden depths of the human mind. In this connection, it should never be forgotten that for a modern psychologist, mind and spirit are the same thing, designated by the Greek word for soul (*psychē*).

In Christian terms, however, the spirit is something quite different from the mind. Indeed, it is not part of the physical constitution of a human being at all. It is true that the Bible uses the word in a number of different ways, and that it sometimes means more or less the same thing as soul, but the apostle Paul in particular also thought of humanity as sharing in a spiritual realm which stood over against that of the mind or the soul. For him, to be spiritual is to partake of the nature of the God who is spirit. The sending of the Holy Spirit into our hearts reinforces the view that in human beings there is a

239

capacity for knowing God (Rom. 8:16). Now it is quite clear from the overall tenor of the Scriptures that this capacity must be linked to the image of God in humans, which is closely connected with the idea of the human 'person', even if not identical with it.[6] It is because modern psychology discounts the divine that it cannot absorb this concept, and we are faced with a fundamental conflict of ideas which amounts at bottom to a conflict of religious principles. We can get a good idea of what has happened by looking at the way the word 'personality' has changed its meaning under the impact of modern psychology. Whereas this word was once synonymous with 'personhood', it now tends to mean the sum total of an individual's psychological attributes.

The significance of this shift in meaning can be measured by asking one simple question: does a Christian who lapses into a permanent (irreversible) coma lose his relationship with God? If his mind cannot function, a modern psychologist would have to say that his spirit is inoperative, and it becomes a legal question as to whether such a 'human vegetable' is still a person. Indeed, most of the legal battles which have been fought in recent years over the question of euthanasia have revolved around precisely this question: is it wrong to terminate the life of a body which the law, but not most modern science, says is still a person?

In debates of this kind, the Christian position is usually fairly clearly stated. 'Human vegetables' are persons whose lives must be respected, although whether they should be prolonged artificially is of course another matter. On the other hand, it is seldom clearly argued that the Christian position rests on a theological assumption, which is that all human beings are persons created in the image of God, and that the failure of parts of our human nature to function as they should does not alter that fact. On the contrary, Christianity teaches that human nature *must* cease to function in death, but that when that happens the human person is not affected: 'for me to live is Christ and to die is gain', as Paul so pithily expressed it (Phil. 1:21).

At this point we can no longer avoid the very real parallel which there is between God and humanity. All human beings, whether they are regenerate or not, have a built-in relationship with God by virtue of the fact that they are created in his image. Modern psychology, working on the basis of human nature, has managed to dispense with sin and guilt, and understandably so. Sin, with its attendant guilt, does not inhere in our nature, which remains the same as it was before the fall. Instead, it inheres in our persons. Sin is always a personal act of disobedience against God. We have inherited our basic sinfulness, that is to say the state of rebellion against God, from Adam, because we stand in relationship to him, as well as to God directly. But without this theological understanding of personhood, sin makes no sense. On the other hand, it is because sin is personal that only a personal relationship with God in Christ can take it away, which is why this element is such an important part of gospel preaching.

Today it is of vital importance that we preserve the Christian concept of the person, both in dogmatic theology and in pastoral practice. Without a theological understanding of the person, we shall soon have no theology and no church. The counsellor's couch is already competing with the pastor's pulpit, and the loss of any clear theological understanding of humanity will bring the day of its triumph only that much nearer. A truly evangelical theology must insist that psychology is a branch of medicine and not a substitute for traditional Christian doctrine.

## Evangelical theology

In conclusion, we can only summarize the main points which should form the basis of responsible evangelical theology today. First, *we cannot neglect our past if we want to speak to the future*. In so far as we dwell in time we must accept its conditions and use them to further the cause of the gospel. We believe that God has spoken in time and revealed himself in a way which is comprehensible to human beings. This belief entails the defence of the historical reliability of the Bible, which is a prominent feature of evangelical scholarship today, and also of its continuing relevance. The real battle today is not so much over the character or content of Scripture as over its applicability to present-day needs.

241

We can learn to do this only if we learn how to relativize history without disrespecting it. We can escape being imprisoned in a cultural horizon which is incompatible with that of Scripture only by remembering that *the Bible is the Word of the living God whom we can know only in his ever-present eternity*. Who God is, is thus the hermeneutical key to what the Bible means, and our modern application of the text can be authenticated only by a worshipful obedience to the God who gave it to us. The Bible remains the only locus of God's self-revelation, and for that reason it is the only source for a valid theology. But the weight of Christian tradition must also be taken into account. The evangelical who defends a historical Scripture must also recognize a historical church, which is the communion of saints in every age, saints who rose above the limitations of their time to rejoice in the transcendent majesty of God. For just as God is the interpreter of Scripture, so too he is the interpreter of tradition, guiding us to the light from his Word which has shone forth wherever the gospel has been proclaimed.

A Bible-centred church has no choice but to wrestle with the complex issue of God and time, but it cannot stop there. Pastoral need demands that we probe more deeply, not only the divine nature, but also what it means for him to be three persons, with whom we can develop a spiritual relationship which is both corporate and individual. *We must explore further what it means to be a person*, and how it is that three divine persons dwell together in perfect harmony. This is doubly important because far from asserting themselves at the expense of the others, each of the divine persons manifests perfection whilst containing and manifesting the perfection of the others. This doctrine of co-inherence is perhaps the most important single teaching of the Bible in an age which finds it hard to reconcile individual freedom and dignity with corporate commitment and responsibility. But if we are to grow in spiritual understanding, these complementary opposites must be held together and promoted in the expectation that each will be fulfilled in perfect union with God. Under no circumstances can one overtake the other, for then the harmony of the divine relationships will be lost.

The freedom of the divine persons is revealed most clearly

in the voluntary abdication of the Son, who gave up the rights he was entitled to in order to become man (Phil. 2:5–8). This fact belongs to the very bedrock of Christian belief, and it is important to remember that it is one of the main starting-points which Augustine used in formulating his doctrine of the Trinity. In more recent times the same verses have been quoted as the basis of what has been called a kenotic chris-tology, from the Greek word *ekenōsen* ('he emptied') which appears in verse 8. Unfortunately, kenotic christology has confused the person of the Son with his divine nature, and thus it has interpreted the Son's self-emptying as a surrender of his divine attributes. It does not see that such a surrender is impossible, and some of the advocates of this theory have even gone to the point of saying that the logical contradiction involved in it is merely a paradox which shows how great the power of God's love is. This is a powerful argument, but it does not do justice to the fact that God's love can never manifest itself in a way which contradicts his being, because God himself is love. The Son's self-denial must therefore be understood in a way which harmonizes with everything we know about God.

The answer, of course, as Augustine clearly saw,[7] is that the Son gave up his personal privileges, not his divine attributes. The basis of *kenōsis* is fundamentally legal, not philosophical, and it is in legal terms that we must understand it. This has important repercussions for our understanding of the imita-tion of Christ. We are no more able to give up our human nature than he was; we cannot change what we are. But we *can* give up our rights, and accept a position of humility in which our God-given talents may be used in service to him. Jesus chose that way, which led him to death on a cross in the world of time. But in the world of eternity his submission led to his exaltation, so that his name, which had previously been hidden from the world, would become the name above every name, at which every knee would bow, and which every tongue would confess. The crowned glory of the ascended Christ is in no way a change in his nature, nor is it a change in his person. Rather, it is a revelation of himself as he truly is, the sharing with human beings of a status which had pre-viously been concealed from them.

243

Furthermore, it is because of this status that Jesus was free to offer himself in service. The higher the one is exalted, the deeper the other is seen to be. Reigning in eternal glory, Jesus is an even greater servant of his church, performing by his Holy Spirit works in us which are greater than those which he did on earth (Jn. 14:12). It is the most wonderful truth of Christianity that the persons of the Trinity govern the attributes of God, and in their work use these attributes for the benefit of humanity. They are not bound by a nature which prevents them from entering into relationship with their creatures, just as human beings, created in the image of God, are not prevented by human nature from having a relationship with God. In our persons, both God and human beings are free to sacrifice themselves for one another, and in that self-denial to find the exaltation of our name which makes us heirs of God's eternal kingdom.

Along with this freedom comes also commitment and responsibility, things which are really only the other side of the same coin. The self-sacrifice of Jesus was not an end in itself, but an essential part of God's love for the human race. In the Nicene Creed we are told that the Son of God became incarnate 'for us and for our salvation'. The significance of this is that before he embarked upon his work of salvation, the Son of God came *for us*; it was because God loved us when we were still sinners that he came to do his great work of atonement (Rom. 3:23). God's love for us is not primarily a question of works or of power, but of relationship. Nine out of the ten lepers whom Jesus healed received the blessing of his powerful work, but only one leper moved on from there to establish a living relationship with the Saviour. The gospels constantly remind us that real commitment to Christ cannot be based on signs and wonders or on what we can get out of him. Commitment to Christ is a fruit of the work of the Holy Spirit in our lives, but the Holy Spirit is himself the person who is perfectly committed to the work of the Father and the Son, so much so that his presence in us is their presence also (Jn. 14:17, 23).

The freedom of Christ's fellowship is at the same time the responsibility to obey his commands (Jn. 15:14), and to grow as branches of his vine, bearing fruit for him by cultivating that fundamental relationship (Jn. 15:5). Here we come to the very heart of a truly evangelical theology. The Bible speaks to us about God not in order to frighten us, not even in order to humble us in his presence. The Bible speaks to us of God because it teaches us that our destiny is to live with him in eternity. In God we see the perfect consummation of a life which has become ours through the inheritance of adoption, and which one day will be ours in its fulness. Because this life is present and unchanging, it is also eternal; because it is eternal, it is also divine.

Evangelical theology is distinctive because it is pre-eminently personal. It relativizes the natures of God and human beings so that they become servants, not masters of the person, and exalts the works of the persons which reveal just how the apparent limitations of our nature may be overcome. Evangelical theology is practical, 'ethical' in the best sense. Its characteristic perversion is legalistic morality, but instead of pushing us in the direction of a spiritually-motivated moral relativism, this sad fact should teach us something about the true nature of our faith. The corruption of the best must not make us content to settle for the worst, but ought to spur us to seek correction from the hand of God the Father, the husbandman of the vine in which we abide.

The moral earnestness of evangelical theology has an absolute character, not because it is rooted in a set of abstract principles, but because it is based on a faith-relationship with God. It is at this point that true evangelicals part company with moral reformers of all descriptions, and with the legalism of its own sectarian fringe. The paradox is that a relationship with God is not relative because God is absolute. We who are capable only of relativity cannot enter into a true relationship with God of our own accord. Faith in God can be only a divine gift, which establishes in us a capacity for living in contact with an absolute God. The belief that such a relationship is both possible and necessary is the glory and the scandal of evangelicalism, the faith of people who know they are saved, and know too, that no-one can come to the Father except through Christ (Jn. 14:6). Here is a teaching which sets evangelicals apart from those who lack assurance of salvation just as surely as from those who believe that in

THE DOCTRINE OF GOD

the end, everyone will be saved whether they believe in Christ or not. In both cases, what is missing is the awareness of the central importance of a right personal relationship with God, something which is made both available and inescapable because it is inherent in the being of the God who has revealed himself to us in his Word.

## The importance of the Trinity

Evangelical theology has traditionally emphasized many aspects of the person and work of the Son and the Holy Spirit which might otherwise have been neglected in the church. But if it is to stand alongside the other great traditions of Christianity and claim the catholicity of a truly biblical faith, it must recover and maintain the centrality of the doctrine of the Trinity both in its confession and in the worship of its congregations. Without the Trinity there is no Christian faith, because the specific revelation of God entrusted to us in the New Testament is lost from view. A living relationship with God requires that each of the persons be honoured and adored in the context of their revealed relationship with each other. When this principle is distorted, as it constantly is in our everyday experience, spiritual imbalance and doctrinal controversy are the inevitable result.

We can appreciate this most clearly by looking briefly at some of the problems currently confronting us in relation to each of the persons of the Trinity, and suggesting ways in which evangelicals will be called to reassert the proper weight of biblical truth in our worship of each one of them.

We must begin, as trinitarian formulations usually do, with the person and work of the *Father*. Before the rise of the charismatic movement, it used to be said that the Holy Spirit was the 'forgotten' member of the Holy Trinity, but that designation would now apply much more readily to the Father.[8] Despite our tradition of prayer to him, in preference to the other persons, we are now less and less aware of his specific role as the initiator of action within the Godhead. We no longer see him as the one whom Christ came to make known to us, nor are we often conscious that it is his

246

will which the Holy Spirit comes to make real in our lives. In some quarters we have become so obsessed with spiritual techniques that we have forgotten the object of the whole exercise, which is to know and be known by God.

Since ancient times it has generally been recognized that the Father represents to us the absolute character of the transcendent majesty of God. It is he who reminds us of the incommunicable attributes of the divine essence, of what Karl Barth called the 'wholly other' quality of God. But in doing this he also reminds us of how great the privilege is which we have been granted in the Son: the privilege of being able to sit with him at the right hand of his exalted majesty and share with him in the government of the universe. The calling of the Christian is to be a co-worker with God (2 Cor. 6:1) in the outworking of his purpose for humanity.

But if this dimension is frequently lacking in our preaching, there are two other dangers which have become increasingly prevalent in recent years whenever mention is made of the Father. The first is to confuse the person of the Father, who is identified as such in relation to the Son, with the fatherhood of God over all creation. It may be true that God can be described as 'father' in this more general sense, and that all human beings are his 'children' in the sense that they have been created by him. But we must not allow this to obscure the much more important biblical teaching which says that in covenant relationship with God, the Christian knows the Father as the Father of the Son, and not merely as the creator of the universe.

Nothing in the Bible entitles us to abuse the concept of fatherhood to the point where we are led to state that all religions are the same, or that each offers a valid road to salvation. The revealed fatherhood of God is essentially different from anything which can be deduced from the fact of creation, because it is rooted in personal relationship, not in natural dependence. A theology which bases itself on a feeling of 'total dependence', to use Schleiermacher's phrase, is subtly unbiblical, because it confuses what is true at the natural level with what has become true for us in personal terms: that we are no longer servants but sons and heirs of our Father's kingdom. We must always be on our guard against any attempt to lead us into error by a wrong application of the truth.

Linked to this is another problem which has surfaced in recent years. This is the tendency to interpret the person of the Father in psychological terms. It is alarming to notice how many preachers and counsellors have started to tell people that our heavenly Father is an extension and perfection of our earthly fathers, so that the relationship we have – or should have – with the latter can serve as a guide to the relationship we ought to have with the former. It may be true that some people are hampered in their understanding of God because they have had bad experiences of their own parents, but the answer to this is surely not to regard God as a substitute for human failure. We can know God the Father only to the extent that we know him in relation to his own Son, in whom we have been redeemed. It is that fact, and not some kind of psychological analogy, which provides the basis for our spiritual experience.

Needless to say, the psychological approach has led to another 'problem', this time to one posed by the so-called masculinity of God. Some feminist theologians have even gone to the point of accusing the church of male chauvinism because of this, and have tried to legitimize the use of the female pronoun when referring to him. Quite apart from the fact that there is no biblical or traditional justification for this, the whole complaint is based on a fundamental misunderstanding. God's 'masculinity' is not a projection of human ideas onto the divine, because human sexuality was created after Adam, and out of him. The created Adam initially contained the female principle within him: woman was formed by subtraction from him. Therefore the male cannot claim to be the image of God in a way which excludes the female, nor is the female in any sense underprivileged. Even in the Genesis account, the Bible insists that God created *them* in his image (5:1–2), so that sexuality as such does not enter into the argument.

The use of the masculine pronoun in relation to God, however, is not simply a convention. Like everything else it must be understood in the context of the relationships which God establishes both within the Godhead and with us. These relationships are based on the procreation of nature, which female imagery would inevitably suggest. We can share with Christ in his kingdom because we are sons by adoption – made equal with him by a legal process.

If we had to depend on nature, we would never get anywhere near him. Nor would the Son ever have become man, since it would have been impossible for him to have entered the human race in the natural way. The daughter of a divine mother would not have found it easy to enter the womb of Mary (would she have become a second mother?), nor could her relationship to Joseph have been any closer than Jesus' was. The end result would have been a docetic saviouress, who would have had no real means of becoming a genuine human being.

The question of God's sexual identity brings us naturally to the person and work of the *Son*, who – whatever we think about the feminist argument – was definitely revealed to us as a male. The historicity of revelation is one of the major battlefields of contemporary theology, and evangelicals are united with all orthodox Christians in defending it strongly. But at the same time, we need to look beyond mere defence and examine more closely what the work of the incarnate Christ actually means for us today. In particular, the whole question of his suffering and death needs to be looked at again from the pastoral angle.

We live in a time when it has become fashionable to say that the sufferings of Christ indicate that God is not impassible, that he understands our condition in this life, and even that he shares it. Given the extremely sensitive nature of the whole question, it is very difficult to argue against such a view without appearing to be either heartless or docetic (or both). Yet while we must certainly recognize the good intentions behind the views of those who would deny the impassibility of God, and point to the sufferings of Christ as their justification, we must be very careful to avoid the imbalance to which such a position so easily leads.

The Christian gospel is not just a message of suffering; it is a message of victory and salvation from suffering and death. This is not to deny that God understands our sufferings, but if he is our healer we must respect his primary purpose. As we have already said, a hospital patient would not be greatly

249

THE DOCTRINE OF GOD

comforted by a doctor who got into the next bed and assured him that he understood the patient's sufferings because he had the same disease himself; the patient wants someone who understands but who can also heal. Over-identification does not help in this; it only destroys the healer's credibility. Moreover, the suffering and death of Jesus had a particular purpose in the plan of God in which identification with us played only a secondary role. The Son came to do the will of the Father, which was to take our place on the cross. This is not identification but substitution – an important difference which must not be obscured. The sufferings of the Christian may be said to involve an identification with (or imitation of) the sufferings of Christ, but Christ did not come to share in our sufferings as such; he came to provide the answer to them.

Lastly, we are in great need of a clear reaffirmation of the person and work of the *Holy Spirit* as these relate to the other two persons of the Trinity. Whatever we may think of the charismatic movement and its various streams of 'renewal', there can be no doubt that some Christians have isolated the Holy Spirit from his trinitarian relationships and exalted him as the sovereign Lord without reference to the Father or the Son. Yet the Scriptures make it quite clear that the work of the Holy Spirit is to glorify the other persons of the Trinity, and make their work a reality in our lives. There can be no genuine work of the Holy Spirit if Christ is not thereby glorified, and the will of the Father seen to be done. To put it another way, the supreme work of the Holy Spirit is seen in conversion and in the practical work of sanctification which flows from that. Yet today we hear too much about the signs and wonders, about the extraordinary gifts, about 'ministry' in the Spirit which has only the most tangential relationship to the work of Christ, if it has any relationship to it at all. We find churches in which the pattern of worship has devalued the sermon and the teaching of the Word of God (who is Christ) in favour of an extended period of fellowship and sharing.

Once again, it should be clearly understood that we are complaining about an imbalance of things which are right in themselves, not about wrong practices. It is imbalance which is the greatest danger we face, and which the doctrine of the Trinity helps us to correct. As evangelical Christians we must take up the challenge of a renewal of solid trinitarian theology, which is the only true witness of our confession. May God grant to us the grace and wisdom to recover the proper balance in our relationship with him – Father, Son and Holy Spirit – that together with all the saints we may worship and adore him as his revelation in Scripture calls us to do.

# Notes

## Chapter 1

[1] In recent years, the term 'theology' has come to be applied to particular social problems which have great pastoral significance but whose links with the doctrine of God are at best questionable. Black theology, liberation theology and feminist theology are typical examples of this. Also related is a view of theology in which the concept of God may be altered to suit the circumstances or the predilections of the author. The best-known current example of this is theology from a feminist perspective according to which God is regarded as female – a view which has no objective justification whatever.

[2] The debates of the late mediaeval and Reformation periods are at least partly responsible for this. Anyone who reads Christian theology from about 1300 to about 1700 must be struck by the relative absence of discussion about the doctrine of God, especially when compared with the furious arguments which raged over these other matters. There was some questioning of classical trinitarianism, as can be seen from the careers of Servetus and Socinus, for example, but this was of minor importance when compared with the other questions at issue.

[3] This does not mean that it is impossible to write coherently about the Jewish or Islamic doctrines of God. In recent years there have even been books purporting to be explanations of Jewish or Islamic theology. But it remains true that works of this kind start with a Christian-

inspired definition of terms, and may well be written for a largely Western audience. Works produced within and for adherents of one or other of these traditions are far more likely to concern themselves with questions of philosophy or law, not of theology in the Christian sense.

[4] This is what the 'orthodox' Protestant theologians of the seventeenth century believed they were doing when they revamped mediaeval scholasticism. Both systems spoke of the 'means of grace', but the Protestants placed the preaching of the Word at the head of their list, whereas Catholics were inclined to treat all alike (in theory) and emphasize the administration of the sacraments (in practice). Protestants also stressed the faith of the believer over against Catholic emphasis on the teaching of the Roman Church, but it was not until the rise of romantic liberalism in the nineteenth century that the two positions came to be seen as mutually exclusive, at least among many Protestants.

[5] Here we must distinguish between two different views. The first of these is that God has not fully revealed himself in Scripture, but that as Scripture is the only source of our knowledge about him, we cannot know anything else. The second view is that biblical revelation may legitimately be supplemented from other sources. This is the standard view of both classical Protestant and Catholic theologians, who differ more over what it is that constitutes legitimacy in this case. Protestants argue that it is the Bible itself which legitimates extra-biblical investigation, whereas Catholics are prone to appeal to the light of reason and the weight of tradition as well.

[6] Of course it should not be assumed that this process was anti-religious or anti-theological. In many cases, it was exactly the opposite. See for example R. Hooykaas, *Religion and the Rise of Modern Science* (Edinburgh: Scottish Academic Press, 1972). Even modern secularists may feel an urge to dabble in theology, although their knowledge of the latter may be superficial: *cf.*, for example, Paul Davies, *God and the New Physics* (Hammondsworth: Penguin, 1983).

[7] Those disturbed by the Hegelian-sounding terminology used here should remember that syntheses of this kind have always been challenged, have seldom proved enduring, and have never been canonized as official Christian teaching. Even Pope Leo XIII's famous endorsement of Thomism (*Aeterni Patris*, 4 August 1879) is no longer widely accepted today.

[8] As a description of Christian theology, this term seems to have been revived by J. G. Eichhorn (1752–1827). It has become popular in the wake of the work of Rudolf Bultmann (1884–1976), who tried to 'demythologize' the gospels. The futility of this task is now generally recognized by biblical scholars, but the need to reinterpret biblical myths, sometimes pushed to the point of 'remythologization', is still

regarded as axiomatic by many theologians. It is one of the factors which must be taken into account when assessing the contribution of the so-called 'New Hermeneutic' to theology. *Cf.*, *e.g.*, A. C. Thiselton, *New Horizons in Hermeneutics: The Theory and Practice of Transforming Biblical Reading* (London: Marshall-Pickering, 1991).

[9] A point worth bearing in mind now that it is a commonplace of modern theology is that its mythologization was largely the result of Hellenic influence.

[10] On classical allegory, see Jean Pépin, *Mythe et allégorie* (Paris: Etudes Augustiniennes, 1976).

[11] For a detailed survey of these questions, see R. Morgan and J. Barton, *Biblical Interpretation* (Oxford: Oxford University Press, 1988).

[12] On these matters, see *e.g.* R. E. Clements, *Old Testament Theology* (London: Marshall, Morgan & Scott, 1978).

[13] H. Frei, *The Eclipse of Biblical Narrative* (New Haven, CT: Yale University Press, 1974).

[14] The futuristic orientation of much Old Testament thought is widely recognized by scholars. See *e.g.* J. Bright, *A History of Israel* (London: SCM Press, 1972), pp. 461–467.

[15] See R. T. France, *Jesus and the Old Testament* (London: Inter-Varsity Press, 1971).

[16] The literature on gnosticism is vast. See R. M. Grant, *Gnosticism and Early Christianity* (New York: Columbia University Press, 1959); S. Pétrement, *A Separate God* (London: Darton, Longman & Todd, 1990); G. Quispel, *Gnostic Studies* (Istanbul: L'Inst. Hist. et Archaéologique Néerlandais, 1974); K. Rudolf, *Gnosis: the Nature and History of an Ancient Religion* (Edinburgh: T. & T. Clark, 1983); R. M. Wilson, *Gnosis and the New Testament* (Oxford: Basil Blackwell, 1968); E. Yamauchi, *Pre-Christian Gnosticism* (London: Tyndale Press, 1973).

[17] See C. Andresen, *Logos und Nomos* (Berlin: De Grugter, 1955).

[18] See R. M. Grant, *Greek Apologists of the Second Century* (London: SCM Press, 1989).

[19] See J. Trigg, *Origen* (London: SCM Press, 1985); H. Crouzel, *Origen* (Edinburgh: T. & T. Clark, 1989).

[20] See A. H. Armstrong, *An Introduction to Ancient Philosophy* (London: Methuen, 1947); R. T. Wallis, *Neoplatonism* (London: Duckworths, 1972).

[21] In this respect it is particularly interesting to note that E. R. Dodds, the modern editor of the fifth-century Neoplatonist Proclus' *Elements of Theology* (Oxford: Clarendon Press, 1933), chose his subject largely because he rejected Christianity and regarded Neoplatonism as a possible replacement for it.

[22] This subject has recently been explored at length in a number of important scholarly works. See R. L. Fox, *Pagans and Christians*

(London: Viking, 1986). A favourite figure of discussion has been Synesius of Cyrene (*c.* 370– *c.* 414); see *e.g.* J. Bregman, *Synesius of Cyrene* (Berkeley: University of California Press, 1982); F. Young, *From Nicea to Chalcedon* (London: SCM Press, 1983), pp. 170–177.

[23] On this subject, see D. Allen, *Philosophy for Understanding Theology* (London: SCM Press, 1985); H. D. Blume and F. Mann, *Platonismus und Christentum* (Münster: Aschendorffsche Verlagsbuchhandlung, 1983); H. J. Blumenthal and R. A. Markus, *Neoplatonism and Early Christian Thought* (London: Variorum, 1981); E. von Ivánka, *Plato Christianus*, (Einsiedeln: Johannes Verlag, 1964, in German, and Paris, 1990, in French); D. J. O'Meara, *Neoplatonism and Christian Thought* (Albany: State University of New York Press, 1982); J. M. Rist, *Platonism and its Christian Heritage* (London: Variorum, 1985).

[24] See Pseudo-Dionysius, *Complete Works* (Mahwah, N. J., 1987); R. Roques, *L'univers dionysien* (Paris: Cerf, 1983).

[25] V. Lossky, *The Mystical Theology of the Eastern Church* (Cambridge: James Clarke, 1957); A. Louth, *The Origins of the Christian Mystical Tradition* (Oxford: Oxford University Press, 1981); D. Staniloae, *Theology and the Church* (Crestwood, N.Y.: St Vladimir's Seminary Press, 1980); H. Urs von Balthasar, *The Glory of the Lord*, 7 vols. (Edinburgh: T. & T. Clark, 1982–91).

[26] See L. Thunberg, *Man and the Cosmos* (Crestwood, N.Y.: St Vladimir's Seminary Press, 1984).

[27] See B. Krivochéine, *In the Light of Christ* (Crestwood N.Y.: St Vladimir's Seminary Press, 1986); G. Mantzaridis, *The Deification of Man* (Crestwood, N.Y.: St Vladimir's Seminary Press, 1984); J. Meyendorff, *A Study of Gregory Palamas* (London: Faith Press, 1964); P. Nellas, *Deification in Christ* (Crestwood, N.Y.: St Vladimir's Seminary Press, 1987).

[28] See M. Spanneut, *Le stoïcisme des Pères de l'Eglise* (Paris: Seuil, 1957).

[29] See R. Braun, *Deus Christianorum. Recherches sur le vocabulaire doctrinal de Tertullien* (Paris: Etudes Augustiniennes, 1977); G. C. Stead, *Divine Substance* (Oxford: Clarendon Press, 1977).

[30] This claim must ultimately rest on the fact that it alone does justice to the Old Testament as a historical revelation of God which was fulfilled, but superseded, in Christ. In Protestant thought since the seventeenth century, at least, this has usually been expressed in terms of covenant – another legal term which expresses both the importance of a divine norm (law) and the experience of personal relationship with God (grace). The mystical tradition, by contrast, usually finds itself forced to allegorize the Old Testament, because its concept of the divine norm is purely metaphysical. The law of the covenant can therefore never be any more than an inadequate approximation to the truth. For the same reason, the experience of salvation cannot be fully expressed in the life

of the church. It is only by mystical union with God, which in the final analysis transcends what we call theology, that God can truly be known.

[31] There is a vast literature on this subject. See *inter alia*, C. Boyer, *Christianisme et néoplatonisme dans la formation de saint Augustin* (1920; new ed., Rome: Officium Libri Catholici, 1953); E. Gilson, *The Christian Philosophy of St Augustine* (London: Gollancz, 1961); R. Jolivet, *Saint Augustin et le néoplatonisme chrétien* (Paris: De Noël et Steele, 1932); M. F. Sciacca, *Saint Augustin et le néoplatonisme* (Louvain, 1956); O. du Roy, *L'intelligence de la foi en la Trinité chez saint Augustin* (Paris: Etudes Augustiniennes, 1966); A. W. Matthews, *The Development of St Augustine from Neoplatonism to Christianity AD 386–391* (Washington: University Press of America, 1980).

[32] See J. Pelikan, *The Christian Tradition 3: The Growth of Medieval Theology (600–1300)*, (Chicago: University of Chicago Press, 1978).

[33] See G. R. Evans, *Anselm and Talking about God* (Oxford: Clarendon Press, 1978).

[34] For an introduction to this, see F. Copleston, *Aquinas* (Hammondsworth: Penguin, 1955); E. Gilson, *Reason and Revelation in the Middle Ages* (New York, 1938).

[35] Oxford: Oxford University Press, 1979.

[36] K. Ward, *Holding Fast to God* (London: SPCK, 1982); H. P. Owen, *Christian Theism* (Edinburgh: T. & T. Clark, 1984).

[37] See J. A. Bracken, *The Triune Symbol: Persons, Process and Community* (Lanham: University Press of America, 1985); J. B. Cobb, *Process Theology: an Introductory Exposition* (Philadelphia: Westminster Press, 1976); D. R. Griffin, ed., *Archetypal Process* (Evanston: Northwestern University Press, 1989); G. Jantzen, *God's World, God's Body* (London: Darton, Longman & Todd, 1984); R. Nash, ed., *Process Theology* (Grand Rapids, 1987); J. J. O'Donnell, *Trinity and Temporality* (Oxford: Oxford University Press, 1983); D. A. Pailin, *God and the Processes of Reality* (London: Routledge, 1989).

[38] See A. Vos, *Aquinas, Calvin and Contemporary Protestant Thought* (Grand Rapids: Eerdmans, 1985).

[39] The clearest and most classic example of this is Martin Chemnitz (1522–86), *Examination of the Council of Trent* (St Louis: Concordia, 1971).

[40] See *e.g.* H. O. Old, 'The Homiletics of John Oecolampadius and the Sermons of the Greek Fathers', in Y. Congar *et al.*, *Communio Sanctorum*, Festschrift for J. J. von Allmen (Geneva, 1982), pp. 239–250. See also T. F. Torrance, *The Hermeneutics of John Calvin* (Edinburgh: Scottish Academic Press, 1988). Recently N. Lossky, *Lancelot Andrewes* (Oxford: Oxford University Press, 1991), has demonstrated the close affinity between the English bishop and the Greek Fathers. It is true that Andrewes is usually classed as an 'Arminian' but that description is

misleading, and his preaching owes far more to Calvin than is generally recognized today.

[2] See R. T. Kendall, *Calvin and English Calvinism to 1649* (Oxford: Oxford University Press, 1979) and P. Helm, *Calvin and the Calvinists* (Edinburgh: Banner of Truth, 1982).

[3] P. Hazard, *The European Mind 1680–1715* (Hammondsworth: Penguin, 1964); P. Gay, *The Enlightenment: An Interpretation*, Vol. 1: *The Rise of Modern Paganism* (New York: Knopf, 1966).

[4] Following K. Barth, *Protestant Theology in the Nineteenth Century* (London: SCM Press, 1972).

[5] This is found mainly in his monumental *Church Dogmatics* (Edinburgh: T. & T. Clark, 1936–69), which was never completed. Opinions differ as to how orthodox Barth really was, but his intentions are seldom questioned.

# Chapter 2

[1] See R. Bevan, *A Twig of Evidence: Does Belief in God make Sense?* (Worthing: Churchman, 1986); B. Davies, *Thinking about God* (London, 1985); C. Hartshorne, *Man's Vision of God and the Logic of Theism* (Chicago: Willett, Clark , 1941); *idem.*, *A Natural Theology for our Time* (La Salle, Ind.: Open Courts, 1967); J. Macquarrie, *In Search of Deity* (London: SCM Press, 1984); C. Tresmontant, *Comment se pose aujourd'hui le problème de l'existence de Dieu* (Paris: Seuil, 1966).

[2] H. M. Kuitert, *Gott in Menschengestalt, eine dogmatische-hermeneutische Studie über die Anthropomorphismen der Bibel* (Munich: Kaiser, 1967); J. Neusner, *The Incarnation of God: The Character of Divinity in Formative Judaism* (Philadelphia: Fortress Press, 1988); D. A. Pailin, *The Anthropological Character of Theology: Conditioning Theological Understanding* (Cambridge: Cambridge University Press, 1990).

[3] See R. T. France, *The Living God* (London: Inter-Varsity Press, 1966).

[4] E. Jüngel, *God's Being is in Becoming* (Edinburgh: T. & T. Clark, 1976); *idem.*, *God as the Mystery of the World* (Edinburgh: T. & T. Clark, 1983).

[5] On Marius Victorinus, see M. T. Clark, 'The Neo-Platonism of Marius Victorinus the Christian' in H. J. Blumenthal and R. A. Markus, *Neoplatonism and Early Christian Thought* (London: Variorum, 1981), pp. 153–159; P. Hadot, *Marius Victorinus* (Paris: Cerf, 1971); R. P. C. Hanson, *The Search for a Christian Doctrine of God* (Edinburgh: T. & T. Clark, 1988), pp. 531–556; R. A. Markus, 'Marius Victorinus' in A. H. Armstrong, ed., *The Cambridge History of Later Greek and Early Medieval Philosophy* (Cambridge: Cambridge University Press, 1967), pp. 331–340; M. Simonetti, *La crisi ariana nel quarto secolo* (Rome: Institutum

Patristicum Augustinianum, 1975), pp. 287–298.

[6] A. Grillmeier, *Christ in Christian Tradition*, vol. 1 (London: Mowbray, 1975), pp. 274–296; Hanson, *op. cit.*, pp. 217–235; J. N. D. Kelly, *Early Christian Doctrines* (London: A. & C. Black, 1977), pp. 240–242.

[7] See R. Bauckham, '"Only the Suffering God can Help": Divine Passibility in Modern Theology', in *Themelios* 9/3, 1983–84, pp. 6–12; J. Galot, *Dieu, souffre-t-il?* (Paris: Lethielleux, 1976).

[8] P. Vitz, *Psychology as Religion: The Cult of Self-Worship* (Grand Rapids: Eerdmans, 1977).

[9] This has long been the contention of Catholic (including Anglo-Catholic) critics. See for example, E. L. Mascall, *He Who Is* (London: Longmans,[2] 1966), pp. 23–29 and 201–226; J. Macquarrie, *Principles of Christian Theology* (London: SCM Press, 1977), pp. 17–18. From a Protestant standpoint, see the criticisms in G. C. Berkouwer, *General Revelation* (Grand Rapids: Eerdmans, 1955), pp. 21–57.

[10] See J. Barnes, *The Ontological Argument* (London: Macmillan, 1972); C. Hartshorne, *Man's Vision of God* (Chicago: Willett, Clark, 1941); A. Plantinga, ed., *The Ontological Argument* (London: Macmillan, 1968).

[11] See E. L. Mascall, *He Who Is* (London: Longmans, [2]1966); J. J. Shepherd, *Experience, Inference and God* (London: Macmillan, 1975).

[12] See R. E. D. Clark, *The Universe: Plan or Accident?* (London: Paternoster Press, 1961); T. McPherson, *The Argument from Design* (London: Macmillan, 1972).

[13] See H. P. Owen, *The Moral Argument for Christian Theism* (London: Allen & Unwin, 1965); A. C. Ewing, *Value and Reality* (London: Allen & Unwin, 1973).

[14] See H. Urs von Balthasar, *The Glory of the Lord I: Seeing the Form* (Edinburgh: T. & T. Clark, 1982).

[15] It is notable that the Greek translators of the Old Testament were also subject to this tendency. See C. T. Fritsch, *The Anti-anthropomorphisms of the Greek Pentateuch* (Princeton, 1943).

[16] Clement of Alexandria, *Exhortation to the Greeks* 5–7.

[17] This tendency is extremely widespread, and is increasing at the present time. It may be understandable that some people find it difficult to refer to God in anthropomorphic terms like 'Father' and 'Son', but to replace these by 'Creator' 'Redeemer' and 'Sanctifier', for example, is to introduce an unbiblical division of labour into the Godhead, which makes understanding even more difficult.

[18] Modern manuals of theology generally cover some of the attributes in John's list, though almost invariably in a truncated form and without John's principles of organization. Even Thomas Aquinas (1226–74) is less comprehensive. In his *Summa Theologiae* Ia, 1–11 (Vol. 2, ed. T. McDermott, London: Eyre & Spottiswoode, 1964) he lists the divine

attributes as follows: simplicity, perfection, goodness, incomprehensibility, omnipresence, immutability, eternity and oneness. The Westminster Confession (II, 1) gives a much fuller list, including no fewer than 27 different attributes, of which at least ten have direct correspondences with John's list. Most of the others can be harmonized with John one way or another, although some are quite clearly attributes of the persons of the Trinity rather than of the divine nature (substance). This confusion is a reminder that what is lacking in the Confession's listing is any systematic principle governing the order of presentation – a surprising weakness, given the overall structure of that document.

[19] See R. Nash, *The Concept of God* (Grand Rapids: Zondervan, 1983), pp. 73–83; and more recently, P. Helm, *Eternal God: A Study of God without Time* (Oxford: Clarendon Press, 1988).

[20] Expressed in this way, Luther's view is certainly the more logical, but Calvin rejected it because it was tied to the notion of *ubiquity*, *i.e.* the idea that Christ's body was potentially present everywhere, and could therefore be located 'in, with and under' the species of consecrated bread and wine. It was this implication which made Calvin reject the idea, because he could not accept an objective presence of Christ in the eucharistic elements. See his commentary on Matthew 26:26.

[21] R. Swinburne, *The Coherence of Theism* (Oxford: Oxford University Press, 1977). See also the same author's *The Existence of God* (Oxford: Oxford University Press, 1981) and *Faith and Reason* (Oxford: University Press, 1983).

[22] Among recent studies of this problem, see S. T. Davis, ed., *Encountering Evil: Live Options in Theodicy* (Atlanta: John Knox Press, 1986); P. T. Geach, *Providence and Evil* (Cambridge: Cambridge University Press, 1977); J. Hick, *Evil and the God of Love* (London: Macmillan, 1966); A. Plantinga, *God, Freedom and Evil* (London: Allen & Unwin, 1975); J. W. Wenham, *The Enigma of Evil* (Leicester: Inter-Varsity Press, 1986).

[23] P. Jewett, *Election and Predestination* (Grand Rapids: Eerdmans, 1985) is the best recent study.

[24] For a summary, see R. Bauckham, *loc. cit.*, n. 7.

[25] J. Moltmann, *The Crucified God* (London: SCM Press, 1974). The theme recurs in many of his works.

[26] For a survey of these views, see H. D. McDonald, *The Atonement of the Death of Christ* (Grand Rapids: Baker, 1985).

# Chapter 3

[1] For a discussion of these questions, see H. H. Rowley, *The Faith of Israel* (London: SCM Press, 1956).

[2] For a summary of the main arguments, see R. K. Harrison, *Introduction to the Old Testament* (London: Inter-Varsity Press, 1969), pp. 362–380.

[3] See J. B. Russell, *Satan: the Early Christian Tradition* (Ithaca, N.Y.: Cornell University Press, 1981).

[4] This subject is now a matter of great controversy. See *e.g.* E. P. Sanders, *Paul and Palestinian Judaism* (London: SCM Press, 1977). After a detailed study of the evidence, Sanders concludes that Paul made a decisive break with contemporary Palestinian Judaism. As he puts it (p. 548): '... in all these essential points – the meaning of "righteousness", the role of repentance, the nature of sin, the nature of the saved "group" and, most important, the necessity of transferring from the damned to the saved – Paul's thought can be sharply distinguished from anything to be found in Palestinian Judaism. Despite agreements, there is a fundamental difference .... Further, the difference is not located in a supposed antithesis of grace and works (on grace and works there is in fact agreement, and an agreement which can hardly be called "peripheral"), but in the total type of religion.'

It is still not clear, however, just when Christians were no longer accepted in the synagogue. Acts suggests that the break was foundational in the establishment of Christian communities, at least in the diaspora, though the situation in Palestine seems to have been more complicated, at least before AD 70. See *e.g.* W. H. C. Frend, *The Rise of Christianity* (London: Darton, Longman & Todd, 1984), pp. 121–126. For our purposes, however, it is the theological break, not the social separation, which is decisive, and that must have occurred in the first decade of the church's existence.

[5] This mood has infected Christian theologians to a greater degree than is realized, and not least, those from third world countries. See *e.g.* J. Hick and P. F. Knitter, eds., *The Myth of Christian Uniqueness* (London: SCM Press, 1987); J. Hick and E. S. Meltzer, *Three Faiths – One God: a Jewish, Christian and Muslim Encounter* (Basingstoke: Macmillan, 1989).

[6] See A. Grillmeier, *Christ in Christian Tradition*, vol. 1 (London: Mowbray, 1975), pp. 46–53. The whole subject is very obscure.

[7] E. J. Fortman, *The Triune God* (London: Hutchinson, 1972), pp. 141–142.

[8] J. S. Trimingham, *Christianity among the Arabs in Pre-Islamic Times* (London: Longmans, 1979).

[9] F. P. Cotterell, 'The Christology of Islam', in H. H. Rowdon, ed., *Christ the Lord. Studies in Christology Presented to Donald Guthrie* (Leicester: Inter-Varsity Press, 1982), pp. 282–298.

[10] See H. J. McLachlan, *Socinianism in Seventeenth-century England* (London: Oxford University Press, 1951); G. H. Williams, *The Polish Brethren*, 2 vols. (Chico, Ca.: Scholars' Press, 1980).

[11] See C. A. Patrides, *The Cambridge Platonists* (Cambridge: Cambridge University Press, 1969); J. Redwood, *Reason, Ridicule and Religion: the Age of Enlightenment in England 1660–1750* (London:

Thames & Hudson, 1976); R. E. Sullivan, *John Toland and the Deist Controversy: a Study in Adaptations* (Cambridge, Mass., 1982).

[12] See A. R. Vidler, *F. D. Maurice and Company* (London: SCM Press, 1966).

[13] G. Lampe, *God as Spirit* (Oxford: Clarendon Press, 1978).

[14] See A. A. Hoekema, *Jehovah's Witnesses* (Exeter: Paternoster Press, 1973); G. D. McKinney, *The Theology of Jehovah's Witnesses* (London: Marshall, Morgan & Scott, 1962); M. J. Penton, *Apocalypse Delayed* (Toronto: University of Toronto Press, 1985).

[15] Origen, or more correctly 'Origenism', was officially condemned at the Fifth Ecumenical Council, the second held at Constantinople, in 553. But his influence lingers on, as can easily be seen in Eastern Orthodox treatments of trinitarian doctrine, where the belief that only the Father is *autotheos* is still latent, making it impossible for them to accept the double procession of the Holy Spirit, for example.

[16] R. Williams, *Arius* (London: Darton, Longman & Todd, 1987) is the best recent study of the subject.

[17] It also weakens Athanasius' rebuttal, since he too accepted the legitimacy of a christological interpretation of Proverbs 8. But it does not alter conclusion, which could equally well have been based on John 1:3, a clearly christological verse.

[18] Whether Tertullian even became a Montanist in the true sense must be doubted. Scholars have usually interpreted his sympathy with them in this way, but see G. L. Bray, *Holiness and the Will of God* (London: Marshall, Morgan & Scott, 1979), pp. 54–63.

[19] See R. Braun, *Deus Christianorum: Recherches sur le vocabulaire doctrinal de Tertullien* (Paris: Etudes Augustiniennes, 1977), pp. 199–207.

[20] J. B. Russell, *The Devil: Perceptions of Evil from Antiquity to Primitive Christianity* (Ithaca, N.Y.: Cornell University Press, 1977). Russell demonstrates how dualism, in so far as it occurs in Hellenistic or early Christian thought, is the product of Zoroastrian influences. These were quite strong at times, but were eventually rejected, particularly by the Neoplatonists.

[21] G. F. Hegel, *Early Theological Writings* (Chicago: University of Chicago Press, 1948); *idem.*, *Lectures on the Philosophy of Religion* (London, 1968).

[22] S. Runciman, *The Medieval Manichee* (Cambridge: Cambridge University Press, 1947). See also, A. P. Vlasto, *The Entry of the Slavs into Christendom* (Cambridge: Cambridge University Press, 1970), pp. 227–235.

[23] The portrait of Sabellius painted here is constructed from fragmentary allusions made in other authors, which is all that we have available to us, and may therefore be inaccurate in certain details. See *e.g.* J. N. D. Kelly, *Early Christian Doctrines* (London: A. & C. Black,

[5]1977), pp. 121–123. Sabellius was not himself a 'Western' theologian, but his views, or a caricature of them, came to be ascribed to Western theology in general, may have been due, at least in part, to the fact that Marcellus of Ancyra, who was generally accepted in the West as a faithful exponent of the first Council of Nicaea, was condemned as Sabellian at the Council of Serdica (or Sardica: now Sofia, Bulgaria) in 343.

[24] It has been especially influential in debates on the impassibility of God. See *e.g.* J. Moltmann, *The Trinity and the Kingdom of God* (London: SCM Press, 1981), pp. 21–60.

[25] The first of these views remains the standard, orthodox one. See *e.g.* Calvin, *Institutes*, I, 13. The third was set out as some length by Friedrich Schleiermacher, *The Christian Faith*, pp. 170–172. The second, which is in some sense a mediating position, is characteristic of Karl Barth, *Church Dogmatics* (Edinburgh: T. & T. Clark, 1936), I/1, p.12. At the present time it would seem that most serious students of the subject subscribe to Barth's view in theory, whilst inclining to Calvin's position in practice. Presumably those who would subscribe to Schleiermacher's teaching have lost all interest in the subject.

[26] An obvious example would be the use of Old Testament theophanies as evidence for the pre-existence of Christ; see Calvin, *Institutes*, I, 13, 9–10. These would not normally be used today as evidence either of the divinity of Christ or of the existence of the Trinity.

[27] London: SPCK, 1952.

[28] Augustine (*On the Trinity*, II, 10) also mentions the story, but he is very cautious about ascribing any trinitarian implications to it.

[29] Calvin, *Commentary on Genesis*, 18, makes no mention of it at all, but H. Bavinck, *The Doctrine of God* (Edinburgh: Banner of Truth, 1977), pp.257–258, mentions something similar in connection with other Old Testament passages.

[30] This is now universally agreed by all commentators. For a brief history of the question, see J. L. Houlden, *The Johannine Epistles* (London: A. & C. Black, 1973), p. 42.

[31] This is the considered opinion of the two most recent studies of the subject. See J. A. T. Robinson, *Redating the New Testament* (London: SCM Press, 1976), pp. 86–117 and J. Wenham, *Redating Matthew, Mark and Luke* (London: Hodder & Stoughton, 1991). Wenham puts Matthew as early as AD 40.

[32] Commentators seem to avoid this question entirely. See *e.g.* F. F. Bruce, *The Acts of the Apostles* (Leicester: Inter-Varsity Press, 1990), pp. 214–231, who does not mention it.

[33] See P. E. Hughes, *The Second Epistle to the Corinthians* (Grand Rapids: Eerdmans, 1962), pp. 488–490.

[34] See D. A. Carson, *The Gospel according to John* (Leicester: Inter-

Varsity Press, 1991), for a full discussion of the relevant passages.

[35] See P. E. Hughes, *The Book of the Revelation* (Leicester: Inter-Varsity Press, 1990).

# Chapter 4

[1] A good example of this is the opening clause of the Apostles' Creed, which traces its origins to about AD 200. The phrase 'I believe in God the Father Almighty, Maker (Creator) of heaven and earth' reflects a time when the words 'almighty' and 'maker' were used of the Father alone, although they are now recognized as equally appropriate for all three persons of the Trinity.

[2] Gregory of Nyssa, *Against Eunomius* I, 42; John of Damascus, *Exposition of the Orthodox Faith*, I, 8.

[3] This idea can be found in John Chrysostom, *On the Annunciation and Against the Arian*, PG 11.842E; also in Cyril of Alexandria, *On the Trinity* 9. But the classic expression of it is in John of Damascus, *op. cit.*: 'we believe also in one Holy Spirit, the Lord and Giver of Life, who proceeds from the Father and rests in the Son'.

[4] For a detailed examination of this complex subject, see C. Stead, *Divine Substance* (Oxford: Clarendon Press, 1977).

[5] See G. L. Bray, 'The *Filioque* Clause in History and Theology', in *Tyndale Bulletin* 34, 1983, pp. 91–144; L. Vischer, ed., *Spirit of God, Spirit of Christ* (Geneva: World Council of Churches, 1981).

[6] On this subject see R. Haugh, *Photius and the Carolingians* (Belmont, Mass.: Nordland, 1975). On the wider question of Photius' relations with the Western Church, see the classic study by F. Dvornik, *The Photian Schism* (Cambridge: Cambridge University Press, 1948).

[7] On this subject, see J. N. D. Kelly, *Early Christian Doctrines* (London: A. & C. Black, [5]1977), p. 264.

[8] An exception may perhaps be made for Gregory of Cyprus, Patriarch of Constantinople from 1283 to 1289. His views have been studied by A. Papadakis, *Crisis in Byzantium* (New York: Fordham University Press, 1983).

[9] See V. Lossky, *The Mystical Theology of the Eastern Church* (Cambridge: James Clarke, 1957); *idem.*, 'The Procession of the Holy Spirit in Orthodox Trinitarian Doctrine', in *In the Image and Likeness of God* (London: Mowbrays, 1974), pp. 71–96.

[10] On Augustine's trinitarianism see C. C. Richardson, 'The Enigma of the Trinity', in R. Battenhouse, ed., *A Companion to the Study of St Augustine* (Oxford: Oxford University Press, 1955), pp. 235–256.

[11] On this whole subject see I. Chevalier, *St Augustin et la pensée grecque: Les relations trinitaires* (Fribourg (Suisse): Collectanea Friburgensia, 1940).

[12] See the discussion of this subject in O. du Roy, *L'intelligence de la foi en la Trinité selon Saint Augustin* (Paris: Etudes Augustiniennes, 1966), pp. 61–72.

[13] See R. Wallis, *Neoplatonism* (London: Duckworth, 1972). Marius Victorinus is treated at length by R. A. Markus in A. H. Armstrong, ed., *The Cambridge History of Later Greek and Early Medieval Philosophy* (Cambridge: Cambridge University Press, 1970), pp. 331–340. See also, R. P. C. Hanson, *The Search for the Christian Doctrine of God* (Edinburgh: T. & T. Clark, 1988), pp. 550–556.

[14] They may both have been students, at different times, of the philosopher Ammonius Saccas, who taught at Alexandria about AD 200–220. Matters are complicated because it seems that there was another Origen, who was both a student of Ammonius and an acquaintance of Plotinus. See J. W. Trigg, *Origen* (London: SCM Press, 1985), pp. 259–260.

[15] It is usually said that this took place at the Third Council of Toledo in 589. However, this cannot be right. The word must have been included shortly before or shortly after this Council. See G. L. Bray, *op. cit.*

[16] See C. C. Richardson, *op. cit.*

[17] *On the Trinity* V, 8, 10.

[18] The Latin phrase is '*tamquam ab uno principio et unica spiratione procedit*'. It is found in the decree *Laetentur Coeli* proclaimed at the sixth session of the Council of Florence on 6 July 1439.

[19] On Boethius, see H. Chadwick, *Boethius* (Oxford: Clarendon Press, 1981), especially pp. 190 ff.

[20] On this controversy, see J. Pelikan, *The Christian Tradition 3: The Growth of Medieval Theology (600–1300)* (Chicago: University of Chicago Press, 1978), pp. 59–61.

[21] On Gilbert, see M. E. Williams, *The Teaching of Gilbert Porreta on the Trinity as found in his Commentaries on Boethius* (Rome, 1951).

[22] On Anselm, see G. R. Evans, *Anselm and Talking about God* (Oxford: Clarendon Press, 1978). On this particular question, see E. J. Fortman, *The Triune God* (London: Hutchinson, 1972), pp. 173–176.

[23] See E. J. Fortman, *op. cit.*, pp. 204–210.

[24] The word 'subsistent' began to replace 'substantial' in the fourth century, because of the need to find a translation for 'hypostatic' which would not be confused with 'essential'. It did not become universal until after the time of Boethius, so that when he spoke of 'person' as a *substantia rationalis* he was using *substantia* to mean *hypostasis*. Later writers would have replaced this word with *subsistentia*.

[25] See E. J. Fortman, *op. cit.*, pp. 191–194.

[26] *Ibid.*, pp. 212–217.

[27] See H. Meynell, *An Introduction to the Philosophy of Bernard Lonergan*

(London: Macmillan, 1991). Unfortunately, Lonergan's main works on the Trinity were written in Latin, and have not yet been translated into English. They are scheduled to appear, however, in his *Collected Works*, currently being prepared by the University of Toronto Press.

[28] K. Rahner, *The Trinity* (London: Burns & Oates, 1975).

[29] See H. U. von Balthasar, *Mysterium Paschale*, in J. Feiner and M. Löhrer eds., *Mysterium Salutis III* (Einsiedeln: Benzinger Verlag, 1969); *idem.*, *Christlicher Stand* (Einsiedeln: Benzinger Verlag, 1977).

[30] E. Jüngel, *The Doctrine of the Trinity* (Edinburgh: T. & T. Clark, 1976).

[31] Of the many works devoted to Karl Barth, see especially, R. Roberts, 'Karl Barth', in P. Toon and J. Spiceland, eds., *One God in Trinity* (London: Bagster, 1980), pp. 78–94; R. Williams, 'Barth on the Triune God', in S. Sykes, ed., *Karl Barth – Studies of his Theological Method* (Oxford: Clarendon Press, 1979).

[32] J. Moltmann, *The Trinity and the Kingdom of God* (London: SCM Press, 1981).

# Chapter 5

[1] This is one of the great unexplored areas of theology. For some indication of what is involved, see *e.g.* H. O. Old, 'The Homiletics of John Oecolampadius and the Sermons of the Greek Fathers', in Y. Congar *et al.*, *Communio Sanctorum*, Festschrift for J. J. von Allmen (Geneva: Editions Labor et Fides, 1982), pp. 239–250. See also the hints given in T. F. Torrance, ed., *Theological Dialogue between Orthodox and Reformed Churches* (Edinburgh: Scottish Academic Press, 1985).

[2] The movement began in the fifteenth century when it was known as the *Devotio Moderna*. For a full account, see R. R. Post, *The Modern Devotion: Confrontation with Reformation and Humanism* (Leiden: E. J. Brill, 1968).

[3] In a reference to the Pseudo-Dionysius, Calvin admits the breadth of his vision, but criticizes him for going beyond the witness of the Bible to develop a theology based on fantasy as much as on fact (*Institutes*, I, 14, 4). The mystical tradition proclaimed the inadequacy of a theology based on revelation to do justice to the essence of God, and therefore it went beyond the former in pursuit of the latter. The Reformers, on the contrary, although they agreed that the Scriptures do not reveal God's essence to us, believed that it was necessary to stay within the bounds of biblical theology and avoid speculating about things of which we have no revealed knowledge.

[4] On the Athanasian Creed, see J. N. D. Kelly, *The Athanasian Creed* (London: A. & C. Black, 1964), also G. L. Bray, *Creeds, Councils and Christ* (Leicester: Inter-Varsity Press, 1984), pp. 172–194.

[5] B. B. Warfield, 'Calvin's Doctrine of the Trinity', in *Calvin and Augustine* (Philadelphia: Presbyterian & Reformed, 1956), pp. 189–284.

[6] *Institutes*, II, 12, 6: '... the image of God constitutes the entire excellence of human nature, as it shone in Adam before his fall, but was afterwards vitiated and almost destroyed, nothing remaining but a ruin, confused, mutilated and tainted with impurity, so it is now partly seen in the elect, in so far as they are regenerated by the Spirit. Its full lustre, however, will be displayed in heaven.' For a full discussion of this question, see G. L. Bray, 'The Image and Likeness of God in Man', *Tyndale Bulletin*, 42, 1991.

[7] This includes mental processes, the sub-conscious and the complex set of characteristics which go to make up a human 'personality'. As a quick rule of thumb, we may say that anything which can be altered or destroyed by physical means (*e.g.* drugs, hypnosis, brainwashing, *etc.*) must be subtracted from Calvin's notion of the soul and transferred to the category of flesh and blood.

[8] The mediaeval theologians had thought of grace as a spiritual substance which transforms mere humanity into something else, but Calvin understood it – more correctly – as the free favour of God accorded to sinners without regard to their natural condition.

[9] See Alan Sell, *The Great Debate* (Worthing: Walter, 1982).

[10] See A. Clifford, *Atonement and Justification* (Oxford: Oxford University Press, 1990).

[11] L. Berkhof, *Systematic Theology* (London: Banner of Truth, 1958), p. 64.

[12] H. Bavinck, *The Doctrine of God* (Edinburgh: Banner of Truth, 1977).

[13] See G. L. Bray, *Holiness and the Will of God: Perspectives on the Theology of Tertullian* (London: Marshall, Morgan & Scott, 1979).

[14] In the eighteenth century a pietistic form of Protestantism emerged which emphasized 'practical sanctification'. This came to mean in the twentieth century a particular type of sober living, identified with renunciation of the 'world'. Dancing, drinking, smoking, cinema and theatre going, card-playing – all these were rejected as 'unchristian' activities, and in pietist circles offenders were easily ostracised, even though none of these prohibitions can be found in Scripture. That did not stop the more zealous, however, and a word like 'temperance' came to mean 'abstinence from alcohol' – a change of meaning which gives a typical picture of the way this school of thought interpreted Christian values.

[15] But if the unbelieving partner wishes to leave, that is permitted, because the tie of holiness does not apply to those who do not share faith in Christ.

[16] On Christian Science see A. A. Hoekema, *The Four Major Cults* (Exeter: Paternoster Press, 1964).

# Chapter 6

[1] For the differences between 'fundamentalism' and conservative evangelicalism, see D. Edwards and J. Stott, *Essentials* (London: Hodder & Stoughton, 1988), pp. 89–104.

[2] On this whole subject, see A. Thiselton, *The Two Horizons* (Exeter: Paternoster Press, 1980).

[3] J. Pelikan, *The Christian Tradition*, 5 Vols. (Chicago: University of Chicago Press, 1971–89); see also his *Jesus through the Centuries* (New Haven, 1985).

[4] J. Ellul, *The Humiliation of the Word* (Grand Rapids: Eerdmans, 1985), p. 51.

[5] See T. J. Burke, ed., *Man and Mind: A Christian Theory of Personality* (Hillsdale: Hillsdale College Press, 1987), pp. 198–222; M. S. van Leeuwen, *The Person in Psychology: A Contemporary Christian Appraisal* (Leicester: Inter-Varsity Press, 1985).

[6] For this, see G. L. Bray, 'The Image and Likeness of God in Man', *Tyndale Bulletin* 42, 1991.

[7] Augustine, *On the Trinity* I.

[8] It has formed the title of at least one book: T. Smail, *The Forgotten Father* (London: Hodder and Stoughton, 1980).

# For Further Reading

## Chapter 1: Our knowledge of God

Among recent books dealing with this subject, *The Science of Theology* by G. Evans, A. McGrath and A. Galloway (London: 1986), provides a good introduction to the subject. Those interested in philosophical questions ought to read D. Allen, *Philosophy for Understanding Theology* (London: SCM Press, 1985) and I. U. Dalforth, *Theology and Philosophy* (Oxford: Blackwell, 1988). The mystical tradition has been well covered by A. Louth, *The Origins of the Christian Mystical Tradition* (Oxford: Oxford University Press, 1983) and V. Lossky, *The Mystical Theology of the Eastern Church* (Cambridge: J. Clarke, 1957). For a general history of Christian theology, the best introduction is the five-volume work by J. Pelikan, entitled *The Christian Tradition* (Chicago: University of Chicago Press, 1971–89).

## Chapter 2: The nature of God

The material covered in this chapter has provoked more debate in recent years than anything else in this book, and the literature is vast! Reformed and evangelical works include the classic study by Herman Bavinck, *The Doctrine of God* (Edinburgh: Banner of Truth, 1977), and G. C. Berkouwer, *The Providence of God*, (Grand Rapids: Eerdmans, 1952). From the English-speaking world have come important works like J. Houston, *I Believe in the Creator* (London: 1979); D. B. Knox, *The Everlasting God* (Welwyn: Evangelical Press, 1982); C. B. Kaiser, *The Doctrine of God* (London: 1982) and R. Nash, *The Concept of God* (Grand Rapids: Zondervan, 1983). The last of these in particular deals with some of the philosophical problems posed by God's attributes.

Among non-evangelical works, there is the important trilogy by R. Swinburne, *The Coherence of Theism* (Oxford: Oxford University Press, 1977); *The Existence of God* (Oxford: Oxford University Press, 1981) and *Faith and Reason* (Oxford: Oxford University Press, 1983). There is also D. Braine, *The Reality of Time and the Existence of God: The Project of Proving God's Existence* (Oxford: Oxford University Press, 1988) and K. Tanner, *God and Creation in Christian Theology* (Oxford: Blackwell, 1988) in which she makes a plea for a return to classical theological discourse in our attempts to resolve problems in this area. Finally, a good Roman Catholic presentation of the subject can be found in B. Davies, *Thinking about God* (London: Churchman, 1985).

Continental theology can be followed in J. Moltmann, *God in Creation* (London: 1985) and also *The Trinity and the Kingdom of God* (London: SCM Press, 1981), where he deals specifically with the question of the relationship between Jewish and Christian perceptions of God. Also important is E. Jüngel, *God as the Mystery of the World* (Edinburgh: T. & T. Clark, 1983). For those who can read French, there is a valuable discussion of divine impassibility in J. Galot, *Dieu, souffre-t-il ?* (Paris: Lethielleux, 1976), and the wider issues are fully discussed by C. Tresmontant, *Comment se pose aujourd'hui le problème de l'existence de Dieu* (Paris: Seuil, 1966).

On the specific problem of Muslim theology, see S. M.

Zwemer, *The Muslim Doctrine of God* (Dart Publishers, 1987) and more recently, W. M. Watt, *Islamic Philosophy and Theology* (Edinburgh: Edinburgh University Press, 1987).

## Chapter 3: One God in Trinity

The classic study remains A. W. Wainwright, *The Trinity in the New Testament* (London: SPCK, 1962) which includes helpful sections on the Old Testament and on Jewish literature as well. Another good survey including the early church period is E. J. Fortman, *The Triune God* (London: Hutchinson, 1972). Other than that, and apart from occasional remarks in commentaries, there is remarkably little which has been written recently on the subject of the Trinity in the New Testament. Here more than anywhere else, we can sense the failure of the present generation to integrate Biblical Studies and systematic theology in a constructive way.

## Chapter 4: The persons and nature of God

In contrast to the position outlined under chapter 3, there is a substantial literature covering the material in this chapter. For purely historical material dealing mainly with the Arian controversy, see R. P. C. Hanson, *The Search for the Christian Doctrine of God* (Edinburgh: T. & T. Clark, 1988). The Eastern position is stated clearly by V. Lossky, *The Vision of God* (Crestwood, N. Y.: St Vladimir's Seminary Press, 1984). The Augustinian tradition is outlined and defended by E. Hill, *The Mystery of the Trinity* (London: 1985). On Karl Barth, see the article by R. Williams in S. Sykes, ed., *Karl Barth – Studies of his Theological Method* (Oxford: Clarendon Press, 1979). Attempts to unite the different positions can be found in J. Moltmann, *The Trinity and the Kingdom of God* (London: SCM Press, 1981) and E. L. Mascall, *The Triune God* (Worthing: 1986). The *Filioque* question is treated at length in L. Vischer, ed., *Spirit of God, Spirit of Christ* (Geneva: World Council of Churches, 1981).

Recent attempts to reconstruct the doctrine of the Trinity can be found in J. Mackey, *The Christian Experience of God as Trinity* (London: 1983); R. W. Jenson, *The Triune Identity*

(Philadelphia: 1982) and most ambitious of all, D. Brown, *The Divine Trinity* (London: 1985).

## Chapter 5: The primacy of the persons in God

Despite its obvious importance, very little has been written on this subject. Apart from some classical Reformed theologies and more recent Eastern Orthodox works, which have made this a central theme of their approach to ecumenical dialogue with the Western churches, there is really only B. B. Warfield's masterly study of 'Calvin's Doctrine of the Trinity', published in his *Calvin and Augustine* (Philadelphia: Presbyterian & Reformed, 1956), pp. 189–284.

## Chapter 6: Constructing an evangelical theology today

Recent attempts to do this include Carl Henry's six-volume work, *God, Revelation and Authority* (Waco: 1979–83) and M. J. Erickson, *Christian Theology* (Grand Rapids, 1983). Mention may also be made of J. M. Boice, *Foundations of the Christian Faith* (Leicester: Inter-Varsity Press, 1986), which deals with most of the issues in passing.

# Index of Subjects

# Index of Names

## DATE DUE

| | | | |
|---|---|---|---|
| OCT 21 1997 | | | |
| NOV 1 2000 | | | |
| | | | |
| | | | |
| | | | |
| | | | |
| | | | |
| | | | |
| | | | |
| | | | |
| | | | |
| | | | |
| | | | |
| | | | |
| | | | |
| | | | |